THIS PROBLEM-SOLVING BOOK
HAS THE ANSWERS

Should you run a small business?

What's the right small business for you?

Is there anyone who will give you financial backing?

What kind of help can you afford, and what kind of person should you hire?

How do you get free publicity? And which of the other best things in business life are free?

How do you appeal to the customers you serve, including targeted ethnic groups?

The difference between success and failure in a small business is access to the right information. And this knowledgeable book has exactly that—plus the names, addresses, phone and fax numbers of people, agencies, and organizations who can help you.

SUCCEEDING IN SMALL BUSINESS®
The 101 Toughest Problems
and How to Solve Them

D1022879

JANE APPLEGATE founded and runs the Applegate Group, a small business publishing and consulting firm. Her nationally syndicated column, "Succeeding in Small Business,®" reaches over 17 million people. She was named Advocate of the Year in both 1990 and 1991 by the L.A. district of the U.S. Small Business Administration, and in 1990 by the L.A. chapter of the National Association of Women Business Owners. She is also a winner of the Gerald Loeb Award for investigative business reporting. She and her family live in Sun Valley, California.

JANE APPLEGATE

SUCCEEDING IN SMALL BUSINESS®

THE 101 TOUGHEST PROBLEMS AND HOW TO SOLVE THEM

A PLUME BOOK

DISCLAIMER: This publication is designed to provide accurate and authoritative information in regard to the subject matter covered. It is sold with the understanding that the publisher is not engaged in rendering legal, accounting, or other professional service. If legal advice or other expert assistance is required, the services of a competent professional person should be sought.

PLUME
Published by the Penguin Group
Penguin Books USA Inc., 375 Hudson Street,
New York, New York 10014, U.S.A.
Penguin Books Ltd, 27 Wrights Lane, London W8 5TZ, England
Penguin Books Australia Ltd, Ringwood, Victoria, Australia
Penguin Books Canada Ltd, 10 Alcorn Avenue,
Toronto, Ontario, Canada M4V 3B2
Penguin Books (N.Z.) Ltd, 182–190 Wairau Road, Auckland 10, New Zealand

Penguin Books Ltd, Registered Offices: Harmondsworth, Middlesex, England

First published by Plume, an imprint of New American Library, a division of Penguin Books USA Inc.

First Printing, May, 1992
10 9 8 7 6 5 4

Copyright © Jane Applegate, 1992
All rights reserved

Ⓟ REGISTERED TRADEMARK—MARCA REGISTRADA

LIBRARY OF CONGRESS CATALOGING-IN-PUBLICATION DATA
Applegate, Jane.
    Succeeding in small business : the 101 toughest problems and how
to solve them / Jane Applegate.
    p.   cm.
    "A Plume book."
    ISBN 0-452-26886-9
    1. Success in business—United States.   2. Small business—United
States—Management.   3. Small business—United States—Finance.
I. Title.
HF5386.A626   1992
658.02'2—dc20   91-39508
                                                               CIP

Printed in the United States of America
Set in Times Roman and Futura

Designed by Steven N. Stathakis

This book is dedicated to my family.

Especially to Joe, who stands by me through everything. To Jeanne, who keeps me in line, and to Evan, who brightens our lives. And to Julie, who taught me not to be afraid of anything, ever.

CONTENTS

JANE APPLEGATE'S TEN COMMANDMENTS OF SMALL-BUSINESS SUCCESS

I. If you use what you have, you have what you need.
II. Before buying anything, ask yourself:
   - Do I really need it?
   - Can I buy it used?
   - Can I borrow or rent it?
III. At least once a day, tell yourself: "I can't do it all." Then, get help.
IV. No matter how busy you are, take a break for lunch.
V. Every day, see your business as others see it. Walk out of your office, factory, or store and walk back in again.
VI. Always thank the people you work with. Thank your employees, customers, and vendors for doing business with you.
VII. Get to know a little about the people you do business with. People like to feel special.
VIII. Take a few minutes at the end of the day to praise yourself for all you have accomplished.
IX. Take a few minutes to forgive yourself for all your mistakes.
X. At the end of each day, make a list of all the things you've accomplished. Then, list a few things you need to tackle the next day.

INTRODUCTION

Owning your own small business is like performing as a plate-spinner at the circus. You know him: the guy racing back and forth between a half dozen china plates dizzily spinning and teetering on spindly poles. His challenge is the same as yours: to keep everything from crashing down on your head.

At times, running a small business seems as impossible as plate-spinning. But when the plates are spinning in synchronized circles and the crowd is roaring, there is nothing as exhilarating as being in control of your life.

You bought my book because you either own a small business or believe you have a future as a plate-spinning small-business owner.

Surprisingly, the number one reason why people start small businesses is to be their own boss—not to make money. Yet, when you are working hard for yourself, it is much easier to make more money than you probably ever dreamed of.

Maybe you once worked for a big company and got tired of feeling small. Maybe you got fired or your job was eliminated. It hurt when it happened, but it's time to start feeling good again.

With corporate contractions squeezing hundreds of thousands of people out of work, you are not alone. In 1991, layoffs were big news. Citicorp: up to 17,000; Sears: 30,000; Hills Department Stores: 3,000; Hughes: 3,000; General Dynamics: 1,200; IBM announced 20,000 in addition to the 65,000 jobs eliminated since 1986.

Once burned by a big company, most people vow never to go back. So what do they do? They either go to work for a small business or start their own.

More people are starting businesses today than during any other time in U.S. history. Approximately 750,000 new businesses opened in 1991.

Just who are these new business owners?

In addition to the thousands of corporate cast-outs, many talented new business owners are middle-managers who were promised a position in top management that never quite materialized. Women and minorities make up a big part of this group. In fact, the number of black-owned businesses grew five times faster than the U.S. population between 1980 and 1987. And, women, who are starting businesses twice as fast as men, are expected to own about half of the small businesses in the country by the end of this century.

Small-business owners are a growing and powerful economic force. Small-business owners in America employ about 49 million people and create two-thirds of all new jobs each year.

And small businesses outpace corporate behemoths every day when it comes to innovation, technology, and guts. Small-business owners like you brought the world soft contact lenses and personal computers. You make everything from satellite dishes to Kung Pao chicken dishes.

The most common trait among small-business owners is a powerful commitment to do-it-yourself. But that same stubborn streak that keeps you motivated in the face of failure frequently contributes to the death of a business.

Why? Because no one, especially a stubborn entrepreneur, likes to admit they need help.

Your business is like your child. And no mother or father wants to admit their child is faltering. But after nearly 1,000 interviews with small-business owners and consultants, I am absolutely convinced that more small businesses fail because of a lack of information rather than a lack of money.

You can't make the right decisions if you don't have the right information at hand. And how can you get the information when you are busy keeping the plates from crashing?

That's why I wrote this book. It offers quick, concise answers to the most common small-business problems.

There are certainly more than 101 problems facing today's entrepreneur, but I have picked the problems that crop up time and time again. I can't promise to solve all your problems, but I will point you in the right direction.

Whenever possible, you will also find telephone numbers and addresses to help you reach the resources yourself. For more comprehensive information, my Resources for Small Business guide is at the end of the book.

The advice here is not all mine. You'll meet scores of business owners and business consultants from around the country.

Some of the solutions are based on my own experiences as a small-business owner. Writing about how to run a successful small business inspired me to jump in and start my own publishing and consulting company, The Applegate Group. Our company owns the rights to my syndicated column and works with small-business experts to provide help as well as workbooks and how-to booklets for small-business owners.

I meet with people like you every day. Once I know what's bothering you, my mission is to figure out where to send you for affordable help. I welcome letters and story suggestions and hope to hear from you after you have finished my book.

We begin with the dream, the first stirrings that push you toward pursuing your own small-business success. The chapters help you make your dream a reality and are loosely organized by subject for easy reference.

You can read this book from beginning to end, or use it as a handy reference guide when you are on the run. The book ends with a detailed resource guide to help you find the affordable help you need in your area.

Here's to *your* "Succeeding in Small Business."

—JANE APPLEGATE
Sun Valley, California

1. DO I HAVE WHAT IT TAKES TO RUN MY OWN BUSINESS?

The working world is dividing itself into two camps: people who own their own businesses and people who work for others. If you're in one camp and want to cross into the other, you need to figure out whether you have the temperament for being an entrepreneur.

Being motivated and energetic is not enough. You need confidence, stamina, and vision. And you need to be able to build a team of people who share your dreams.

Dr. Robert Maurer, a Santa Monica clinical psychologist who has studied the psychological and physical traits of successful people, says that truly successful people are not only successful in business, but in life. On the basis of years of animal and human research, Maurer, who teaches family practice at Santa Monica Hospital Medical Center and lectures frequently at universities on the subject of success, offers these four success traits:

1. An awareness of the need for attention as well as a generosity in giving and receiving appreciation.
2. An awareness of and respect for FEAR; a willingness to feel it and to reach for comfort—emotional and educational.
3. A built-in nurturing voice that automatically offers as-

surance that it's okay to make mistakes, okay to be afraid, okay to ask for help.

4. A sense of mission or vision—successful people are clear about their goals and the sense of purpose sustains them in crisis.

If you feel you have these traits, you have an excellent chance of being successful.

Now ask yourself a few questions to figure out whether or not you are suited to run your own business:

- Do you enjoy tackling new projects?
- Do you take the initiative, or do you usually wait for someone to tell you what to do?
- Do you like people?
- Are you well organized?
- Do you stick with things, or do you get discouraged easily?
- Can you visualize yourself at the helm of your own business?
- Do you have a lot of energy?
- Do you keep going even when things are crashing around you?

If you answered yes to more than half of these questions, give starting your own business a try.

Before you quit your job—if you have one to quit—set up some appointments to meet a few small-business owners who are doing something similar to what you want to do. Most people are quite willing to talk about themselves. They will be flattered by your questions and probably tell you more than you want to know.

Jerry Durgerian, owner of Carousel Baby Furniture in Pasadena, California, suggests that would-be entrepreneurs volunteer to work in a business similar to the one they want to start. Working for free is a great way to get an inside peek at your prospective future. Be honest and tell them why you want to work with them so they don't expect you to stay forever. Or, if the owner won't have you for free, how about a part-time job?

When you get to know successful small-business owners, you'll find one very common trait: small-business owners are doers, not watchers. Although they want to make money, their greatest motivation is exerting control over their lives.

The other common trait is that to small-business owners, the business is not a job. When you own it, you are either working or thinking about your business seven days a week. Thus, when friends and family say you have lost your marbles, you must be willing to defend what you are doing—even at times when you think they are right.

When people ask me what kinds of businesses to start, I answer that it doesn't matter what you do—but you must be passionate about it. The business becomes you. You can't get away from it. So, you'd better love what you are doing.

If you can't picture yourself involved with your business all the time, it's the wrong business. For some wonderful, offbeat business ideas, read *555 Ways to Earn Extra Money* by Jay Conrad Levinson (see "Books" in Resources guide).

Once you have decided what to do and have proven to yourself and others there is a market for it, plan to spend about three times as much money getting started as you expect to. Starting a business is much harder—and more expensive—than you imagine. But, fortunately, the initial euphoric stage of entrepreneurship lasts for quite a while and gives most entrepreneurs boundless energy.

At first, you will feel excited about being the boss. But the stress that goes along with freedom can be debilitating.

Each day, your responsibilities increase. At first, you are only responsible for yourself, and maybe your family. But when you hire your first employee, you become responsible not only for your own family, but for the families of the people who work with you.

You are responsible to your customers, your clients, and your vendors. Without them, you have no business.

One day, you'll wake up and realize your life, your reputation, and possibly all your savings are on the line.

It's a terrifying moment. But it's okay to feel this way and if you don't dwell on it, rest assured, this too shall pass.

Everyone is counting on you to keep those plates spinning. And it's hard. And it is okay to consider giving up once in a while. But if you are ready to own your own business, you know you could never be happy working for someone else again.

Good Advice for New Business Owners

"Most new businesses are typically undercapitalized," says Jerry Durgerian, owner of Carousel Baby Furniture. "They think a dollar in the cash register is like a dollar in your pocket, but they don't think of the overhead involved."

He suggests apprenticing to someone in a business similar to the one you want to start.

"Work for free, get involved, and ask people their opinions about their own business."

The hardest thing about owning a small business:

"When the business isn't making money, it's hard to be happy," he says, laughing.

---

2. HOW CAN I USE THE SKILLS I'VE GOT TO START MY OWN BUSINESS?

Sometimes the easiest way to take control of your life is to parlay the talent and energy you customarily give to someone else's business into your own business. It all depends on whether your skills, contacts, and experience are transferrable into a money-making venture—and whether you love what you do enough to continue doing it on your own.

If you operate a pneumatic drill along an assembly line, there is probably little chance of building a business around that skill. But if you have a special talent you can take with you when you quit, read on. For instance, Patsy Sultan and Lynne Cohen took what they learned while working at the Los Angeles County Museum of Art and started their own successful art rental gallery, Art Dimensions, Inc.

Sultan worked in the museum's rental gallery for seven years. Cohen served as a docent for 10 years. "We had the background and motivation to do something together in the arts community," says Sultan.

When they decided to leave the museum, the pair began contacting well-known modern artists, including Laddie John Dill and Billy Al Bengston, to see if they would be interested in leasing their art through Art Dimensions. They decided to go for major talents because they figured they didn't have anything to lose. "We went out to lunch with Laddie John Dill and we couldn't stop talking and trying to convince him to give us a try," says Lynne, laughing.

Once Dill agreed to let them rent out his work, many other top artists followed suit.

The gallery presently has work available from about 100 artists and is constantly being approached by artists looking for the steady income the leases provide, as well as the exposure. "The artists also have a good shot at selling what we send out because we have sold about half of what we have leased," reports Lynne Cohen.

For clients, leasing takes the fear out of investing in contemporary art. "Contemporary art is very frightening to a lot of people," remarks Lynn Cohen. "It usually takes time to get used to it."

Art Dimensions' leases run for six months and cost up to 2.5 percent of the purchase price. If the renter decides to buy the piece, 60 percent of the fee applies to the cost.

"At first, we thought we could work out of our homes and work by sending out slides," says Lynne. "But we realized people needed to see the art so we opened up a gallery." The gallery opened in June 1990 and has been flourishing ever since.

Most clients are renting the art to decorate their offices. The main benefit for the gallery's corporate clients is that they can write off the payments as a business expense, "like a coffee machine or typewriter," according to Sultan. This means a toney law firm can impress its clients with a $10,000 piece of art by a well-known artist for about $250 a month. In fact, renting art was the perfect solution to the 14 partners in a law firm who could not reach a decision on how to decorate their offices. "For three years, they had hideous etchings," says Sultan. "Then, they leased about 25 to 30 pieces and eventually purchased the 18 they could all agree on."

To protect the art while it is out of the gallery, Sultan and Cohen require clients to provide adequate insurance coverage. The gallery also insists that every piece be professionally installed to protect it from being damaged.

"We started this business with the bottom falling out of the contemporary art market, a major recession, and the Persian Gulf War," says Lynne. Which proves that even when times are tough, if you have talent and the guts, you can transfer your expertise to a successful small business.

Are you wondering if your skills are transferrable to your own business?

Take a few hours off, away from your job, your family, and your friends to assess your talents.

Bring along a pad and pencil and answer these questions:

- Are my job skills transferrable to a service or manufacturing business?
- Do I need additional training?
- Do I need a partner whose skills complement mine?
- Will I have to sign a noncompete agreement with my former employer or deal with other legal issues?
- Do people need done what I know how to do?
- Would it be easy to promote my talents to the public?

If you have more yes answers than no's, you should consider setting off on your own. Getting some free advice from a counselor at your local U.S. Small Business Administration office or Small Business Development Center is a good way to get some feedback on your idea.

Interview a few owners in a similar business to find out how they got started. Starting a skill-based business is easier than starting a business you know nothing about. The secret is to market your talents properly, to charge the right prices, and to make sure you have enough energy to complete the work you bring in.

Some of the easiest skills to transfer into your own business are word processing skills, computer programming, paralegal skills, interior design, graphic design, editing, writing, and drafting. Or perhaps your best skill is dealing with people. I've written columns about several entrepreneurs who have started successful errand businesses to help people too busy to run their own lives. Another people-oriented person I met runs a nanny network, placing child-care and senior-care providers with private families around the country.

Turning your talent into dollars takes energy, enthusiasm, and contacts.

The big question is whether you are prepared, emotionally and financially, to make it on your own, without benefits, without job security, and without a regular paycheck. A tough call, but if you've come this far, read on and you'll learn what it takes to succeed in small business.

3. HOW CAN I TURN MY HOBBY INTO A BUSINESS?

Turning your hobby into a business sounds like a good way to make money while having fun. But if you're not careful, you'll lose your shirt—and your interest in what was once your passion.

People who successfully transform hobbies into small businesses say no matter how much you love something, you must be able to treat it like a business. Having a clear vision of the potential market and enough money in hand to last at least a year are essential to your success.

"I think it is the dream of most collectors to make their hobby into a business, but most are not successful," says Larry Whitlow, who began collecting stamps and coins as a child. He's speaking from experience. At 18, Whitlow paid $35 a month in rent for his first coin shop. He knew a lot about coins and was sure he could make some money. But, within three months he was broke.

Whitlow now owns Galleria Unique, an elegant coin, fine arts, and antique gallery in Oakbrook Terrace, Illinois. Over the years, he says, he learned to separate his passion for collecting beautiful objects from the business aspects of selling them at a profit. Today, he surrounds himself with experts in the objects he sells and has brought in outside advisers to help him run the business side of the operation.

Bob Marriott was a real estate developer who learned about the fly-fishing equipment business by hanging around a friend's store. Fly-fishermen shun live bait in favor of handmade flies designed to resemble insects and other natural materials. When high interest rates hurt his real estate business, Marriott bought the business from his friend in 1983. It has flourished, as fly-fishing continues to gain popularity as an international sport.

"I got into the business for the business more than the sport," says Marriott. "But I knew if I wanted to do some fishing, I had to create enough volume to keep this going while I'm away." His three fly-fishing stores currently employ about 14 people and feature workshops taught by celebrity fishermen.

"Most people say 'Don't turn your hobby into a business because you won't like it anymore,' " says Larry Alperin, Marriott's partner in one of the stores. But Alperin and Marriott still seem to like their hobby—and make money at it too.

Sometimes a hobby inspires an idea for a big business. Two Los Angeles real estate and hotel developers, Bo and Robert Zarnegin, opened the Los Angeles Fine Arts & Wine Storage Co. to house their personal art and wine collections.

They thought if they needed a safe place to store their valuables others would as well. "Our own collections had begun to overflow our ability to display them in our homes and offices," says Bo Zarnegin. So, he and his brother invested about $8 million in the 45,000-square-foot, high-security complex. Here, wealthy collectors can park their treasures for $20 to $700 a month.

TIPS

- Make sure your hobby has business potential.
- Talk to owners of similar businesses to see what worked for them.
- Consider working part-time at your hobby business while keeping another job.

■

4. HOW DO I BRING MY INVENTION TO LIFE?

Inventors are a special breed of entrepreneurs. They are passionate, creative—and traditionally awful businesspeople. Meet one of my favorite inventors, Bob Ayers.

Ayers, a professional actor and inventor, is a driven man who struggles every day with the business of being in business for himself.

He never set out to be an inventor. His life changed one day when he was shooting a movie in an Iowa nursing home. To brighten their day, the residents were invited to watch the filming. Between takes, Ayers noticed an elderly woman in a wheelchair. She rocked incessantly by pushing her wheelchair back and forth, back and forth, with her feet. At home that night, after a long day in the nursing home, Ayers could not stop thinking about the woman trying to move while trapped in her immobile wheelchair.

From that day on, Bob Ayers, the actor, became Bob Ayers, the inventor. When he couldn't find a rocking wheelchair on the market, he decided to invent one.

He bought used wheelchairs, tore them apart, and tinkered with them for hours. He jury-rigged models with a variety of springs. He struggled with the mechanics. He talked to every wheelchair-bound person he met.

His obsession nearly drove his wife Becky and their kids crazy. But they stood by him. And still do. For years, Becky has supported the family with her screen- and copywriting skills.

In the late 1980s, when Ayers finally perfected the rocking wheelchair mechanism, the struggle for financing began in earnest. No one wanted to lend this wild-eyed actor/inventor any money. So, like many small-business owners, the Ayerses maxed out their credit cards and are still paying them off several years later.

During his quest for financial backing, Ayers was wined and dined by a major wheelchair manufacturer whose executives led him to believe they really wanted to build his rocking wheelchair. It turns out that, in truth, they were doing everything they could to keep him from building it. His negotiations with them brought no deals—only months of anguish and disappointment.

His hopes were crushed again and again. At one point, while living in Des Moines, Iowa, Ayers was a top candidate for obtaining a state economic development grant to build rocking wheelchairs in Iowa. But at the very last minute, his application was rejected. Why? Because the factory in which he planned to build the chairs was just outside the prescribed "Golden Circle" geographic zone. The grant money went instead to an ice cream parlor, which failed several months later.

Bitter and discouraged, Ayers packed up his family and moved to southern California to pursue both his acting career and his rocking wheelchair. "We've encountered every problem you could possibly have with this business," says Becky Ayers, who has backed away from taking a day-to-day interest in things.

Eager for capital to boost production, the Ayerses sold a share of the company to foreign investors, who ended up trying to take over the company. He and his two partners eventually ended up buying them out—but only after a sticky and costly legal battle.

"We learned you have to choose your partners very carefully," says Becky Ayers, who believes, "America is a really tough place for a small-business owner right now."

Because they don't have money for advertising, the patented Rx Rocker is continually omitted from product guides that purport to list all wheelchairs on the market—but are really just paid advertisements. "It's been frustrating because people really flip out over the chair—they love it," says Becky. "But people have to know it's there before they can buy it."

They also found that having the lowest price doesn't work to their advantage. Bob wanted to keep the chairs really affordable, but he found that the dealers were more likely to push chairs they could make more of a profit on.

The lightweight Rx Rocker costs $995; the classic is $795. "Our lightweight model is $200 to $300 less than any other lightweight model," says Ayers. "I'd rather have 1,000 people buy my chair between now and Christmas than spend $1 million and sell only 500."

He is frustrated because although he needs to get the word out, he'd rather keep the price down than to spend the money on advertising.

"Bob would like to give them away free, that's how much we believe in it," says Becky, with a sigh.

After all these setbacks, Bob is still upbeat.

"I'm out selling 99 percent of the time," says Ayers. "I meet all the time with head nurses, rehabilitation people—anybody who will listen, I will talk to."

His sales approach is great: "I roll the chair into the office and sit them in the chair—this way they can see just how comfortable it is."

Seven years after meeting the woman in the nursing home, Bob Ayers is still obsessed about his invention.

"It bothers me that thousands of people are sitting in uncomfortable wheelchairs," says Ayers, who is still seeking new investors to help launch a national advertising campaign for his Newbury Park, California, company.

PATENTS—BRINGING AN IDEA TO REALITY

Before you can patent an idea or product, it must meet three tests. First, you must be the first to conceive the idea. Then, you must be able to build a working model and test it in the environment in which it is supposed to work. After publicly disclosing your idea or trying to sell it to someone, you have one year to file for a patent. Obtaining a U.S. patent costs between $1,000 and $100,000, depending on the complexity of your idea.

TIPS FROM AN EXPERT—GARY LYNN:

■ *Document your idea* from the beginning in a log book with permanently bound pages. This record is critical to prove the evolution of your idea.

■ *Find out if there are similar patents.* Ask the research librarian at a major library to help you conduct your search. Document the search in your log book.

■ *Build a working model* of your product if at all possible.

■ *Find a qualified, experienced patent attorney* to help you apply for the patent.

■ *Do your own market research.* Ask at least thirty people who could be potential buyers of your product to answer these questions: What do you like about this product? How much would you pay for it? Where would you buy it? Would you buy it? Make sure they agree in writing not to discuss your idea with anyone else.

■ *If the response is favorable,* decide whether you are in a position to start your own company or license someone else to make the product for you.

■ *Seek letters of intent* from store buyers who are interested in stocking your product. These letters are invaluable when you are ready to approach potential manufacturers or financial backers.

(Gary Lynn's book, *From Concept to Market,* sells for $17.95. It is published by John Wiley and Sons, 605 Third Avenue, New York, NY 10158-0012.)

■

5. WHAT KIND OF BUSINESS CAN I START PART-TIME?

What can you do if the entrepreneurial bug bites you, but you're not yet ready to quit your job and pursue your dream full-time? Most entrepreneurs—including me—continue working for someone else while they lay the foundation for their own business.

There are hundreds of money-making part-time ventures that provide a taste of what it's like to run your own business without jeopardizing your financial security. Many good ideas are listed in Jay Conrad Levinson's book, *555 Ways to Earn Extra Money* (see "Books" in Resources guide).

The book is wacky, entertaining, and packed with great ideas. Here are a few of them:

Have you considered becoming a "chain monkey"? If you live near a ski area you can charge lazy motorists $20 or more for putting on and taking off snow chains.

How about setting up a coffee route to serve small businesses that can't afford a big coffee-service company?

Why not apply for a notary license and work as a mobile notary serving people who don't have time to get to the bank to get a signature notarized?

If you like tropical fish, Levinson suggests cleaning aquariums for other people. It's a nasty job, somebody's got to do it, and others are willing to pay someone else to make sure it's not them.

If you like throwing parties, why not set yourself up as a busi-

ness-party planner and organize block parties and other events for
small-business owners too busy to do it themselves?

I could go on and on, but the best thing to do is read Levinson's
book.

With so many people now competing for a limited number of
jobs, Levinson predicts, more people will soon be pushed into making money by doing several different things at once. "Although
many of these are part-time ventures, with some you could earn a
living wage if you devoted all your time to it," notes Levinson, a
former advertising executive and author of a series of "guerrilla"
marketing and financing books. (See Resources guide.)

If you prefer to try a tested money-making venture, hundreds
of low-cost franchises and licensing arrangements are available. For
example, for a basic fee of $495, you can be licensed to represent
Money for College Inc., a Granada Hills, California, educational
consulting firm that helps students track down scholarship money
and provides other services. Many former schoolteachers, administrators, and educators sell the firm's services, according to Harold
Maroz, president and founder.

Various janitorial franchises are also available for a modest
investment. San Diego-based Coverall Cleaning Concepts offers
packages beginning at under $5,000. (See Resources guide for fran-
chise directories.)

If you prefer having more structure and a built-in support system, try selling just about anything at an indoor swap meet or flea
market. Unlike the traditional outdoor weekend swap meets, today's indoor swap meets are lively, colorful indoor shopping malls.
They tend to attract a multicultural mix of vendors and shoppers.

Starting a retail business at a swap meet is much cheaper than
renting space on the street. You can usually rent a booth for between $300 and $1,000 a month, including utilities, parking for your
customers, and the advertising support provided by the owners.
And if you try selling one thing and it doesn't work, you can always
switch to something else—without losing much money.

How do you find something to sell? If you think about it, you
probably already know somebody who knows somebody who makes
something you can buy to resell—hopefully at a profit!

At the Woodland Hills, California, Indoor Swap Meet, considered one of the biggest and best in the country, you can find every-

thing from African arts and crafts and designer jackets to a store that sells nothing but all-purple gifts, T-shirts, and stationery.

Visit a few swap meets for several days each to get the feel for what is selling and what isn't. You might also try to get a job working for someone else for a while to learn the ins and outs of the business.

Once you've tried a few low-risk, part-time ventures, you'll have a better feel for what kind of business to start. You may also find that being an entrepreneur is *not* for you!

6. SHOULD I START A HOME-BASED BUSINESS?

Working at home conjures up visions of flexible hours and long lunches in front of the television. But working at home only works if you are a highly motivated self-starter.

There are a lot of you out there. More home-based businesses will be started in the 1990s than during any other period of economic history. About 600,000 new home-based businesses opened in 1990 alone, according to Paul Edwards, a home-based business consultant and author.

If the skills or products you have to offer can be handled from home, the next question is whether you can do the work safely, legally, and professionally from your home.

All kinds of businesses, ranging from auditing to a window-washing service, can be easily set up in a spare room or garage.

Local zoning laws in most cities prohibit many kinds of business activity from being conducted in residential areas. Ask the local zoning officials about the rules in your neighborhood. The main concern about home-based businesses is whether your enterprise will create traffic and parking problems for your neighbors. But unless you are dealing with customers and accepting deliveries all day, odds are that nobody will even know you are there.

Before you get started, it is essential to read a few good books on home-based businesses.

One of the best books is *Working From Home*, by Paul and Sarah Edwards (see "Books" in Resources guide). The Edwards are home-based authors, radio personalities, and business consultants who probably know more about working at home than anyone else in America.

According to Paul Edwards, the three most significant problems faced by home-based business owners are: dealing with zoning difficulties, finding affordable health insurance when you are self-employed, and the virtual impossibility of obtaining merchant card-processing services.

The zoning problems differ from area to area. And finding insurance is possible if you join a group such as National Small Business United or the National Association for the Self-Employed (see Resource guide).

But the credit card issue *is* sticky. Bankers tell me they do not like to offer credit card privileges to home-based business owners because they have been burned too many times by fraudulent home-based mail-order ventures. Nevertheless, if you have a separate business account and a good relationship with your bank, it wouldn't hurt to apply. The banker will probably visit your home to make sure you have the proper business licenses and permits. He or she will also want to see whether you are really doing what you say you are doing.

If you cannot obtain your own merchant credit card services, try working with a fulfillment company that can take orders on an inbound, toll-free 800 line. Companies like these, including 800-Direct in Canoga Park, California, will run your credit card billings through their account for an additional fee.

Once you establish a financial support system, you still have to deal with your friends and family. A veteran public relations person who has been working at home for 10 years still has neighbors ask his son why his father can't get a job. In fact, many home-based business owners complain that their friends and family members do not take them seriously. The Edwardses offer these tips for combatting prejudice and working in the midst of chaos:

■ *Maintain a regular work schedule.* Choose your own hours, but stick to them.

■ *Use rituals to begin work.* Pick a pleasurable or easy task to begin your day. If you are on the West Coast, try making long-distance calls to the East to get going. (You'll also save on lower-cost phone rates.) Set your first appointment early enough to get you out of the house before you get stuck, or set a time to do some exercises and move into the office right after you finish.

■ *Set goals* and figure out what you want to accomplish by the end of the day. You might also begin where you left off the night before, if that helps.

■ *Set deadlines.* This helps you focus and concentrate, even if you don't make every deadline you set.

■ *Bribe yourself.* Take yourself to the movies or on a short trip as soon as you complete a major project.

■ *Inspire yourself.* Tell yourself you are doing a great job. Try affirmations, which are positive things you tell yourself aloud several times every day. A good one is, "I am a productive and successful person."

■ *Pretend you are away at the office.* Put a door on your office if you don't have one. Think of how you would handle distractions at the office and do the same.

If your household duties interfere, the Edwardses suggest setting a timer and giving yourself 10 minutes or so to run around the house to tidy up. Then, it's back to work!

Since working at home on a daily basis can be very isolating, try to get out at least once a week. Set a lunch date, or visit your suppliers, vendors, or customers. Get dressed up and go to a professional meeting. It is important to stay in touch with the world, even though your telephone and fax machines keep you plugged in.

Despite the drawbacks, working at home is a great way to start a business or even run a growing one. I work at home. My business manager works at home. And my public relations person worked at home until he outgrew his house.

7. HOW CAN I MAKE MONEY IN A MAIL-ORDER BUSINESS?

Make MILLIONS IN MAIL ORDER!!!

Almost everyone dreams of opening the mailbox and collecting stacks of checks and orders for what they sell. But that dream rarely comes true in the real world, according to one of America's most successful mail-order entrepreneurs.

"If you think you can start a mail-order business at home, in your spare time, and with about $10,000—forget it," says Ruth Owades, founder of Gardener's Eden and Calyx & Corolla, two upscale botanically oriented catalog companies. Owades, who built Gardener's Eden into a $15-million-a-year business before selling it, says it takes both marketing savvy and heavy capital to crack the $120-billion-plus mail-order marketplace.

It's easy to see why starting a mail-order business seems so attractive. Nearly 92 million people did some of their shopping by mail in 1991, according to the Direct Marketing Association in New York City. Those shoppers bought everything from outdoorsy clothes from Lands' End in Dodgeville, Wisconsin, to fossil skull replicas from Skullduggery, a Tustin, California, company.

And specialty catalogs are growing in popularity, not only because they provide unique merchandise, but because mail-order companies can cut costs by targeting specific groups of consumers. "Our customers are busy, upscale shoppers, who are primarily women," says Owades, who founded Calyx & Corolla, her San Francisco-based mail-order flower company in 1988. By dealing directly with growers and providing special, stay-fresh packaging for shipping via Federal Express, Owades says 98 percent of their orders arrive fresh and on time.

A 1975 graduate of the Harvard Business School, she was working as marketing director for a major catalog company in Boston when she proposed a new, upscale catalog for gardeners. She spent six months developing the catalog, convinced it would be a hit. At the last minute, her bosses nixed the project. Disappointed and angry, Owades made an appointment to meet with the chairman. "I asked him if I could pursue the idea on my own," recalls Owades. "He patted me on the head and signed a letter drafted by my attorney. I think if I were a man, he wouldn't have said yes."

In 1978, she raised $200,000 from a group of businessmen to launch Gardener's Eden. In 1982, Owades sold the company to Williams-Sonoma and moved from New England to San Francisco to continue at the helm for a few years.

In 1987, she began exploring the feasibility of shipping fresh flowers directly from the grower to the consumer. Everyone she met told her she would be crazy to sell fragile and perishable flowers by mail. But careful market research confirmed her belief that there was room for a new method of flower distribution to compete with retail flower shops, supermarkets, and national wire services such as FTD.

She turned to a group of private investors to provide the $2 million necessary to launch Calyx & Corolla in May 1988. (The company is named for two parts of a flower.) Each year, the company sends out about 5 million catalogs, offering everything from roses to orchids.

Potential mail-order entrepreneurs should be aware that U.S. postal rates are expected to increase about 20 percent in the next few years to keep pace with escalating costs. But there are ways to keep costs under control, including making sure the mail lists you create or rent from others are up-to-date and accurate.

It also pays to address and label catalogs carefully to insure their prompt delivery. Your local postmaster can answer any questions you have about rates, discounts, and ZIP codes.

Mail-order experts recommend computerizing your new business from the start. More than a dozen computer software packages are designed for mail-order businesses. Choosing the right one depends on many factors: how many orders you plan to process each month, how many products you offer, how many order takers you have, how orders will arrive, how long it will take to process orders, and whether or not you will be mailing products overseas.

TIPS FOR MAIL-ORDER ENTREPRENEURS

■ Begin with comprehensive marketing research to make sure what you want to sell is what consumers want to buy.

■ Have enough money. Owades recommends having at least $1 million in start-up capital.

■ Feature a complete product line, with at least 75 items that represent your catalog's theme.

■ Feature nothing under $10 and aim for an average sale of at least $30.

■ Rent mailing lists from reputable list brokers and do some test marketing before a major mailing.

■ Mail at least 200,000 catalogs.

■ Expect about 1 percent return on orders, increasing to 1.5 percent later.

■ Have at least 25 percent of all the items you expect to sell on hand.

■ Fulfill orders promptly. The Federal Trade Commission (FTC) requires orders to be shipped within 30 days.

■ Send at least two but ideally four catalogs a year.

Because many mail-order shoppers prefer to call in their orders, training your staff to answer the phone correctly is essential, according to Nancy Friedman, founder of The Telephone Doctor, a consulting firm in St. Louis, Missouri. "You only have four to six seconds to make a good impression on the phone," says Friedman. "The message to your customers has to be, 'You have called the right place!' "

Whether you contract with an outside company to take orders or hire your own, it's important to train your salespeople to share information about other products in the catalog. "I may not want to buy anything else, but I think, 'Boy, is that person sharp,' " Friedman says.

8. HOW CAN A MACHINE PUT ME INTO BUSINESS FAST?

When Alison Weinberg married her husband Robert, he was practicing law in Dallas. Today, he runs margarita machines in Los Angeles. Robert Weinberg chucked his law career to make slushy frozen drinks with a high-tech machine that he rents for about $165 a day, plus drink supplies. About 40 times a month, partners Alison and Robert Weinberg can be found serving drinks made from a Frozen Drinks Unlimited machine at private parties, golf tournaments, food shows, and sporting events. They cart around the 160-pound machines in a specially designed black minivan decorated with grinning limes and bananas in bow ties.

The Weinbergs are among the thousands of entrepreneurs who believe that a machine-oriented business is the way to go—especially if the machine is affordable, does what it is supposed to do, and the manufacturer provides the right kind of technical support and training.

For decades, American entrepreneurs have bought machines that put them instantly into business: Sewing machines, washing machines, film processing machines, vending machines, video games, and copying machines are just a few of those available to launch a venture for a relatively modest investment.

Machine-based businesses are also attractive if you want to begin working for yourself on a part-time basis before making a total commitment. For example, people who buy street-sweeping machines often work part time in the evening and on weekends, says Bill Burr, founder of Ven-Co in Ventura, California.

Burr never set out to be a professional street sweeper; he just sort of fell into it. Newly married at 18, Burr was looking for something he could do with his father, also named Bill. "I had a strong back and energy, and my father had a little money," Burr says.

In 1975, a friend who sold sweepers introduced the Burrs to a widow who wanted to unload her husband's failing sweeping business. They paid her $50,000 for the business, which was generating only $3,200 a month. The machine that came with the business fell apart. They immediately had to buy a new one—for $8,000.

If you wanted to start a sweeping business today, you'd need $20,000 to $40,000 to buy a machine; a machine's size and power dictate price. The smallest parking lot sweepers, known as beer can sweepers, are mounted on the back of light pickup trucks. A top-of-the-line street sweeper runs about $110,000. "It takes about a year of hard work to build a new route for one machine," says Burr. One sweeper can generate $6,000 to $9,000 a month in revenue if busy seven days a week.

In southern California, where rates are highest, sweepers charge customers about $25 an hour for their service. A skilled operator, who earns about $10 an hour, can make about six stops a night.

"Sweeping is really dirty work with nasty hours," Burr says. "Not a lot of people are attracted to used baby diapers at 3 A.M." But because it is relatively easy to buy a sweeper and get started, Burr says, the competition for local sweeping jobs is fierce. "Every year, five to eight new companies start out in Ventura County, but most don't last a year," according to Burr.

Today, Ven-Co's sweeping division has 22 machines and 36 employees. The company also provides landscaping services, employs a total of 80 people, and grosses about $4 million a year.

If cleaning up parking lots, streets, and construction sites does not appeal to you, consider renting frozen-drink machines.

"The machines are relatively easy to maintain and are so small we can work out of our home," says Robert Weinberg. And the couple's drink business compliments their catering service, which specializes in lobster dinners and clambakes.

A single machine, which produces 128 drinks per hour, lists for about $4,000; a twin-dispenser, major-event model runs about $7,600. Frozen Drinks Unlimited, based in Dallas, sells the machines through distributors such as the Weinbergs. It costs about $30,000 to buy the van and five machines, plus an additional $50,000 or so for promotion and overhead to get the business off the ground.

The machine, half the size of a two-drawer filing cabinet, is a mini-refrigeration unit hooked up to metal canisters of drink mix. Within 10 minutes of turning it on, alcoholic or nonalcoholic margaritas, daiquiris, and piña coladas begin flowing nonstop into the glasses of thirsty people. "We fill the machine up with as many drinks as the client needs," Robert Weinberg says. "One 55-gallon tank can make 880 drinks nonstop."

Hard-drinking Dallas party-goers have turned their passion for the frozen drinks into a $3-million-a-year industry in that area, according to Robert Weinberg. On a visit to Los Angeles, he called party rental companies trying to rent a frozen-drink machine. He was surprised that no one he called had even heard of one. Seizing the opportunity, the Weinbergs headed West to educate southern Californians about frozen party drinks. They've been partying ever since.

9. HOW DO I BUY AN EXISTING SMALL BUSINESS?

Sometimes the best way to go into business is to buy an existing business. At any given time, thousands of small businesses are for sale around the country. How do you find them?

You can check out the classified ads under "Businesses for Sale." You can contact a business broker in the area you want to look, or spread the word that you are looking for a certain kind of business. Many sellers also advertise in trade magazines and national publications such as *USA Today* and the *Wall Street Journal*.

The goal should be to buy a business suited to your talents, interests, and bank account. In other words, if you're not technology-minded, it's best not to go out and buy a high-technology business unless the management team plans to stick around.

The secret is to find out everything you can about the business so you don't end up buying a big headache.

Once you find a business that fits your interests and your price range, plan to spend several weeks or months digging into its financial history. Sellers are notorious for painting a very rosy picture, even if the company is in deep financial trouble.

Unless you have a strong analytical background and can really tear apart a balance sheet, this is the time to bring in a good accountant and a good attorney. You want to keep your emotions out of the way when you are doing what is called "due diligence." The biggest mistake a prospective buyer can make is to fall in love with the business before carefully checking it out.

Here's how one southern California woman bought an existing business:

When Azmina Kanji was asked to computerize the real estate development firm where she worked, she spent three weeks teaching herself how to use the software program. "It cost my company about $5,000 worth of my time and it seemed silly," says Kanji, who vowed to buy her own computer software training business someday.

Although she and her husband, a pharmacist, had founded three day-care centers and purchased a pharmacy, buying a computer business wasn't easy. Steve Lampert, a business broker, eventually introduced Kanji to Contracted Computer Training in Marina del Rey, California. While the training business was thriving and serving many major companies, the owner was burned out and ready to sell.

With help from an experienced accountant, Kanji spent seven months examining every aspect of the company. Finally satisfied the business had ongoing contracts with stable companies, potential for growth, and an enthusiastic staff, Kanji made an all-cash offer for about $250,000. She was glad she spent the time checking out every detail and feels she made a wise purchase.

"Most people look at the numbers too quickly, fall in love, and get burned," says Joseph Krallinger, author of *How to Acquire the Perfect Business for Your Company* (see "Books" in Resources guide). "In real estate, it's location, location, location. In business, it's market share, market share, market share," says Krallinger, a certified public accountant based in Palm Desert, California, who once helped a conglomerate acquire 27 companies.

Once you find the kind of business you would like to run, Krallinger advises you to take a very close look at the products or services produced by the business. Ask yourself these questions:

- Does the quality match what you and your customers expect?
- How many years has it been since the company introduced a new product or service?
- Does the company have any patented technology or valuable trade secrets?

It is critical to determine why the owner wants to sell the business and to keep searching for "the fatal flaw." It is also essential to find out how the company ranks against its competitors and whether it has growth potential in the current economy.

Don't try to save money by doing all this research yourself. Bring in an experienced accountant to review three to five years' worth of financial statements. If you are thinking of buying a corporation, rather than just its assets or name, an accountant can help you uncover such hidden liabilities as unpaid taxes, employment agreements, or short-term leases.

"If the seller's business has multiple locations, make sure he is not consolidating sales to bolster sales from a weak location," advises Mel Poteshman, managing partner of Levine, Cooper & Spiegel in West Los Angeles. Your accountant can help you check the inventory and review the existing financing or credit lines. Poteshman also advises buyers to ask the seller for an indemnification agreement to protect them against future liabilities.

When you are ready to draft a sales agreement, be sure to consult with an experienced lawyer who can keep you out of trouble. You also want to structure the deal to your advantage, taxwise. If the seller agrees to finance the sale, that adds another twist or two.

"It's a buyer's right to ask as many questions as possible," says Lampert, a principal of Biz Brokers in Sherman Oaks, California. "Buying a business is an emotional thing—the buyer is operating out of fear of the unknown." Lampert advises prospective buyers to spend a few days observing how the business operates if the seller will allow them to hang around.

Although it is proper to collect as much information as possible about a company from public or industry sources, Lampert advises against speaking directly with customers or vendors until the deal is completed. Many sellers will also ask potential buyers to sign a letter of confidentiality, which should be treated very seriously: If you breach the agreement and release information, you could be subject to legal action.

"When you are looking at buying a business today, ask how strongly that business will be affected by the recession," suggests Lampert, who is advising clients to avoid buying any business related to new construction or luxury items. "Stick with the basics," says Lampert. Currently, he is helping buyers in the market for messenger services, auto parts stores, medical laboratories, flower shops, and health-food stores.

Lampert and other business advisers say it is important to know exactly where the business fits in the industry and what kind of reputation it has with customers, vendors, and suppliers.

It is also important to figure out whether the owner has such a hold on the business that it would be impossible for you to step in and take over successfully. "I would recommend working in the industry for a while so there are no surprises," says Kanji, who also helped her husband revitalize the ailing pharmacy they bought in the late 1980s.

Kanji was lucky enough to retain most of the original staff. The transition wasn't easy, though. One key manager quit in a fit of emotion after the sale, but later asked Kanji for her job back.

Despite the rocky start, Kanji's business has flourished under her leadership. And she realizes she got a lot more value for her investment than if she started a business from scratch.

BUYING SMART

Buying a business is a major, life-changing decision. Take the time to evaluate every aspect of any business you are thinking about buying. Then, hire professional advisers to double-check your research.

Find out as much as you can about the company's:
- Profit and losses
- Cash flow
- Salary and wage levels
- Financial strength and stability of customers
- Availability of raw materials
- Patented or proprietary technology
- Corporate income taxes
- Payroll taxes
- Value of the assets and liabilities
- Reputation in the industry
- Customer base and growth potential

- Existing leases
- Employment agreements
- Union contracts

Valuable information is available from:
- Competitors
- Vendors
- Customers
- Distributors
- Neighboring business owners
- Trade or industry associations
- Trade journals or magazines
- Secretary of state's office
- Franchise or other tax boards
- Current and former employees

10. HOW CAN OLDER ENTREPRENEURS GET INVOLVED IN A SMALL BUSINESS?

Freed from the responsibilities of working for a living, hundreds of thousands of older Americans are actively pursuing second careers as small-business owners or contributing their know-how to fledgling small businesses around the country. Although there are no firm statistics on the number of older entrepreneurs, more than 1.9 million early retirees are willing and able to work, according to a study by the Commonwealth Fund, a philanthropic foundation.

One of the most inspiring older entrepreneurs I've ever met was Helen Edwards MacAfee. At 84, she signed a long-term lease on her insurance office and opened a classic car company with a friend—even though she doesn't drive. The car business was one of several MacAfee has started in the past 50 years, including a charm school, an employment agency, and an insurance company that provides insurance for American tourists visiting Mexico.

"I don't plan to die—I'm too busy," joked MacAfee when I met her. "If you have goals and skills, age shouldn't be a hindrance."

If you've spent your life working for a big company or just working for someone else, the thought of starting a business after 50 or 60 may be scary. But starting a business late in life may be easier than starting one at 30. Why? Because many retirees have money to invest in a venture that will supplement their pensions. Many are also able to take advantage of long-standing banking relationships and strong personal credit history to help capitalize a new business.

"A lot of people have dreams and fantasies about starting a small business," says Samuel Small, author of *Starting a Business After 50* (see "Books" in Resources guide). "When you are older is a wonderful time to try it."

Small's list of popular businesses for older entrepreneurs includes opening a gourmet food store, becoming a flea market vendor, and running a messenger service, travel agency, or gift shop. If starting from scratch is too daunting, consider buying a franchise. There are hundreds of service franchises that do not require a lot of physical labor on your part.

Another possibility is working full- or part-time for a small business, which traditionally employ more older workers than big businesses do, and small-business owners appreciate employees with sharp skills and reliability.

For instance, the ACS Management Group in El Segundo, California, has 5,000 "graybeards" in its data base, according to Mills Spangberg, director of business development. ACS, which also has an office in Houston, specializes in placing retired or laid-off aerospace workers into new jobs.

"Older workers serve as a great role model for younger workers," says Spangberg. "And a retiree brings between 20 and 45 years of experience to your business." Other advantages are that older workers have fewer political ambitions to rise through the ranks in your company.

Contrary to popular belief, older workers tend to be a hiring bargain. For example, Spangberg can place an experienced engineer with a Ph.D. at your company for a rate of between $35 to $45 an hour, which is usually less than what you would pay for a younger, less experienced engineer.

Let's dispel some common myths about older workers to help you figure out how they can fit into your employee mix. This information was provided by Career Encores in Los Angeles, a company that places older workers in a variety of jobs.

Myth: Older workers are often sick and have many health problems.

FACT: The majority of older people have no serious health problems that limit their activities, at least into their seventies. Most health problems can be controlled by diet or medication.

Myth: Older workers are frequently absent and have more accidents.

FACT: Studies show 18 to 37 percent perfect attendance for older workers, versus 10 percent perfect attendance for the labor force as a whole.

Myth: Older workers cost more in health insurance premium payments.

FACT: Older workers may be eligible for Medicare. A 65-year-old is actually less expensive to insure than a 30-year-old with two dependents. A 55-year-old can cost half as much as a 30-year-old.

If you are an older entrepreneur or about to reenter the workforce, I recommend reading Robert Redd's *Achievers Never Quit*. Redd's book discusses every aspect of planning for retirement, including starting your own small business.

TIPS FOR OLDER ENTREPRENEURS

■ Figure out what kind of business your skills and expertise would best apply to.

■ Determine how much money you are willing to risk without jeopardizing your financial security.

■ Talk with your banker to find out if he or she would be willing to extend credit or make a loan for your new venture.

■ Consider buying a reputable franchise to minimize the financial risks and increase your potential for success.

11. IS RUNNING A BED AND BREAKFAST THE SMALL BUSINESS FOR ME?

Many entrepreneurs who love to cook and like people dream of running a bed-and-breakfast inn. But beware: behind the romance lurk long hours, stress, and relatively little money.

Two veteran innkeepers share the truth to help you make your decision:

After downing enough eggs, pineapple soufflé, fresh fruit, and coffee to fuel a day of Civil War country sightseeing, guests at Boydville slowly disperse.

Many guests imagine innkeepers Ripley Hotch and Owen Sullivan spending the rest of the day on the porch swing, sipping frosty gin and tonics. In truth, the minute the guests depart, the work begins. There are dishes to wash, bed linens to change, laundry to do, general tidying up, and more than 10 acres of lush West Virginia grounds to tend.

"I used to work 38 hours a week and make a living," says Sullivan, who worked as an interior designer before buying the inn with Hotch in 1987. "Now I'm working 75 hours a week and not making any money."

After five years at Boydville, The Inn at Martinsburg, Hotch and Sullivan are finally breaking even.

The partners still rely on Hotch's full-time editing job to keep financially afloat. Although they love their guests, they still face harsh financial realities. For instance, it costs at least $200 a day to run Boydville, whether or not one guest has checked into the 1812 vintage stone mansion. The inn, which can accommodate 14 guests, commands about $115 a night for a spacious room filled with antiques.

Despite the challenges, however, owning an inn or B-and-B has great appeal as a small business. Industry experts believe that there are 12,000 to 15,000 inns across the United States, concentrated mainly in the West and Northeast. Travelers relying on the myriad of guidebooks can find inns in every state. Although most are located in rural areas or small towns, there are bed and breakfasts located in most major cities, even in downtown Los Angeles.

If you've thought about chucking it all for an idyllic life in the country, though, make sure your bank account and energy level match your dreams. "People suffer from what I call the green velvet skirt or smoking jacket syndrome," observes Pat Hardy, a veteran innkeeper and codirector of the Professional Association of Innkeepers International in Santa Barbara. "They don't know that underneath that green velvet skirt are tennis shoes because you are running as fast as you can to keep the old building going and the people happy." Hardy, who teaches seminars to aspiring innkeepers, warns people to expect a negative cash flow for the first three years.

Buying an existing inn with repeat customers and a reputation is often the best way to go. Although the softening real estate market in the early 1990s pushed inn prices down, expect to pay between $35,000 and $135,000 per guest room, depending on the location.

"It's a lousy time to think about starting up a new inn, but an okay time to buy one," says Sandra Soule, author of a series of guidebooks called *America's Wonderful Little Hotels and Inns*. "A lot of people go into innkeeping naively and undercapitalized," she says. "First the romance and then the bank carries them away."

The most successful inns are found in college towns with lots of visitors or near popular tourist attractions. But you want to avoid opening an inn too close to a major tourist attraction such as Disneyland or Epcot, where visitors spend money at the attraction rather than on their accommodations.

Hotch and Sullivan believe that Boydville has flourished because Martinsburg is not only in the heart of Civil War country but home to the Blue Ridge Outlet Center, a shopping complex that attracts about a million visitors a year.

There are ways to succeed in the business if you are energetic, have a good sense of humor, love people, are skilled at fixing things, and are willing to work very, very hard.

For more information on becoming an innkeeper, contact the Professional Association of Innkeepers International, P.O. Box 90710, Santa Barbara, CA 93190, or call (805)965-0707.

So, You Want to Be an Innkeeper: The Complete Guide to Operating a Successful Bed and Breakfast Inn, by Davies, Hardy, Bell, and Brown, is published by Chronicle Books; it's available by mail by writing to the association.

Boydville can be reached at (304)263-1448.

The Bed & Breakfast Innkeepers of Southern California can be contacted by writing P.O. Box 15425, Los Angeles, CA 90015-0385.

For information on the industry itself and a new inn rating program underway, write to: American Bed & Breakfast Association, 1407 Huguenot Road, Midlothian, VA 23113.

12. HOW CAN I BE AN ENTREPRENEUR AND A DOCTOR, TOO?

When he was learning to do hip replacements, Dr. Hank Wuh, a young orthopedic surgeon, was frustrated by the slow and potentially harmful method used to remove the cement securing an old artificial joint before replacing it. "Taking out the old cement was tedious, the blood loss was high, and there was always the risk of fracturing the femur or thigh bone," says Wuh. After much experimentation, Drs. Wuh and Albert Chin developed a patented cement extraction system marketed worldwide by Origin Medsystems Inc. in San Mateo, California.

"The operating room is my fountain of inspiration," says Wuh, who is one of thousands of physicians and dentists who divide their time between treating patients and running small businesses. In recent years, their numbers have increased as health-care cost-containment policies have cut into physicians' income.

"Economic problems have forced doctors to be more astute and aware of the business opportunities in their fields," says F. T. Jay Watkins, president of Origin Medsystems. "The words *licensing*, *royalties*, and *investments* are no longer foreign to surgeons." Since Origin opened in 1989, Watkins's staff has reviewed 500 product ideas—95 percent of them developed by surgeons.

Major universities and medical schools are also encouraging their faculty and staff to license their inventions and transfer technology to industry as a way to boost income. Stanford University's Office of Technology Licensing, for example, collected about $24 million in fiscal 1990–1991, up from $14.1 million a year ago. Seventy-one percent of the total was generated by projects at the School of Medicine, according to Sally Hines, administrator of the licensing office.

Wuh, who licensed the cement extraction system to Origin, chose orthopedic surgery because "it is the field with the greatest room for innovation." At work on another invention aimed at preventing transmission of the AIDS virus, Wuh claims that healthcare professionals are in an excellent position to develop marketable solutions to common problems. "I've found that a simple solution is often the best for a difficult problem," advises Wuh.

Once you develop, document, and test your idea, Wuh suggests sharing it with potential investors who specialize in funding medically oriented ventures. "There is a tremendous interest in medical innovations from venture capitalists and private investors—especially in northern California," notes Wuh.

He raised several million dollars from a group of Far Eastern investors to create his own company, Pharmagenesis, in Palo Alto, California. Pharmagenesis's goal is to pinpoint the active ingredients in ancient herbal remedies and eventually work with major drug companies to produce and market new versions of the drugs.

Wuh and his associates, orthopedic surgeon Nick Pliam and research scientist Dan Henderson, assembled a renowned team of biomedical researchers to analyze the properties of the herbal medicines. "Seventy percent of the world practices this form of traditional medicine, which has been around for 4,000 years," says Wuh, who was born in Taiwan.

Surgeons aren't the only ones busy running companies. Many dentists have set up their own entrepreneurial ventures.

Dr. Robert Ibsen, who still sees patients twice a week, is founder and chief executive of Den-Mat Corp. in Santa Maria, California, a $30-million-a-year maker of cosmetic and restorative dental materials.

"I found that just going to the office, treating patients, and earning a good living was not as satisfying to me as I thought it might be," Ibsen says. "So, I kept looking beyond common knowledge to see if there were ways to solve problems that didn't have solutions."

Ibsen said one of Den-Mat's secrets of success has been to

market products directly to dentists through educational programs, rather than relying on dental products dealers.

He also relies on people more expert than himself to run the day-to-day business operations of his growing company.

"I get other people to do the mechanics of accepting orders, doing research, and communicating with the dentists," Ibsen says.

Den-Mat's consumer products division makes the popular Rembrandt Whitening Toothpaste. The product was once sold only to dentists, but now it is available over the counter.

13. I LOVE TO COOK: IS CATERING A GOOD BUSINESS FOR ME?

Do friends swoon over your strawberry shortcake or cluck over your Chinese chicken salad? Have you ever taken those compliments to heart and thought: "Since everyone loves my cooking, maybe I should become a caterer?"

Well, think again.

Although catering is one of the easiest small businesses to start up—you can begin experimenting with recipes in your kitchen—the competition is cutthroat and the failure rate is staggering. In fact, Persian Gulf War jitters and corporate budget cuts canceled enough holiday parties in 1990 and 1991 to throw hundreds of caterers out of business, according to industry experts.

Suzanne Kallick, founder of The Catering Company in New York City, and her partner, Jim Gilliam, have watched many novice caterers falter because they don't run their business like a business. "You have to run the inside of the business very tightly," says Kallick. "And the spotlight on service is brighter than ever before." To control costs, most small catering firms employ a handful of full-time employees and rely on freelance chefs, waiters, and waitresses to staff events.

Being an excellent cook is just one ingredient in a successful catering business. Stashing away enough money to get through the first year is the biggest challenge. It might take months to book your first profitable party and years to build up a good reputation. So before you make your first mousse, be sure you have established a good working relationship with rental equipment suppliers and food vendors.

Without them, no one will taste a bite.

"You have to have a real passion and bullheaded desire to succeed, other than just loving to cook," says Janet Rosener, founder of Thymes, The Special Events Group, in Garden Grove, California. "You endure tremendous rejection in this business. There are times when it is so horrible you can't bear it. Then, at other times, windows of joy open up," she adds.

Like most successful caterers, Rosener started off doing something else. Although she always wanted to be a chef, she studied business in college and worked as assistant marketing director for a large restaurant chain. When, at another company, she was passed over for a promotion she thought she deserved, Rosener bailed out.

Armed with a business plan, she raised $55,000 from private investors to start her catering company. Today, Rosener's five-year-old company caters between 20 and 30 events each month, ranging from elegant private dinners to company picnics.

Although her company is busy, she admits the competition is tough. In fact, she recently heard there are more than 3,000 caterers in the Los Angeles area alone. "The problem is, anyone can call themselves a caterer, but not everyone has a health department-approved kitchen, a business license, and a million-dollar liability insurance policy," notes Rosener, who has all three.

"The bigger catering companies do complain that the smaller ones aren't licensed and don't have insurance," says Liese Gardner, editor of *Special Events* magazine, which is published in Culver City, California. "Still, most caterers start their businesses at home." Gardner, whose magazine covers catering and other aspects of the event-planning industry, says small catering companies across the country make most of their money by staging private parties, weddings, and bar mitzvahs. "The private parties provide a higher profit margin than the corporate work," she adds.

Keith Birch, a former restaurant chef who owns Piaf's in Los Angeles, thought he'd make his fortune catering upscale events for big companies. But, he soon realized the competition for the upscale jobs—especially in Los Angeles—was fierce. So he changed direction. "When I saw 20 to 25 catering trucks in front of downtown office buildings every day, I realized there was a lot of food to bring in," explains Birch, who caters many lunches for law firms that encourage their busy partners to dine in rather than going out for lunch.

One of Birch's best marketing strategies is to offer potential clients a free meal so his food and its presentation can sell itself.

Successful caterers try to set themselves apart from the pack. For instance, Rick Royce, of Van Nuys, California, describes himself as a "barbeque fanatic." He reaches new clients by participating in food festivals and entering barbeque contests. Royce, a Detroit native, has gone beyond catering to bottle his Rick Royce Sensuous Rib Sauce for sale in supermarkets, including Gelson's and Vons. He also sells a 250-pound, coffin-size Rick Royce Super Q grill to folks who can't get enough of those ribs.

Because Royce's ribs are prepared in a U.S. Department of Agriculture-inspected and approved kitchen, he can also sell his barbequed food to other caterers. To keep up with the demand for his ribs, he's hoping to open a take-out location. "I know there is a demand because strangers who've tasted my cooking show up at my house and want to eat dinner," says Royce.

If you are determined to launch a catering business, make sure you have enough money to live on for a year and begin lining up clients before you jettison your steady income. It also helps to find a niche, such as corporate parties or suburban bar mitzvahs. One ingenious caterer I met specializes in cooking for busy working mothers.

The high risks involved make catering one small business where it makes sense to start out small and work part-time before you take a major leap.

14. HOW DO I RUN A SUCCESSFUL RESTAURANT?

"Everyone seems to have a fantasy of writing a book or opening a restaurant," muses Danny Liberatoscioli, president of The Restaurant School in Philadelphia, which specializes in training people for a second career. Students at the school have ranged from a nun to the cofounder of a major credit card company.

Each year, thousands of entrepreneurs across the country jump into the highly competitive and risky restaurant business without being aware of how hard it is.

Meet Andrew Rakos—a typical second-career restaurateur:

At one point in his life, Andrew Rakos was a tastemaker and trendsetter for Max Factor, dreaming up new cosmetics and spending millions of dollars to promote them. But now, you can find Rakos up to his elbows in fresh fruit and pasta salad, dishing out breakfast and lunch at his trendy Los Angeles café, Who's on Third. "I was working 80 and 90 hours a week, making a lot of money, but something was missing," says Rakos, whose life changed at a New Year's Eve party a few years ago. At the party, a friend told him that the delicatessen next to her boutique was dying and the owner might be willing to sell the business.

Tapping his marketing skills, Rakos sat across the street from the deli for 10 days, counting patrons going in and out. "I realized he had no business," recalls Rakos. "Since there was no clientele to buy, I had to start from scratch."

Rakos did a lot more marketing research than most new restaurant owners; that's why he is successful. In fact, he recently remodeled the restaurant and opened a second store, "Who Makes Sense," nearby, to sell colognes and other body-care products. Rakos says he has never had so much fun—but admits he has never worked so hard.

The Restaurant School's Liberatoscioli agrees. "Owning a restaurant is hard work. It means 12- to 14-hour days, low pay, and a high rate of fatality."

Still, ill-advised people open restaurants every day. Restaurant ownership fits perfectly into the definition of a small business. About 62 percent of all eating and drinking establishments have annual sales below $250,000, according to the U.S. Census of Retail Trade. Eighteen percent of the restaurants had sales between $250,000 and $500,000. Only 8 percent had sales of more than $1 million a year. The message is clear: You should *not* open a restaurant to make money, because you won't—at least for the first few years. In addition, rising food and labor costs have cut deeply into restaurant profits in recent years.

Apart from the tough economics, running a restaurant taxes the skills of even the most energetic entrepreneur. Unlike many other businesses, it requires expertise in purchasing, accounting, personnel, food preparation, and planning. "Those who believe that this is a simple or easy business are doomed to failure," says Gerald Breitbart, a veteran restaurant owner who counsels people interested in opening restaurants.

Breitbart believes there are five keys to determining the location for a new restaurant: population density, accessibility, site dimensions, local zoning, and liquor license availability. After you find a site, you have to prepare a financial plan, asking yourself if cash flow will service your debt and provide any return on your investment. And because most bankers consider restaurants extremely risky, it's best to plan on borrowing money from friends and relatives.

Meanwhile, after more than a year in business, Rakos can laugh about his first weeks. In his first week, he went through six chefs, realized he needed an air-conditioning system, and could not serve runny foods on paper plates. "You have to stay clear-headed because things happen all the time," says Rakos, who takes a nap or heads to a local movie theater between 3 and 5 P.M. every day to recharge his batteries.

What terrifies this former model and marketing whiz?

"Waking up in the morning and wondering if anyone will come into my restaurant that day."

BECOMING A RESTAURATEUR

■ Find a good location with plenty of parking and street access.

■ Set up a reliable system of ordering food and supplies.

■ Plan your menus creatively and completely.

■ Hire experienced help whenever possible.

■ Make sure you have proper insurance coverage.

■ Be sure your operation is sanitary enough to please the local health inspectors.

■ Order enough supplies, dinnerware, utensils, and so on.

■ Train your employees well before you open.

■ Set up a detailed bookkeeping system.

■ To work out all the glitches, begin with limited hours of operation.

15. SHOULD I CONSIDER BUYING A FRANCHISE INSTEAD OF STARTING A BUSINESS FROM SCRATCH?

Here's a startling statistic: A new franchise opens every 17 minutes in America.

Franchising is very big business in this country. About half a million franchises in the United States generated about $716 billion in sales in 1990, accounting for more than a third of all retail sales, according to Info Franchise News, which publishes a directory and newsletter about franchising.

You can buy a franchise for just about any business from a BYOB Water Store to Women at Large, a fitness center for large women. You can set yourself up as a detective or a decorator, make wax castings, sell pizza, run a day-care center, or sell sheepskin from Australia.

This certainly proves that buying a franchise is the way to go for many small-business owners. But it is not for everyone.

Buying a franchise is a good idea if you don't want to start from scratch and if you want someone else to tell you exactly how to run your business.

About a third of all new franchise owners are executives or middle managers who use their severance pay to go into business, according to a study by Francorp and DePaul University.

"The fit is good because the prototypical corporate dropout brings business experience and capital to the table," says Patrick J. Boroian, Francorp's president. "What he often lacks is the entrepreneurial experience to start a business on his own. And, a franchise gives him what he lacks: It provides a business system and an already established name."

The key to success is to make sure you are dealing with a reputable franchiser. Fortunately, both the state and federal government take an interest in franchising. (*Too* much of an interest according to some franchisers.) Most states have rigorous franchise registration processes designed to protect investors from fraud. The federal government, under the Federal Trade Commission, also regulates franchising and requires franchisers to disclose the risks and benefits of their operations.

A great way to start looking for a franchise is to attend one of the many franchise expos held every year around the country. Attending an expo is an affordable way to see what's hot in franchising—tickets are usually $5 to get in.

At the expos, fees are all over the map. You will see janitorial franchises starting for under $10,000. A pet center franchise can run between $150,000 and $200,000. A floor tile franchise is about $30,000. A landscape maintenance business is around $50,000, and a diet center can run as high as $500,000, depending on the location.

In addition to needing money up front to pay the franchise fee and to lease a building and buy equipment, you will be required to pay a percentage of your gross sales to the parent firm. Most franchisers also require you to help pay for advertising and promotional costs. Depending on what kind of business you choose, you will go through some kind of training program for at least a week. Expect to have to pay your own travel and hotel expenses.

Norman Schutzman, founder of the Franchise Brokers Network in Wilmington, Delaware, represents about 60 different franchises. He is very active in promoting consumer awareness about the industry, and he's prepared the following checklists to help prospective buyers.

If you are thinking about buying a franchise, ask yourself these questions:

- Do I have legal, accounting, banking, and insurance counseling available?
- Can I work within a preestablished system, accepting ground rules and advice from a parent company?
- Can I train and direct employees?

- Can I supply a detailed financial statement showing my own and my spouse's personal assets and net worth?
- Can I answer a detailed personal history questionnaire that asks about my interests, hobbies, work experience, credit rating, and community involvement?

Once you find an interesting franchise, Schutzman provides these questions for you to ask the franchiser:

- Who is the parent company?
- Are you successful in my area?
- How long has the franchiser been in business?
- When did you begin selling franchises? How many outlets do you have and where are they? How many more do you plan to open?
- Will you provide a list of current franchise owners? (If not, move on to another company!)
- Do you have any financing mechanisms available to help me get started?
- Do you provide opening advertising, displays, and supplies?
- Do you offer good training and advertising programs?
- Is a well-known personality involved in your advertising campaign? What happens to us if that person ends his or her involvement?
- Do you help me find a site and negotiate a lease?
- Are royalties fixed or tied to sales?
- Does the contract termination clause cover both sides, your right to sell, my right to sell, and an ownership clause in case of death or disability?

If you get satisfactory answers to these questions, then you want to speak directly to other people who own these franchises.

Ask the franchisees (the people who bought the franchises):

- Are you satisfied with the service provided by the parent company?
- Was the precontract information provided accurate?

■ How much cash did you actually need to get the doors open?

■ Were there any unexpected costs?

■ How long did it take you to break even? To show a profit?

■ Have you had problems or disputes with the franchiser?

■ What were they and how were they settled?

■ Is it a hassle to provide the required reports to the parent company?

■ Would you do it again?

Here are some other tips:

■ If you decide to buy a franchise, be sure your family is behind you. Running a franchise is not a 9-to-5 operation, and you will need all the support you can get.

■ Make sure you choose the right industry, because most contracts are long-term—up to 20 years in some cases.

■ Obtain a copy of the company's disclosure statement or the Uniform Franchise Offering Circular. This has 23 detailed sections on the business and how it operates.

■ Ask a trusted accountant and attorney to review ALL documents before you sign them.

■ Watch out for scams. The industry has had its share of fraudulent companies. If you are asked for an up-front fee before you can obtain the disclosure statement, run for the hills.

■ Personally visit at least six franchises to get a feel for what operations are like. Try to find someone who has owned the same location for at least five years to learn from their experiences.

The International Franchise Association offers several publications for prospective buyers. Write to them at P.O. Box 1060, Evans City, PA 16033.

The International Franchise Association headquarters are at 1350 New York Avenue, N.W., suite 900, Washington, DC 20005.

For a schedule of IFA franchising expositions, contact the Blenheim Group, 1133 Louisiana Avenue, suite 210, Winter Park, FL 32789; phone: (407)647-8521.

Info Franchise News Inc. is at 728 Center Street, Lewiston, NY 14092; phone: (716)754-4669. The 1992 directory costs $39.95, including shipping and handling. It provides a comprehensive list of about 5,300 different franchises available in North America.

Francorp, a national consulting firm, has offices in New York, Chicago, and Los Angeles.

16. CAN I CASH IN ON THE GREEN REVOLUTION?

For Jack Cutter, a better mousetrap doesn't just catch mice, it lets them live. Cutter, founder of Seabright Laboratories, invented a green plastic Smart Mouse Trap after disposing of one too many mice mangled by conventional snap traps. Instead of being killed, mice caught in his $10 reusable trap are carried off to a release point and eat their way to freedom through a soda cracker lodged at one end of the trap. (The cracker-release method allows the squeamish to stand clear of the trap during release.) Seabright, based in Emeryville, California, is one of thousands of small businesses across the country attempting to capitalize on renewed interest in protecting wildlife and the environment.

Raising money for an environmentally oriented company may seem easier in the midst of the Green Revolution, but companies still need a sharp business plan and competent management to attract money, says Shelly Guyer, an associate at San Francisco-based Hambrecht & Quist's Environmental Technology Fund. "We probably receive an average of six business plans a week, or 300 a year," Guyer notes. "We are primarily focusing on technology and new ways to do things."

She said many entrepreneurs wrongly believe that they will automatically attract investors and make money on anything related to the environment. "It has to be a good business for venture capitalists to be interested," Guyer says, adding that venture capitalists usually require a 25 percent stake in a company and promise of "a superior return" on their money.

Nora Goldstein, executive editor of *In Business* magazine, which covers environmentally oriented business, says there are investors who are very interested in hooking up with the companies she writes about.

"But I don't have the sense everyone is rushing to venture capitalists the way the computer companies did 10 years ago," says Goldstein, who works in Emmaus, Pennsylvania. Instead, companies caught up in the recycling boom are turning to private investors called angels or to such companies as the Catalyst Group of Brattleboro, Vermont. Founder and president Bob Barton recently said the environmentally oriented management consulting firm plans to arrange about $50 million in financing in 1990. Catalyst also helps smaller companies form strategic relationships with other firms.

Back in California, Seabright is trying to raise $1 million by selling stock to qualified investors at $5 a share. According to the prospectus submitted to the California Department of Corporations, Seabright plans to use the money for new product development and to market existing products. Seabright's growing line of "Earth Friendly" products includes a Yellow Jacket Trap, Sticky White Fly Traps, and a tape that snags snails. Its most televised product is a trap used to catch the bane of California farmers—Mediterranean fruit flies.

Unlike many corporate presidents, who dread the annual shareholders' meeting, Cutter said he expects shareholders to suggest new products and help steer the company along the right course. Cutter provided the start-up capital and has lent the company another $500,000 during the past 10 years. Cutter, who previously founded Cutter Lumber Products, said his interest in developing environmentally safe pesticides stemmed from his involvement with an environmental trust he created called Pacific Waters. The trust helped establish a wildlife refuge, among other projects.

To prosper, Cutter says, any firm developing environmental products or technology must keep its formulas secret.

"You should file for a patent to help keep the competition away," said Cutter, who holds 15 patents.

QUEST FOR CAPITAL

Hambrecht & Quist's Shelly Guyer has these tips for environmental entrepreneurs seeking capital:

- Prove that your technology or products can work in the real world.
- Assemble an experienced management team.
- Research the regulatory environment to see how it helps or hinders your product.

■

17. WHY DOES PASSION EQUAL SUCCESS?

If you don't absolutely adore what you do, you'll never be successful. After interviewing hundreds of successful small-business owners across the country, I'm convinced this is true.

"When we go into work simply for security, the enthusiasm is not tapped," says Marsha Sinetar, author, educator, and organizational psychologist. Her best-selling book, *Do What You Love, The Money Will Follow* (see "Books" in Resources guide), liberated thousands of unhappy workers in the 1980s.

Although Sinetar says she does not advocate "dropping everything and running off to play," she does believe the most successful small-business owners are passionate about their work. A truly "vocationally integrated" person, according to Sinetar, "centers himself in his tasks, is responsible in his relational life, and creates with great force and vitality. . . . He gives all he has to the thing at hand because this giving is the way in which he exists."

Here's one entrepreneur whose passion for work propels his success:

Dave Rochlen still looks like the surfer and lifeguard he was 40 or so years ago. He's big, friendly, and intense. His thriving Honolulu sportswear business was inspired by a photograph he saw years ago in *Life* magazine. "I remember seeing a black-and-white photo layout of a resort on the Black Sea," says Rochlen, formerly a lifeguard at Santa Monica Beach. "The people were wearing their bathrobes and pajamas down to the beach."

Rochlen, who was having trouble finding comfortable surfing attire, felt the light bulb go on over his head when he saw the Russians in the photographs. He bought a few yards of brightly printed fabric and asked his wife, Kea Nue Nue, to make him some swimming pajamas, with these modifications: Forget the top, sew up the fly, and cut the legs off at the knees. As soon as Rochlen started wearing his "jams," as he called them, to the beach, all his surfing buddies wanted some, too. Today, nearly 30 years later, Surf Line Hawaii Ltd., sells about $7 million a year worth of hotly colored beach and sportswear.

Rochlen has no background in fashion or design; the main secret of his success is his passion for what he does. Every morning he's in the office by 5 A.M., using the quiet time to think and dream. "I love what I do and the money follows," says Rochlen, who could have been an archetype for Sinetar's book.

Like most successful entrepreneurs, Rochlen started out doing something totally different. After his lifeguarding days, he worked for about 10 years as a systems analyst for two research organizations, doing top-secret government work. "Then I started to have a bad feeling about the military-industrial complex," admits Rochlen, who moved to Hawaii in the early 1960s.

On Christmas Day, in 1964, the first pair of Jams (which is a registered trademark) hit the beach at Makaha, Hawaii. They were a hit and their popularity landed Rochlen and a group of Jams-wearing friends on the cover of *Life* magazine—the same magazine that inspired him to create the funky, knee-length swimming pajamas.

Today, Surf Line has about 115 employees who are busy cutting, sewing, and shipping clothes from an airy 30,000-square-foot warehouse in an industrial area of Honolulu. And although all the Jams, windbreakers, dresses, shirts, and shorts are made in Honolulu, Rochlen and his design team take a global approach to the fashion business. Four times a year they visit Osaka, Japan, to spend a few days brainstorming with their Japanese designers. When the wild colors and designs are complete, the fabrics are printed by a textile company partly owned by Rochlen's firm. Rochlen also works with a fabric designer in Lyon, France, and makes yearly trips to Italy and Paris to check out the food and fashion.

Rochlen infuses his personal philosophy of life into every piece of clothing he makes. Almost everything in the Jams World line sports a hang tag with a bit of Rochlen's expansive philosophy:

- "Our credo is color, humor, freedom, difference and love. This seems to be what life is all about."
- "We believe in color. Color expresses life, art and the joys of living."
- "Color is a performance. Color isn't fattening. Grab some! Put some color into your life."

"I am deliberately designing to please myself," says Rochlen. "After 14 seasons on the beach as a Santa Monica lifeguard, I have seen it all come and go."

Rochlen offers this advice to other entrepreneurs: "Make a difference. Make a statement. The highest ground is the better ground. Take a position. Allow yourself the freedom to fail," he says. "And remember, success is feeling good about what you do."

18. SHOULD I WORK WITH MY SPOUSE?

For decades, the term *mom and pop* has been synonymous with small business. From grocery stores to bakeries to shoe stores, couples have worked side by side, tending to customers and their children at the same time. But it takes a special kind of couple to be able to withstand the stresses of running a business on top of the day-to-day struggle of keeping a relationship together.

In their book, *Running a Family Business* (see "Books" in Resources guide), Joe Mancuso and Nat Shulman delve deep inside both successful and troubled family businesses of all sizes.

The authors describe couples who go into business together as "copreneurs." According to Mancuso, "It isn't the money that drives copreneurs—it's the gratification they receive from working together." Mancuso says, "Copreneurs are entrepreneurs who never need to go home and explain to an uninvolved spouse what's going on with work. The inevitable late hours, setbacks, and losses (as well as the discoveries and triumphs) are all understood and shared equally between these partners."

True enough, as far as it goes, but couples who work together also reveal a darker side. They talk about the perils of too much togetherness. The constant battles over money and how to spend it. And the difficulty of getting away from work when the work is brought home with them every night.

Meet two couples who have worked together for years. You may be surprised at their differing views of being "copreneurs."

Lee and Myles Lieberstein were celebrating their forty-third wedding anniversary the week I interviewed them. They have been working together since 1975, raising their son, Darryl, and daughter, Terry, in between running two complementary businesses. The family owns a PIP printing franchise in Canoga Park, California, and Myles Advertising, which specializes in direct mail and is based in their nearby home.

I interviewed the Liebersteins separately.

"I would not do it again, nor would I advise other couples to work together," says Myles, quickly adding that he is not unhappy about the way his life has turned out. "It's much too stressful," he says. "I'm the physical and psychological head of the family. I also take care of the 11 other people who work for us. I have 11 families to feed every time I wake up in the morning." Myles says the biggest negative factor "is not being able to walk away because it's a family thing."

Although he runs his advertising agency from home, and leaves the printing business to Lee and son Darryl, Myles carries all the financial responsibilities of both businesses. Still, he says, he can't imagine doing anything else but owning two family businesses. "I was a lousy company man, when I was a company man," asserts Lieberstein.

What does he like about working with his wife and son? "I like being able to watch them work," he says. "I'm proud of my family."

While Myles describes himself as a loner, Lee Lieberstein is outgoing and people-oriented. For years she taught elementary school and was involved in the teachers' union. She finally got tired of fighting the Board of Education and bailed out. While she was figuring out what to do next, she attended a printing convention with Myles and thought, "Gee, I could do this." Soon after, they mortgaged the house and bought the PIP franchise in 1975.

Lee admits the first year in business was very difficult.

"We went to PIP's two-week training course, but then had to face the reality of running a business," she recalls. "For the first three years, I could not fire anybody—I had Myles do it," Lee admits. "I leaned on him tremendously. I knew something about printing, but not the nitty-gritty."

After a couple of years working closely, their clashes intensified. "We found our personalities were too strong," says Lee. "We each had our own way of doing things. So, he left the store and went back to running his business for the betterment of the business and our marriage." But Myles is still very much involved. They frequently brainstorm about how to run the PIP and how to jointly market Myles Advertising.

After being the boss for eight years, Lee turned management of the store over to their son, Darryl. "Now, I act as an employee and do outside sales," says Lee. "I treat him as though he is the boss, and he treats me like an employee."

Why?

"If you stay in a mother-son relationship, it won't work," she says. "I was very happy to let go." When it gets too stressful, she stays out of the store for a few days.

Lee is not as pessimistic as Myles about working with a spouse.

"If you've got a good relationship, working together strengthens it," says Lee. "It brings you together personally and emotionally, but you can be together too much."

Any regrets?

"I never dreamt it would be as tough," she says. "But, with all the ins and outs and ups and downs, it has never been dull."

Lee offers this advice for couples considering a joint business venture:

- Be sure you have a very strong marriage.
- Work on having a very open and communicative marriage.
- Don't do it when you have small children—this makes it twice as hard.

Jerry and Ann Durgerian, owners of Carousel Baby Furniture in Pasadena, California, share a brighter view of husbands and wives in business together.

Jerry, who has a business degree from UCLA, has been in the toy business since 1957. Ann joined him in the family business in 1964. They have two grown sons. The family first opened a large bike shop, which prospered for many years. They eventually switched to selling baby furniture and now employ 15 full and part-time people.

"Working together as a team, you are with each other a lot," says Ann. "Having a business is like having a child: You give birth to it, nurture it, and are constantly watching out for it."

While Jerry runs the day-to-day operations, Annie, as he calls her, does all the public and community relations work, including demonstrating car-seat safety at local hospitals. She also attends trade shows and makes most of the buying decisions.

Who is the boss of their family business?

"Jerry is the boss," says Ann simply. "We do challenge each other at times, but I tell people he is the boss."

"If it's 50-50, you won't get too far," says Jerry.

One secret of their success is that Ann and Jerry complement each other's skills and experiences. "I look at things from a woman's point of view and he looks at things from a man's point of view," explains Ann. She admits "some of our friends are surprised the business has lasted and we are still married." Ann credits good role models—her parents. From the age of 9, Ann worked in their grocery store, watching them work things out every day.

What secrets can these successful small-business owners share with couples considering working together?

Have faith, they say.

Although they are not regular churchgoers, Ann, who says she does most of her praying in the car, believes, "God has worked overtime for us."

If you decide to try working with your spouse, here are some additional points to consider from accountants who deal with family businesses.

- Treat your spouse as you would any other employee, paying the same salary you would pay an outsider.
- Be sure to file all the appropriate tax forms and deduct the proper amounts of state and federal taxes.
- Pay your spouse with company checks, just like everyone else.

If you do these things right, you should have no trouble taking legitimate tax deductions for life insurance, medical and dental expenses, accident insurance, and travel and entertainment expenses for business purposes.

WHY MOST FAMILY BUSINESSES FAIL

The average lifespan of a family business is 23 years, according to John Ward, a respected family business expert who teaches at Loyola University in Chicago.

Ward conducted a study of 200 family businesses that were around in 1924. By 1984, 78 percent of them were history.

According to Ward, about 39 percent of family businesses reach the second generation and only 15 percent reach the third.

There are several reasons these businesses die. Most common: a lack of communication and an unwillingness for the founder—traditionally the father—to share the dream with people he loves.

The family's desire to take care of everyone often conflicts with the painful decisions necessary to run a successful business.

Family business owners also tend to resist change at every turn. They refuse to recognize changes in the marketplace and resent any changes suggested by children who return to the business after graduating from school or working for a nonfamily business.

———————————————————◼———————————————————

ALL IN THE FAMILY

Dennis Jaffe, author of *Working With the Ones You Love* (see "Books" in References guide), has five tips for successfully bringing new family members into your business. Jaffe, cofounder of the HeartWork Group in San Francisco, counsels business owners around the country.

■ Set clear expectations about what the person will do. Don't assume anything.

■ Base salary on service to the business and make it comparable to other employees doing the same work.

■ If possible, heirs should be supervised by a nonfamily member who can become a mentor.

■ The new person should be responsible for certain areas of the business and performance should be regularly reviewed.

■ Give siblings different areas of focus and rotate them into different areas so they can learn all aspects of the business.

———————————————————◼———————————————————

19. SHOULD I CONSIDER WORKING WITH MY MOTHER OR MY DAUGHTER?

"Before you decide whether or not to go into business with your mother, ask yourself: Do you want to ride the roller coaster or do you want to ride the merry-go-round?" This advice comes from Lilly Walters, executive director of Walters International Speakers Bureau in Glendora, California.

Walters, who has been working with her mother, Dottie Walters, since she was eight, joined her mother's company on a full-time basis about seven years ago. "I felt all kinds of trepidation, but where else would someone automatically give me this kind of opportunity?" asks Walters, who not only runs the speakers bureau, but oversees the design and production of *Sharing Ideas*, a magazine for professional speakers and meeting planners. Walters and her mother often disagree about how to run their thriving home-based business, but they share the same goals and work hard to treat each other as professionals.

"When Lilly came to work with me, I said, 'Sit down beside me and I'll teach you,' " says Dottie Walters. "She said, 'Get out of my way.' " Walters, a professional speaker, writer, and consultant, admits she and Lilly get angry with each other, "but an hour later we are friends."

One thing is clear: Dottie Walters is not only president of the company, but the undisputed boss. And deciding who is boss is critical to running a successful mother-daughter business, according to Ross Nager, executive director of Arthur Andersen's Center for

Family Business in Houston. "You have to decide who is in charge from the beginning," says Nager. "And it is often a more difficult situation when the mother is the founder and the daughter comes to work for her."

Dividing up the responsibilities and power is also essential to a strong mother-daughter enterprise. Nager, who is currently creating a succession plan for a mother and two daughters involved in a retail business, said he is dealing with the mother's reluctance to relinquish control over her daughters and everything they do. "In this case, I've got a very strong-willed, overpowering mother and two fairly nonassertive daughters," says Nager. "Right now, they are getting along because they don't have much to do with each other."

Since American women are starting small businesses twice as fast as men, it's easy to understand why more mothers and daughters are going into business together. And mothers and daughters who are close and share common interests are also more likely to form a successful partnership.

"You have to try to treat each other as business associates, not as family," advises Lilly Walters. "The fact that you didn't make your bed when you were 10 years old doesn't matter."

While Lilly joined her mother's successful speaking and publishing business, Jean Renfro did the opposite: she joined her daughter's new business. Renfro moved from Indiana to California to help make earrings for "Rachel's Mom," her daughter Connie's children's earring business.

Connie Dichtel created a small business that not only taps her creativity but provides a way for her mother and daughter to spend more time together. Dichtel's five-year-old daughter, Rachel, was the inspiration for "Love U's" pinch-on earrings. Like most little girls, Rachel loves earrings, but she doesn't have pierced ears and was always frustrated by the short life of the popular children's stick-on earrings.

Dichtel remembered wearing a kind of pinch-on earring when she was younger and set out to design a modern version. The family's two-sided earrings feature tiny hearts, butterflies, and pearls. After a successful test marketing campaign, the orders started rolling in. When the earring business appeared to be taking off, Renfro moved to Chatsworth. By the time she arrived, she was already a skilled earring maker. "When I was still in Indiana, Connie made a videotape to teach me how to make the earrings," says Renfro. Just about every day, Jean visits with Rachel while putting together the tiny, decorative earrings.

"My mother and I are very well-matched," says Connie Dichtel, who makes earrings as well as doing everything else for the business. "We are very detail-oriented and we are both workaholics."

Apart from making money, Dichtel says the best thing about her business is that "Rachel has a chance to get to know her grandmother."

Dichtel and Renfro say they have yet to have a fight over the business. That doesn't surprise Renfro. "I know Connie is the boss," she says.

20. HOW DO I WRITE AN EFFECTIVE BUSINESS PLAN?

If you are looking for investors, you'll need more than a lavish dream to share with them. You'll need a well-written business plan. Even if you are not looking for financing, your detailed business plan serves as a personal and professional road map.

Unfortunately, most people are a bit hazy about what a business plan is. The best way to find out is to read a few produced by small-business owners like yourself. If possible, ask a fellow business owner if you may read a copy of his or her plan. Your banker or accountant might also be willing to share a business plan, providing that confidentiality is not a problem. Or ask a counselor at an SBA-sponsored Small Business Development Center if he can show you some real business plans. Once you've read a few, you'll understand how to put one together.

Several resources are available to help you get started. Most major accounting firms offer free business planning guides. In addition, there are many good business planning books on the market. And there are consultants and technical writers who specialize in writing business plans on an hourly or project basis.

Investors tell me their biggest problem with most small-business plans is that the plans are written from the enthusiastic entrepreneur's viewpoint. It's a natural enough mistake, but a big one!

A good business plan is written for bankers or potential investors who may be acquainted with you but know little about your plans and expectations. They don't want to read about your goals and rosy projections; they want a realistic assessment of whether your business concept can make money for them if they decide to support you. Thus, while your business plan should be upbeat and optimistic, it must include truthful and realistic answers to questions raised by skeptical, outside observers.

Even if you are not a great writer, it is important for you to complete a rough draft of the plan yourself. Writing the draft will help clarify your thoughts and focus your personal vision for the company. Write it in your own words, and don't worry about the grammar or structure. Most small-business owners then hire a free-lance business writer or consultant to rewrite, edit, and proofread the plan. The finished plan should be free of typographical errors, printed on nice paper, and put together in a professional manner. A stack of loose papers caught with a paper clip won't do it!

A business plan's most important element is the part you should write last: the executive summary. A well-written and convincing summary, which is the first part of a business plan, is critical because most people who read business plans never make it past the executive summary.

According to a business planning outline prepared by Ernst & Young, a well-written summary will:

1. Outline the purpose of the plan
   a. to attract investors
   b. to outline a plan for managing the business
   c. to test the financial feasibility
2. Present an overview of the company
   a. the needs your company will fill
   b. the products and services you plan to offer
3. Provide detailed market analysis
   a. who will buy your products or services
   b. size of the market
4. Discuss product research and development
   a. major milestones
   b. ongoing efforts
5. Analyze marketing and sales
   a. marketing strategy
   b. sales strategy
6. List organization and personnel

   a. key managers and owners
   b. key employees
7. Provide financial data
   a. funds required and what they will be used for
   b. historical financial data
   c. prospective financial summary

Once you have this general outline, fill in the sections themselves with as much detailed, specific information as possible. You'll find yourself distilling the elements of the plan for quick reading.

Remember, many people will read your plan before they meet you. This critical document has to reflect your intelligence and integrity. Do your homework. Know what you are talking about and *don't* fake it. Above all, make sure the plan sells you and your capabilities.

"Management is the factor most frequently cited by investors in determining whether they are willing to put money in a particular business," says Frank Kilpatrick, an investment banker who counsels many entrepreneurs. "Highlight your qualifications," he advises. Relevant experience, commitment, time, and personal resources available. "You might also include job descriptions and organizational charts with staffing strategies noted for each stage of your venture's development."

Kilpatrick, who teaches business planning at the university level, recommends these business planning books: *Business Plans That Win $$$*, by Stanley R. Rich and David E. Gumpert; and *Guide to Creating a Successful Business Plan*, by David E. Gumpert (see "Books" in Resources guide).

You might also contact any of the major accounting firms (Ernst & Young, Price Waterhouse, Arthur Andersen) and ask for their business planning brochures for entrepreneurs. They are usually available at no cost.

21. HOW DO I RAISE MONEY TO START MY SMALL BUSINESS?

Money. Money. Money.

Finding the money to fuel your dream is the biggest challenge. But it is possible if you have a clear and convincing business plan (See 20. How Do I Write an Effective Business Plan?) and are willing to devote all your energy to making it work.

The first rule of finding money: You must be willing to invest your *own* money and put your personal assets on the line before asking others for help.

Why? Simply put, if you are not willing to take a serious financial risk, why should anyone else?

The amount of money you need depends on what kind of business you plan to start. If you plan to open a retail store, you not only need money for rent, but to buy merchandise and pay a staff even before the first customer walks in the door. A service business usually needs less capital to get started.

A good rule of thumb is to put away two and a half to three times the amount you think you'll need. Raising that sum may sound impossible, but it's essential to keep you from running out of cash and going under before you really give yourself a chance to succeed.

After figuring out how much money you need, spend time making a list of all the people you know who might want to participate in your venture. In most cases, we are discouraged from borrowing money from relatives, but when it comes to starting a small business, family members are a key source of money. But don't borrow from a cousin who is always broke, no matter how enthusiastic he or she is about your idea. Rather, approach well-to-do relatives who have other investments and are comfortable with taking risks. See if they may be willing to make you a loan at the prevailing interest rate, or possibly a bit below if they are willing to give you a break. I wouldn't recommend taking in partners at the beginning. You don't need the aggravation of your investors telling you how to run the business—at least not until you figure out how to do it yourself.

Private investors are usually the best place to start, after you have tapped yourself and your relatives. They generally offer better interest rates than banks and fewer strings than venture capitalists.

Many entrepreneurs still think that professional venture capitalists provide seed money for most new businesses. But this is a myth, according to Robert J. Gaston, author of *Finding Private Venture Capital for Your Firm* (see "Books" in Resources guide). Gaston contends venture capitalists—who reject about 99 percent of the deals they consider—invest in only about 2,000 of the 600,000 to 700,000 new businesses opening up every year in the United States.

This means most entrepreneurs are getting money from private investors, relatives and "business angels," as Gaston calls them. "Angels put almost six of every ten dollars in very small firms with less than four employees and sales of under $150,000 per year," says Gaston, who based his book on a five-year study of 435 angels who invested $60 million between 1982 and 1987. Gaston, a banker and an economist, believes about 700,000 angels invest in 87,000 new ventures a year. This translates into about $56 billion in risk capital.

Who are these business angels and how do *you* find one?

The typical angel is a white male, 47 years old, with a college degree in business or engineering. He is a business owner with an income of $90,000 a year and a median net worth of $750,000. Angels like to keep an eye on their money and usually invest in businesses within a 50-mile radius of their home.

"Angel investors will usually have some degree of familiarity with the business or industry," says Frank Kilpatrick, a Manhattan Beach, California, business consultant and investment banker.

"They feel they can contribute something tangible to the enterprise."

An engineer who raised about $1.5 million from angels tried this route after striking out with venture capitalists. "I suggest you spend two days with your address book, writing down the name of everyone who may have money," he advises. "Then, contact them."

He cautions against paying professional finders to find investors. "I'd say do not spend money to get money unless you are completely lost."

He and others recommend finding an angel in your field through your trade association or professional group. This way you will not only get the money, but the expertise to go along with it. If you are not a member of an alumni association or industry trade group, this is the time to join. Your local reference librarian can help you find the right organization by looking through a directory of associations.

The least attractive way to finance the start-up costs is to use your credit cards. The high interest rates can really take a toll on your financial health. But I've met scores of business owners who were forced to use plastic to start their companies.

If you must use a credit card, try to set a limit and only use one card for business purposes. Then, do your best to pay off the balance every month to avoid the high interest charges.

Money is essential to your business, but energy and enthusiasm can help you through the tough times. It also helps to have the support of friends, your spouse, and your family, since most bankers aren't interested in talking to you if you want a loan to start a new business. (See 22. How Can I Convince a Banker to Lend Me Money?)

QUEST FOR CAPITAL

Tips for entrepreneurs seeking capital:

■ Prove that your technology or products can work in the real world.
■ Assemble an experienced management team.

■ Research the regulatory environment to see how it helps or hinders your product.

■ Determine the size of your potential market.

■ Check out the competition and understand why customers should buy your products over someone else's.

22. HOW CAN I CONVINCE A BANKER TO LEND ME MONEY?

Many small-business owners believe bankers hate them. But this isn't true. Bankers don't dislike entrepreneurs, they just don't like the way entrepreneurs tend to approach them to ask for loans.

Here's the problem: Bankers are taught to be very conservative and not to take risks with other people's money. Entrepreneurs, in contrast, are dyed-in-the-wool risk-takers and can't understand why bankers don't share their enthusiasm for their ventures. Once you realize the basic problem, you can develop a new strategy that will increase your chances of getting a loan.

Here's how one small-business owner wooed his banker.

Jim Morris, chief executive of Envirotech International in Houston, had a problem. He needed a way to establish credit for customers who wanted to finance his company's water treatment systems. His initial discussions with local bankers were discouraging. Envirotech had only been in business two years, and bankers traditionally require three years of financial statements before considering a business loan application.

In his ultimately successful quest for financing, Morris learned a big lesson: You can never tell a banker too much about your business.

Many small-business owners think that bankers know everything about all kinds of businesses, but that isn't true. You need to make sure the banker understands what your business is all about and why the money about to be borrowed is so critical to the venture's success. For instance, Morris was able to tell bankers that the unique feature of Envirotech was that their systems didn't use chemicals.

As Morris persisted, he finally met Joel Pearson, an assistant vice-president at First Interstate Bank of Texas, who agreed to review Morris's customer list and equipment brochures. "With that information, I was able to show Pearson how we differed from other water companies," says Morris.

"They went through their sales pitch," says Pearson, who later agreed to consider loan applications from Envirotech clients. "They were enthusiastic, excited, and knowledgeable about their products."

Bankers who do business with small-business owners say they wish more entrepreneurs would find out what a banker needs to feel comfortable. And they emphasize that the very best time to set up a banking relationship is long before you need the money.

"Invest time talking with prospective bankers," advises Douglas Freeman, former executive vice-president of Wells Fargo Bank's business loan division in San Francisco. "Explain your business, its cycles, and its cash needs." Adds Frank Mynard, chairman of the American Bankers Association's small-business banking unit, "If problems develop, don't wait until the last minute to call your banker. The worst thing a small business owner can do is beg his banker for help on a Thursday because he can't meet a Friday payroll."

Williams Arant, Jr., president and chief executive officer of First National Bank of Knoxville, Tennessee, agrees. "Bankers don't like surprises," says Arant. "The worst thing in the world is to hear something is wrong with a client's business through the grapevine or to read it in the newspaper."

Besides open communication, Arant stresses, the thing that makes a banker most comfortable is the "feeling that the customer really knows his business."

If you want to gain a banker's confidence, ask for something specific. Do you need a long-term loan to refinance existing debt, expand your business, or introduce new products? Do you need a credit line to provide short-term working capital? How about a business credit card for keeping track of travel and entertainment expenses?

Once you've figured out what you need the money for, be prepared to present three years' worth of financial statements, business and personal tax returns, a historical summary of the business, and a secondary source of repayment. You will also need a clearly written current balance sheet, profit-and-loss statement, cash-flow projections, and information on accounts receivable and accounts payable.

If your business is incorporated, your banker needs to know if the stockholders will cover the losses. If you are in a partnership, the bank usually requires all principals to sign a personal guarantee for the loan. Sole proprietors will usually be asked to back up the loan with personal assets such as a home.

Bankers are not magicians, and there is little mystery concerning how they decide whether to lend you the money. In addition to historical and industry factors, lenders rely on ratios to determine short-term liquidity. A quick way to figure your liquidity is to add up the cash on hand, accounts receivable, and marketable securities, then divide that sum by your current liabilities, including accounts payable, loans outstanding, and salaries. But remember, every industry has its own ratios. If your ratio is 3 to 1 and the industry average is 7 to 1, you won't look like a very good risk to a loan officer.

If you want to please a banker, read *Steps to Small Business Financing* before applying for your next loan. This fact-filled booklet is published jointly by the American Bankers' Association and the National Federation of Independent Business. Single copies are available for $2.50 by sending a check to Small Business Financing, NFIB Foundation, Box 7575, San Mateo, CA 94403.

HOW TO MAKE YOUR BANKER LOVE YOU

■ Think of your banker as a business partner.
■ Invite your banker to visit your business to see exactly what you are doing and how you do it.

■ Communicate regularly—the good news as well as the bad.

■ Remember, bankers hate surprises.

■ Find out exactly what kind of documents a banker needs to process a loan—because inadequate documentation creates unnecessary delays.

■ To generate enthusiasm for a proposed product or service, ask your banker what he or she thinks of it. An involved banker is more likely to make a good presentation to the loan committee.

———————————————————■———————————————————

23. HOW DO I INCREASE MY CHANCES OF GETTING A BANK LOAN?

When you're looking for a loan, it helps to understand that bankers prefer the known to the unknown, so even before you plan to borrow any money, get to know as many people as you can in your bank branch. Being cordial to the tellers you deal with is not enough. Introduce yourself to the loan officer and the bank manager, as well as to his or her support staff. It also helps to move all of your accounts into one bank to show that you trust them with all your personal and business funds. Remember, if they know you, if they consider you a good customer and a loyal one, they'll be more likely to listen to your pitch for funds when you need them.

Bankers, as I'm sure you realize, are conservative by nature. Thus, a loan officer is generally not interested in lending you money until your business is two years old and profitable—although certain banks that specialize in small-business loans, such as Mechanics National Bank in Paramount, California, will often make riskier, "seed money" loans to borrowers with good personal credit.

A major problem is that too many entrepreneurs try to dazzle bankers with their plans and dreams. Your enthusiasm might impress private investors or potential employees, but enthusiasm is worth very little to a loan officer concerned with prompt repayment based on cash flow.

Thomas Timmons, a former banker and turnaround expert, works with many small companies seeking financing. "You need to sell your banker on the future cash-generating capabilities of your business," says Timmons, founder of Business Directions in Mission Viejo, California. "Your banker must be convinced that the loan will be paid off with adequate cash flow generated by anticipated business operations, rather than a fire sale-type forced asset liquidation."

But before you fill out a single piece of paper, set up an appointment to meet the loan officer you plan to deal with. The loan officer is the one who makes a presentation about your loan request to the bank's loan committee, and unless you convince this one pivotal person to support your request, you won't get a dime.

Timmons and other experts say that too many loan requests from small-business owners contain the wrong information or not enough of the right information. For instance, says Timmons, "It's a common mistake to use past income tax returns to convince the banker that your business can handle the requested debt."

The problem is that most small-business tax returns are designed to legally minimize taxable income and reduce taxes. As a result, the tax returns don't reflect the real ability of your business to service the debt. So although you will probably be required to provide the tax returns, consider them just one element of your financial statement. Work with your loan officer to put together the right package.

Timmons offers these six steps for putting together a loan package. His suggestions are followed by a small-business loan checklist from Hawkeye Bank in Des Moines, so you can see what a real bank asks for.

1. Prepare a written summary of the loan you want, including the amount requested, the security provided, and terms and method of payment. Most banks require a secondary source of repayment.

2. Provide a mission statement outlining the core purpose of your business and where you are headed. Bankers want to know what makes your company different from the competition and what motivates you and your management team.

3. Include a brief version of your business plan to share your vision with your potential lenders.

4. Provide credible financial projections for the term of the loan.

Communicate honestly how much cash you believe the business will generate.

5. Provide information on your earnings and cash flow for the past three years.

6. Include other selling points, such as brochures and literature about your products, profiles of your top people in management, and credit references.

ESSENTIALS OF A SMALL-BUSINESS LOAN APPLICATION

If you own or manage a small business, you know the importance of organization in order to stay on top of business activities. Applying for a small-business loan requires the same organization and planning. By completing the checklist below, your business plan will include the items most lenders need for evaluation during a small-business loan application process. As you complete each step, check that item and move on to the next element.

—— Cover Letter Describing Request
　—— Dollar amount
　—— Terms and timing
　—— Type of collateral proposed

—— Summary of Business
　—— Description
　—— Name
　—— Starting date
　—— Location and plan description
　—— Product and competition
　—— Market and competition
　—— Management expertise
　—— Significant company history
　—— Business goals
　—— Summary of financial needs and application of funds

—— Market Analysis
    —— Description of total market
    —— Target market
    —— Current market position
    —— Competition

—— Products and Services
    —— Description of complete product/services offered
    —— Proprietary position: patents, copyrights, legal and technical considerations
    —— Comparison to competitor's products/services
    —— Product/service objectives

—— Manufacturing Process (If Applicable)
    —— Materials
    —— Sources of supply
    —— Production methods
    —— Production time
    —— Type of equipment and degree of productivity

—— Marketing Strategy
    —— Overall strategy
    —— Pricing policy
    —— Sales terms
    —— Method of selling, distributing, and servicing products

—— Management Plan
    —— Form of business organization
    —— Board of Directors composition
    —— Officers: organization chart and responsibilities
    —— Résumé of key personnel
    —— Staffing plan/number of employees
    —— Facilities plan/planned capital improvements
    —— Operating plan/schedule of upcoming work for next one to two years

—— Financial Data
    —— Financial history (three years to present)

—— Three-year financial projections (first year month by month; remaining years annually)
  1. Projected Profit and Loss statements
  2. Pro forma balance sheets
  3. Cash-flow projection
  4. Capital expenditure estimates
—— Explanation of projections
—— Key business ratios
—— Explanation of use and effect of new funds
—— Contingent liabilities (leases)
—— Personal financial statements for each owner (plus two years tax returns)

Courtesy, Hawkeye Bank of Des Moines

24. SHOULD I DEAL WITH VENTURE CAPITALISTS?

It used to be that every entrepreneur was hungry to attract venture capital to their doorstep. Not anymore.

The honeymoon ended in the late 1980s, when venture capitalists began shunning all but the snazziest high-tech deals. In fact, venture capital investment for small companies sank to about $1 billion in 1991, less than half of 1990's $2.1 billion, according to Venture Economics Publishing Co., a Needham, Massachusetts, research group. In the first half of 1991, only 15 venture capital firms raised money from investors—a combined total of $541 million, down 43 percent from the $954 million raised in the first six months of 1990.

And too many small-business owners were stung by the realities of dealing with investors who had not one shred of emotion attached to their business instincts.

One Iowa entrepreneur learned this very painful lesson when his one-time sugar daddy turned out to be a sourpuss and eventually forced the company into bankruptcy.

When Philip Akin was a student at the University of Iowa, he noticed students constantly had trouble finding a washing machine and dryer in working order. Figuring he didn't have much to lose, he got his fraternity house to agree to let him install a washer and dryer. Soon, he was installing machines in frat houses and sororities around the campus.

Buoyed by his success, Akin decided to open laundromats unlike any others. He wanted to make doing the laundry *fun*. So, each Duds 'N Suds store featured refreshments, games, snacks, and a clean and bright place to bring the family. By popular demand, Akin and his family began selling franchises. In August of 1985, Akin and his father were invited to meet with A. E. ("Gene") Rouse, a Phoenix millionaire who was the coinventor of the Water Pik toothbrush. "At 21, I was overwhelmed by what he was talking about," recalls Akin. "We were just family members putting up laundries."

Filled with enthusiasm and big plans, Rouse convinced the Akins to sell him 33 percent of the company for about $500,000. For his investment, Rouse was named chairman and immediately began expanding the company, hiring a group of his friends to come in and help enlarge the business.

Rouse moved the headquarters from a cramped warehouse to a modern, 3,000-square-foot office. Rouse wanted to move the headquarters to Arizona, but that's when the Akin clan put their feet down. They did not want to leave Iowa. Next, Rouse hired a team of investment bankers and underwriters to begin planning to take Duds 'N Suds public.

In early 1986, Rouse raised more capital by selling 16 percent of the company to his friends and gained control of the company. He eventually brought in $2.7 million. "In three months, the stock price rose from 30 cents a share to $4," recalls Akin.

In the first year of his control, Rouse opened 18 stores and was planning a national expansion. Then, in October 1987, the stock market crashed, obliterating all plans for the initial public offering.

Minor frictions between Rouse and the Akins began to increase to major disagreements.

"When the experts said the IPO (initial public offering) market was dead for three to four years, he had absolutely no interest in the company," says Akin.

By January 1988, Rouse had pretty much checked out of the operation. Akin said he was forced to lay off all of Rouse's expensive managers in his scramble to pay off a $350,000 bank loan.

Between January and March, Duds 'N Suds managed to pay down the bank debt to $150,000. But they still owed nearly $600,000 in fees to the accountants and lawyers who had worked on the stock offering.

To raise more cash, Akin sold off nine company-owned stores. Then, one day, his banker called and said the $150,000 loan was being called and he had to pay off the balance immediately. Akin was in shock. "They seized our operating accounts and never gave an explanation," says Akin.

On April 5, 1988, Akin's board agreed the best strategy was to file for Chapter 11 bankruptcy protection. Nine months later, the company emerged, owned by another, friendlier venture capitalist—the Iowa Venture Capital Fund.

The bankruptcy court approved a restructuring of the company, which allowed the state fund to take over the struggling enterprise. Duds 'N Suds recovered enough to have about 70 stores operating around the country in 1992.

"The second group of venture capitalists helped us get straightened out," says Akin, who learned many painful lessons.

Akin, much wiser at 29 than he had been at 21, offers this advice for other entrepreneurs considering a deal with venture capitalists:

"Realize your venture partner is someone who wants to make a very large profit on their investment and they will control that process.

"I would suggest working with a professionally managed fund, rather than an individual so you can take the emotion out of it.

"Never, ever overstate your business plan goals. In fact, underestimate what you think you will earn because the first six months are very important."

And, he says, "Call it adventure capital, because you will have one!"

25. IS IT POSSIBLE FOR ME TO RAISE MONEY FROM THE PUBLIC?

Until recently, it was virtually impossible for a small business to sell stock to the public. The expense of hiring attorneys and accountants to prepare the stock offering for review by the Securities and Exchange Commission would drive most small companies right out of business.

But a few years ago, a savvy group of state securities administrators decided to create a way for smaller companies to raise money from the public. They created the Small Corporate Offering Registration, or SCOR, for short. So far, approximately 20 states have approved this method of stock registration.

Although SCOR requires that you prepare a hefty form, resembling a detailed business plan, you do not have to deal with federal securities regulators at all.

Maybe this program is just what you need. Here's how it works:

Like many small-business owners, Elizabeth Gillenwater-Gould relied on family funds to launch her children's designer-clothing business. But when her brothers were no longer able to support the venture, she knew she had to look beyond her kin for capital. "Our business started going crazy, but we ran out of money to grow," says Gillenwater-Gould, whose Designs by Egg, Inc., is based in Phoenix.

At first, she turned to a local underwriter to raise $100,000 through a private placement offering. In 1991, she dropped that idea in favor of a public stock sale via SCOR—an undertaking that lets companies raise up to $1 million a year by selling shares at a minimum price of $5 each.

Notice of the offering must be filed with the Federal Securities and Exchange Commission. Beyond that, the federal government is not involved in the review or registration process. Instead, the states that have approved the program—among them Arizona, Washington, North Dakota, and Texas—handle the regulatory aspects.

Advocates say these state-approved securities are less risky than traditional private placement offerings—or the penny-stock offerings frequently employed by small firms—because companies must provide investors with more detailed information about the risks involved. "Investors can feel more confident because these securities have been subject to scrutiny by the state," says Fred Schaffer, the Phoenix attorney who helped draft the offering for Designs by Egg.

State-by-state registration is designed to reduce the steep costs of public stock offerings, according to its supporters. "Many companies are far too small to go to a big securities house and do a Securities and Exchange Commission-approved public offering," says Dee Harris, director of the Arizona Corporation Commission's securities division. "This allows a company to have a public offering without spending a third of the gross proceeds on the expenses involved."

The 30-page disclosure form, which must be reviewed and approved by state securities officials, serves as a detailed business plan. By answering the questions, corporate executives explain exactly how they plan to spend the money that they raise.

"Over time, we expect to see very widespread use of this program," says Scott Stapf, investor education adviser for the North American Securities Administrators Association in Washington, D.C., which developed the mechanism. "This is an effort by the states to come up with a simplified and streamlined way for small companies to raise capital."

To qualify for the program, companies must have fewer than 500 individual stockholders and assets below $3 million. Although an offering can be registered in several states, shares may only be purchased by investors living in states where the offering is registered.

Marvin Mears, president of Corporate Capital Resources, Inc., in Westlake Village, California, is working with entrepreneurs in putting together these new stock offerings in Washington, Illinois, Missouri, and Massachusetts. "This is an opportunity disguised as a lot of work," cautions Mears. "Companies putting together these offerings face a huge responsibility which comes along with raising money from the public."

Washington State is credited with pioneering the small-corporate-offering concept in the late 1980s. Of the 36 filings reviewed by state officials, 25 have been approved. "We are pleased with the number and quality of applicants we've had," says Deborah Boartner, assistant securities commissioner for the state. "We've dealt with wineries, title companies, mortgage pools, a garbage recycling center, and land development companies."

Although the offering process is simplified, it appears that small corporations are still struggling to raise funds. The handful of Washington State companies that sold stock raised about $3 million by the middle of 1991, according to Greg Toms, an analyst for the state securities division.

Meanwhile, Gillenwater-Gould, who started the children's clothing business in the basement of her Colorado Springs home, is using the money she raised to grow her company. Designs by Egg infants' and children's clothes sell in better department stores around the country. In 1990, revenues were around $90,000. With the infusion of between $250,000 and $350,000 in working capital, Gillenwater-Gould says she hopes revenues will jump to $250,000 in 1991 and more in 1992.

Mark Howells, the broker selling the Designs by Egg stock, says most of the shares have been purchased by wealthy individuals in blocks of $3,000 to $5,000.

For more information on small public stock offerings contact: Karen O'Brien, North American Securities Administrators Association, 555 New Jersey Avenue, N.W., Suite 750, Washington, DC 20001.

STATES THAT HAVE ADOPTED SCOR

1. Alaska
2. Arizona
3. Colorado
4. Idaho
5. Indiana
6. Iowa
7. Kansas
8. Maine
9. Massachusetts
10. Mississippi
11. Missouri

12. Montana
13. Nevada
14. North Carolina
15. North Dakota
16. South Dakota
17. Tennessee
18. Texas
19. Washington
20. West Virginia
21. Wisconsin
22. Wyoming

26. HOW CAN I BORROW MONEY IF I DON'T QUALIFY FOR A STANDARD BANK LOAN?

Small-business owners tired of dealing with bankers too nervous to lend them a penny can arm themselves with two effective financial tools: U.S. Small Business Administration loan guarantees and asset-based financing.

Once considered the court of last resort for high-risk borrowers, the SBA's $3.5-billion loan guarantee program became the darling of bankers across the country in the 1990s because of its solid government guarantees.

"The banking industry likes SBA loans these days," says Daniel Feiman, vice-president of Western Bank in Beverly Hills. "In the last few years, the stigma of getting an SBA loan has been blown away." Chuck Hertzberg, assistant administrator for financial assistance for the SBA in Washington, says bankers are much more receptive to making the loans in a tight lending market if the loan is guaranteed. "As the bank regulators got tougher, the lenders saw more value in the SBA program," says Hertzberg.

In mid-1991, 93 percent of all SBA-guaranteed loans were current and performing—a percentage that would make many a banker envious. Under the SBA program, the government guarantees 80 percent to 90 percent of the loan value. The participating banks can also sell the guaranteed portion of the loan on the secondary market for a premium price, although they continue to service the loan.

Qualified small-business owners like SBA loans, too. The interest rates are competitive and the borrower often has up to 10 years to pay off a machinery or working capital loan and up to 25 years for a real estate loan.

"Usually getting loans is such a pain in the neck, but this one went very smoothly," says Scott Webley, who obtained an SBA-guaranteed loan to buy the 13,000-square-foot building housing his Van Nuys, California-based ShowBiz Enterprises. "When I started looking for money, most banks only wanted to lend me 75 percent of what I needed," says Webley, whose firm posted about $2.5 million in sales in 1991. "With the SBA guarantee, I got 85 percent."

Webley put down 15 percent and borrowed $840,000 to buy the building where he and his 20 employees make theatrical draperies for television shows, rock tours, and other attractions. His loan was packaged and presented to General Bank by Jennifer Leathers, an SBA loan specialist and president of Money Source in Huntington Beach, California.

"It's the bank you have to sell on lending you the money, not the SBA," says Leathers, who is paid by the bank, not the borrower, for putting together SBA loan packages.

Despite the growing popularity of SBA loans, however, there are still myths to be dispelled. One myth is that struggling start-ups can qualify for the loan guarantees. Not so. In most cases, your business must be stable and profitable to qualify for the SBA approval. Leathers said small-business borrowers must be willing to put up virtually everything they own to collateralize the loan. "The SBA has a mission to help small-business owners, but the program has to make sense for the bank or they won't do the loan," she says.

"Another myth is that it takes a long time to get the money," says Leathers. "In fact, when I'm working with the SBA office in Los Angeles, I can get verbal loan approval in a week."

Mechanics National Bank is the number-one SBA lender in the Los Angeles area. "We have been quite busy," says Kiyo Kaneshiro, senior vice-president of the SBA division. (Mechanics' SBA division is at 8225 Alondra Boulevard, in Paramount, California.) "There seems to be quite a demand." For the nine months ending June 30, 1991, Mechanics National Bank processed 103 SBA-approved loans, with the SBA guaranteed portion totaling $29.7 million.

For detailed information on SBA loan guarantees, ask your banker or contact your nearest SBA office.

If your business doesn't qualify for an SBA loan guarantee, join the thousands of business owners around the country turning to asset-based lenders. These lenders, who are not subject to state and federal bank regulations, make higher risk loans if you have the collateral to secure them. "We are busier than we were a year ago and I think we will be even busier in the next few years," says Bron Hafner, president and owner of Celtic Capital Corp. in Santa Monica, California.

Celtic and other asset-based lenders act as middlemen, borrowing money from their banks and lending it out at higher rates. Most of Celtic's loans are in the $500,000 range, and the money is not cheap. Borrowers pay 2 to 3 percent interest on the average balance each month, compared with a commercial bank loan made at a few points over the prime rate. But for companies with credit or cash-flow problems, asset-based lenders provide an alternative to selling off a piece of your business to an equity investor or even worse—going out of business.

"Once people get over the psychological barrier of paying higher interest rates, companies like ours can be a good source of funds to help their business grow," says Hafner, who is currently lending funds to a temporary help agency, a hot dog manufacturer, a few trucking companies, and a plastics manufacturer. Typically, the amount of money advanced is based on a borrower's accounts receivable.

Hafner says most clients repay their high-interest loans within 18 months, improving their financial picture enough to move on to bank financing.

27. HOW CAN A FACTOR HELP FINANCE MY BUSINESS?

One of the keys to finding money for your business is to widen your search far beyond nervous bankers and skittish venture capitalists. Another financing option for many small-business owners is the "factor."

The original factors supervised trade conducted by the British East India Company and ran the North American trading posts for the Hudson's Bay Company, which was chartered in 1670 by Charles II of England to settle the Hudson Bay area of North America. By law, factors were entrusted with other people's goods and could act on their behalf.

Long a tradition in the textile and apparel trades, factors provide comprehensive financial services to thousands of importers, toy, shoe, and furniture manufacturers. If you are willing to pay more than the going rate for your money, a good factor will provide a steady source of cash, credit, and timely credit information on your customers.

Here's how a factor works:

The client submits a customer's order to the factor for credit approval. If the order is approved, the factor advances the client some cash, typically 80 percent of the face value of the receivables. The remaining 20 percent is credited to the client as the factor collects it.

The service that factors provide and the money they lend is not cheap: Most factors charge betwen 2 and 3 percent above the prime rate for this short-term financing. They also charge commissions ranging from 0.5 to 1.5 percent, which means that a company with

$2 million in sales could spend about $25,000 a year on commissions.

Factors point out, however, that they save companies money by virtually eliminating the need for hiring a credit and collection staff. And if a customer is insolvent and cannot pay, the factor absorbs the loss.

"The industry lends itself to products sold on short terms, usually consumer products which end up in a store," says David Rubin, president of Republic Factors Corp., one of the nation's largest factors with 400 clients and offices in Los Angeles, New York, and Charlotte, North Carolina. Rubin, who has been in the factoring business for 39 years, says traditional bankers are especially wary of lending to apparel and textile companies because these businesses are usually highly leveraged and undercapitalized. Although the factor takes a risk by lending to high-risk businesses, factors also protect themselves by buying credit insurance. (See 79. How Can I Protect My Business If My Customers Fail?)

Republic and other major factors, including Heller Financial Factoring Group and Bankers Trust, prefer to deal with companies with $200,000 in capital and annual sales of about $3 million. However, smaller companies rejected by the larger firms can turn to second-tier factors, which deal with smaller, riskier firms.

As good as it sounds, factoring does have its dark side, according to Richard Reinis, a Los Angeles attorney who represents dozens of apparel makers. "A factoring agreement is a very Mephistophelian deal," warns Reinis. "It is very easy to get into and very difficult to get out of."

Reinis said it is especially hard to change factors because they are so involved in your company's day-to-day operations. One of his clients once paid $60,000 in legal fees to disentangle herself from a factoring agreement.

He urges business owners to be aware of the tremendous control the factor has over your business. "You should know that the advances, which become the mother's milk of manufacturing, can be altered at any time if there has been a material adverse change in your financial condition," says Reinis.

FACTORS

Attorney Richard Reinis offers these tips on choosing a factor:

■ Take 10 to 20 orders and give them to three or four differ-ent factors to see how much credit they will give you. Choose the one that gives you the most credit.

■ Choose a factor that understands your niche in the market and may even represent your competitors.

■ Choose a factor that has a credit staff large enough to properly review your accounts. The more accurate they are, the better off you are.

■ Try to include a bailout clause in your agreement, permit-ting you to end the agreement after giving a 60- to 90-day notice.

■ Keep careful track of all your credit approvals and ad-vances. Document all conversations with follow-up letters to your account representative to protect yourself.

28. HOW CAN I CHECK OUT MY COMPETITION?

I'm amazed by how many new business owners jump into a venture without knowing if someone else is already out there selling similar services or products. Remember: The most successful small businesses flourish not only because they produce a great product or provide a great service, but because they fill a *specific* gap in the marketplace. That's why it is essential to learn everything you can about the competition before jumping in.

There is *no* excuse for not doing market research; saying you don't have the time or the money just doesn't wash. You don't need to hire a team of researchers. You can do it yourself by visiting your competitors' stores and buying their products. If you can't afford to keep their products, buy them, examine them, and return them.

Ask friends and neighbors who use similar products what they think about them—what they like and don't like. Listen carefully.

A trip to the library will provide recent newspaper and magazine articles about your particular industry. Don't be surprised to find others busy at work on ideas similar to yours; the old saying, "great minds think alike," is very true when it comes to entrepreneurs. You'd be surprised how many inventors send me similar devices. In 1991, for instance, I was swamped with aluminum can crushers as recycling became fashionable again. But the world doesn't need 10 different can crushers and the market cannot support that many. So before you invent another can crusher, or whatever it is you want to sell, *check out your competition*.

In marketing my syndicated "Succeeding in Small Business" column and the spinoff projects created by its success, I've learned that keeping abreast of the competition is critical. Really knowing what was already on the market worked to my advantage. If the world was glutted with small-business columns, there wouldn't have been room for mine.

In 1988, *Los Angeles Times* editor Shelby Coffey III and former *Times* business editor Martin Baron asked me to develop a management column for business owners. Although I was a veteran financial writer who specialized in reporting on white-collar crime, I didn't have a clue about how to run a small business. I knew the only way to make the column work was to turn to successful business owners for the advice.

When appreciative letters and phone calls from business owners poured in, we knew that small-business owners were hungry for practical, inspirational information they could use every day. This proved the column filled a need in the marketplace.

With the column well-established in the *Times*, Howard Bragman, a friend, mentor, and savvy public relations counselor, suggested that I try to syndicate the column to other newspapers. "If it's a hit in Los Angeles, it can be a hit in Chicago and Des Moines," said Howard.

Dubious at first, I agreed to make a presentation to the *Los Angeles Times* Syndicate, my first and most likely choice for a syndicate. Based on the letters sent from readers in other states, I knew the column was being pulled off the *Los Angeles Times-Washington Post* News Service and published regularly in other newspapers; as news service subscribers, the editors had access to my column at no additional charge. The question was: Would they pay for it once it was syndicated?

Before making a presentation to the Syndicate, I consulted a syndication directory and found very few small-business columns out there. My closest competitor was Mark Stevens, a self-syndicated writer who claimed his work appeared in more than 100 papers. To make sure my product—the column—was different, we planned to include graphics (tip boxes) and black-and-white photographs produced by the *Times*. I knew these extras would appeal to business editors, who are always struggling to illustrate their pages.

Confident that the market would welcome a fresh, new, real-world column for small-business owners, I made my pitch to Syndicate president Jesse Levine and executive editor Steven Christensen. My presentation included a marketing plan, much like one you would write for your business. Within 18 months we had far exceeded the goal of selling the column to 10 newspapers. (The exact number is confidential—a quirk of the syndication business.)

With the syndication growing, I revised my marketing plan. The next step was this book, because readers were always asking where they could buy my books.

Before putting together the book proposal, I spent hours reading every book I could find on small-business management. I saw what was on the market. I figured out what I could do that was not only different, but would fill a gap in the marketplace. Beyond the weekly column and books, my market research revealed a real demand for affordable, how-to booklets for small-business owners. Responding to the need, my husband, Joe Applegate (a skilled writer and editor), and I have put together a series of "Succeeding in Small Business" booklets (see Resources guide).

I use myself as an example to emphasize that no matter what you plan to sell, you must first make sure someone is out there to buy it.

You will not succeed if you start your business in a vacuum. So introduce yourself to other people in your industry. Join a business organization or drop by the Chamber of Commerce for a mixer. Spend time and money attending conferences, seminars, and trade shows for your industry. Talk to potential customers, vendors, and brokers about your idea, unless it is top secret. You'll be amazed at the information you can pick up without making much of an effort.

For instance, people who already deal with your competitors can provide you with a treasure of valuable information. I don't mean you should ask them for trade secrets, but for general information about whether or not your competitors have new products on the way. Find out whether their business is going up or down. Are they hiring, firing, building a new plant, moving out of town, or slashing inventory? Just knowing whether your competitor has hired or laid off the second shift is extremely important to your new business.

If you need help, the marketing department of any college or university usually has students eager to do research projects. Or you can hire the best professional researchers you can find.

Seena Sharp, a veteran researcher and principal of Sharp Information Research in Hermosa Beach, California, offers what she calls "direct competitive intelligence" to business owners. Sharp actually contacts people at the company you want to know about and asks them detailed questions about their businesses, products, and strategies. "It constantly surprises me that we get responses to 95 percent of the questions," says Sharp, who always identifies herself as a professional researcher. "We start with people at the lower levels and work our way up to the president."

She was recently astonished by one series of interviews she did for a client interested in what his competitor was up to. "People at the competing company told us everything about a product that was due to be released in a year and a half," marvels Sharp. "It was unbelievable."

A note of caution: If you don't want your competitors to know what you are doing, instruct your employees *not* to discuss company secrets or strategy with people who call in for information. If appropriate, ask key employees to sign secrecy agreements or noncompete agreements. And if you give tours of your plant to the public, don't include any area where proprietary work is being done.

Remember, your valuable secrets can easily end up in a competitor's hands!

TIPS

Here are some affordable research tips from *Inc.* magazine's special 1991 "Small Business Success" issue:

- Find out where the managers of your competing firms congregate. Visit those restaurants or work out in the same gyms. You'll be surprised how much people will say about their business dealings in a casual setting.
- If you are in a fast-changing, high-technology field, read the *Official Gazette*, a government publication that reports on newly patented products.
- If you can afford it, hire a clipping service to collect newspaper and magazine articles about your industry for a few months. Clipping services can cover a wide field or a very narrow one, depending on how much you want to spend.
- Stockbrokers and security analysts can be very helpful in providing a sense of what is happening in your particular industry. It may be worth buying a few shares of stock in a competitor's firm if it is publicly held, just so you can receive the annual and quarterly reports.

29. HOW DO I GET MYSELF AND MY BUSINESS ORGANIZED?

For three days, Sally Bishop and Tom Brohard examined and sorted every single piece of paper stacked in Brohard's disorganized office.

"We unpacked two moving boxes filled with papers I hadn't looked at in five years," admits Brohard, an owner and manager of Willdan Associates, an engineering and planning firm in the City of Industry, California. "I had stacks of paper, but I couldn't put my hands on what I needed," says Brohard, who is paying Sally Bishop, a partner in Insight Consulting Group, based in Santa Monica, California, thousands of dollars to get himself and his 145 employees better organized.

Getting organized is on just about everyone's "things to do" list, but few people, especially busy entrepreneurs, actually take the time to do something. Yet professional organizers say business owners overwhelmed with undone paperwork lose money and business because they have lost control over their lives—surely a major consideration when it's *your* money and *your* business.

"If you really dread approaching your desk, that feeling of dread will impact on what you do that day," warns consultant Beverly Clower, owner of Office Overhaul, in Santa Monica. "If you are not processing things daily, you will forget appointments and begin missing out on important things."

Professional organizers say many entrepreneurs are overwhelmed with paperwork because they are so busy running the business they don't have time to deal with it.

Time-management consultants estimate the typical manager has 35 to 42 hours' worth of work within arm's reach of his or her chair, yet only 10 hours available each week to do it.

"If you are under an avalanche, it doesn't feel too good," says Sally Bishop. "We help people dig themselves out from underneath the avalanche and set up monitoring systems to get them from A to B."

Bishop and others say being better organized not only alleviates stress by giving you control over your time, but frequently results in increased profits because you spend less time on paperwork and more time making strategic decisions.

Stephanie Winston, author of *The Organized Executive* and founder of The Organizing Principle in Manhattan, often calculates exactly how much money her clients lose each year by spending valuable time looking for lost papers or proposals. While digging through her clients' stacks of unread material, she often finds letters and proposals that add up to lost business—and lost profits.

Once she straightens out the physical surroundings, Winston teaches people how proper delegation can free them up to make more money. "One of my clients, whose company produces newsletters for banks, felt he was spending far too much time putting the newsletters together instead of bringing in new business," says Winston. By shifting some of his production tasks to others, he gained seven free hours a week. He used the time to solicit new customers and within a few months increased his business by one-third.

Professional organizers—and there are hundreds around the country—all have their own pet systems for handling paperwork. Organizers' theories differ, but all advocate handling a piece of paper one time only. Winston says there are only four things to do with a piece of paper: "Toss it, refer it, act on it, or file it." She calls this her TRAF system.

Stephanie Culp, author of *How to Conquer Clutter*, suggests setting up four baskets, marking them: "To Do," "To Pay," "To File," and "To Read." The "To File" basket might be a large wicker basket stashed under your desk.

The "To Do" and "To Pay" baskets should sit on your desk for immediate attention, but the "To Read" basket should be kept behind or beside your work area to be carted off later. Some people also like to add a "Calls to Make" basket and a "To Buy" basket. Culp suggests forgetting a "Pending" basket—work could languish there forever.

The last, and probably most important, basket is the trash basket, which should be big and easy to carry. In the spirit of conserving our natural resources, many businesses have begun to recycle paper.

Insight Consulting's Russell Bishop encourages clients to use task assignment forms, which are 8 × 11–inch sheets of paper attached to material you want to refer to others. The full-size sheets provide ample space to write instructions, due dates, and follow-up requests. Bishop says it shouldn't take more than five minutes to review and decide what to do with each piece of paper on your desk.

Although learning to properly sort, toss, and file paper is a big step toward getting organized, organizers say busy entrepreneurs must also learn to delegate certain tasks to others if they want to succeed. If you can't afford full-time help, try a part-time assistant, temporary worker, or student intern from a local business or professional school.

Professional organizers recommend spending 15 minutes at the end of each day preparing for the next day. Taking time to clear off your desk and plan ahead is essential to staying in control and better organized. (See the Ten Commandments, page xiii.)

GETTING ORGANIZED

If you can't afford to hire a professional organizer, some terrific books are available. There is also a myriad of nifty filing systems, organizers, and office supplies designed to streamline your office and your life.

Try these books:

- *The Organized Executive*, by Stephanie Winston, Warner Books, $8.95.
- *How To Conquer Clutter*, by Stephanie Culp, Writer's Digest Books, $10.95.
- *Organized to Be the Best!* by Susan Silver, Adams-Hall, $12.95.
- Also, *How to File and Find It* is an excellent free booklet available from the Quill Corp. Business Library. Write or call Quill Corp., 100 Schelter Road, Lincolnshire, IL 60069. Phone (708)634-4850.

To find a professional organizer, contact the National Assn. of Professional Organizers, 1163 Shermer Road, Northbrook, IL 60062. Phone (708)272-0135. The group's membership directory is available for $15.00.

Author Susan Silver offers these tips for getting your life together:

- Write a list of business and personal goals.
- Adopt a time-management system to help you keep track of details, deadlines, and demands.
- Develop a company-wide paperwork system and a well-organized filing system.
- Regularly clean out and organize your computer files.
- Redesign your work space to make it more comfortable.
- Buy equipment designed to make your work life easier, including a telephone headset if you are on the phone more than one hour a day.

■

30. WHAT KIND OF EQUIPMENT DO I NEED TO RUN A BUSINESS FROM HOME?

This is an important question. There are things that everyone needs and equipment that might make *you* especially productive. But be careful: The glossy brochures might label as "essential" something that doesn't work and eats up cash.

The exact make and models you need depend on what you want the machines to do, but you will definitely need:

■ *One to three separate phone lines:* One for the phone, one for the modem in your computer, and one for the fax machine. It is possible, but a real hassle, for the telephone and fax machine or fax and modem to share a line. It is worth a few dollars a month to leave the fax permanently hooked up to its own line.

■ *A personal computer with the appropriate software and possibly a copier.* Many fax machines can copy a document if you don't need a plain paper copy.

■ *A comfortable desk chair.* This is essential. So is a well-lit work area, desk or table, and some shelves for books.

I also have a map over my computer to figure out where places are when I am writing about them. Reference books, including a dictionary, thesaurus, and style book are also helpful.

Where you work, whether it is in a converted closet or a spacious basement, is not as important as making sure it is comfortable and conducive to work.

It is very important, for tax purposes, that your office be used only for your business. If you want to qualify for the legitimate tax deductions, you must be able to show that the space, and everything in it, is used only for running your business.

Consult a CPA for exact details on home-office deductions.

31. SHOULD I BUY, RENT, OR LEASE MY COMPUTER SYSTEM?

I can't imagine going into business today without some type of computer system. Even the tiniest home-based business can get a flying start with a personal computer and a handful of easy-to-use software programs.

So, don't say "if" you get a computer. Say, "when" and read on to figure out whether you should buy, lease, or rent a system. With all the simple and affordable word-processing and accounting programs on the market, buying a computer may well be the first thing you do, after installing a business telephone.

First, meet Tony Fung, a computer-lover who turned his passion into a thriving small business:

Like many small-business owners, Tony Fung, founder and chief executive of American Cryptronics Corp. in Costa Mesa, California, rents personal computers to run his business. But unlike businesses that rent a couple of machines a month, Fung spends about $5,000 a month renting different models for his engineers to take apart in order to develop new computer add-ons and accessories.

"If we had to buy every one of them, it would cost $20,000 to $30,000 every month," says Fung, whose company develops 40 to 50 new computer products a year. "It would be very difficult to generate that kind of capital, so for us renting is the way to go."

Small-business owners such as Fung are contributing mightily to the growing computer rental business, which is estimated at $500 million a year. Although renting is perfect for short-term needs, including special projects, and for people who want to try out a system before buying one, many business owners also turn to leasing for long-term needs. Consequently, leasing is a growing, multi-billion-dollar industry. IBM Credit Corp., for example, reported nearly $5 billion in leasing business in 1990.

The chief advantage of renting or leasing computers is to free up cash for other purposes. Another benefit is that in most cases, the rental or lease payments are fully deductible as a business expense.

But let's dispel one common misconception about leasing: If you don't have the cash and the bank won't make you a loan, don't count on being able to lease the equipment either.

Because leasing is basically 100 percent financing, your credit history and financial statements will be carefully scrutinized. In many cases, you will be asked to guarantee the lease payments personally, even if your business is incorporated.

"Renting and leasing computers is not just for large companies anymore," says Gary Phillips, senior vice-president of Electro Rent Corp. in Van Nuys, California. "It also benefits small and midsized companies that want to preserve their capital equipment budget." Phillips says his firm is seeing an increase in orders from project-oriented companies, including architectural, engineering, and accounting firms.

When you are just starting out, you can easily be overwhelmed by the amount of computer equipment on the market. Don't be afraid to ask for help. Just because you are an expert in making drivers doesn't mean you know anything about disc drives. Although store salespeople are very helpful, I suggest spending some time and money on an independent computer consultant.

"Our job is to define how the business owner wants to use the computer within their business first, then we choose the software and finally the hardware," explains Mel Mitchell, managing director of System Technology Group, a consulting firm in Encino that works with many small-business owners.

Once you decide what you need, it's time to figure out a budget and a plan to pay for the system.

"There are two basic types of leases," says Neil Leddy, a senior account representative for Apple Commercial Credit in Chino Hills,

California. "In a true lease, the customer can buy the equipment, return it, or continue leasing it," whereas with a "bargain purchase lease" the customer pays a bit more each month for the option to buy the equipment at the end of the lease, often for as little as $1.

A $10,000 computer system, including a high-quality printer, can be leased for about $230 a month. Most commercial lease agreements run three to five years. You should also expect to pay about two months' payments or a security deposit before the equipment is delivered.

In addition to the monthly payment, the customer is responsible for making sure the equipment is properly insured against damage or theft. You must also pay for any service or maintenance costs and for all sales tax due. "Equipment leases are not cancelable," warns Leddy. That means if your business dies, you are still responsible for the lease payments.

When comparing prices, Leddy suggests asking questions to be sure you understand exactly what the agreement covers and if there are any hidden costs, including documentation fees. These fees might be as low as $50 to write up the lease, or as high as 2 percent of the total lease amount.

Leddy says business owners can deal with lease brokers, who generally handle all kinds of equipment, a corporate lessor, such as Apple Commercial Credit, which usually represents one major company, or a captive leasing company, such as one owned by IBM, GE, or AT&T.

A few years ago, most computer rental companies were mom-and-pop enterprises. Today, big companies, sensing a growth opportunity, have moved into the market. Businessland, believed to be the nation's largest personal computer retailer, has rental centers in Chicago, Los Angeles, and San Francisco and is currently expanding to the East Coast. GE Rents, an Atlanta-based division of General Electric, rents equipment by the day, week, month, or year. PCR Personal Computer Rentals, based in Cranbury, New Jersey, has more than 60 franchised locations throughout the United States.

John Doyle, vice-president of marketing for IBM Credit Corp. in Stamford, Connecticut, says most small businesses are more likely to buy their first, small computer system outright. But as the businesses grow and need more powerful and expensive computer systems, they are more likely to finance the next step. He advises small-business owners to think ahead and choose a system that can handle their growth requirements over a two- or three-year period.

Don't overlook one more option: used equipment.

There is a growing market for used computer equipment—stuff that is perfectly good, but obsolete or outgrown. Check your Yellow Pages under computers or visit a computer swap meet.

SMART LEASING

- Determine what kind of computer system you need before you contact a leasing company.
- Compare the cost of down payments, security deposits, and documentation fees.
- Find out whether the lease contains an obsolescence clause and how the company handles requests to upgrade equipment.
- Ask if there are prepayment penalties. It is usually very expensive to pay off the lease early.
- Ask your accountant and your attorney to review everything before you sign any documents. Leases are complex legal agreements.

32. HOW DO I FIND A GOOD ATTORNEY?

When you are starting a business, it is natural to try to save money at every turn. But it doesn't pay to scrimp when it comes to getting solid legal advice.

Most business owners' first encounter with legal forms comes with a DBA, which means "doing business as" and is legally referred to as a fictitious name statement. Beyond this first step, you'll need good legal advice to buy or sell real estate, form a partnership, create job applications, and review employee handbooks.

A good small-business attorney will protect you and your business from legal troubles involving employees, vendors, and customers. He or she can also help when you are looking for investors or dealing with bankers.

Finding a good attorney is not as challenging as you think. There are about 729,000 practicing attorneys in this country, with three out of four working for themselves or a small firm, according to Brad Carr, spokesman for the New York State Bar Association. The best way to find a good lawyer is to ask other small-business owners if they would recommend their own attorney. Your banker and your accountant may have some recommendations; ministers and rabbis are also good sources of referrals, because they know so many people in the community.

Another way to find one is through legal directories. The reference section of most larger public libraries should have the *Martindale-Hubbell Law Directory*. This directory provides brief biographical information about lawyers in your area. Some listings also include the names of other clients so you may call them for references.

Most state bar associations offer free referral services to help people find the right lawyer. Call the bar association in your state (usually located in the state capital) and ask for the number. Most lawyers listed through the referral service charge a modest fee for an initial consultation.

Remember, hiring an attorney is a very personal thing. Be sure to choose someone who you can confide in, who makes a good impression, and who has experience in your industry. Your attorney represents more than your company—he or she represents you to the public wherever he goes.

Don't be shy about discussing the hourly fees and expenses you will be charged. "A lawyer might not be able to determine the exact amount of money you'll have to pay for his services, but he can usually provide an estimate based on past experience," says Carr.

A glut of attorneys, especially in big cities, has forced many attorneys to reduce their fees to beat the competition. Most are happy to work by the project and do not expect to be put on a monthly retainer. Some attorneys who specialize in working with entrepreneurs will take you on as a client in exchange for stock in your company or profit-sharing down the line. If an attorney is willing to work on this basis, consider making him or her a part of your strategic team.

The hourly fees you'll pay depend on where you live. For instance, business owners in New York City and Los Angeles generally pay higher legal fees than those living and working in Omaha.

When you are interviewing prospective attorneys, ask these questions:

- Are you a member of the state bar and licensed to practice law in this state? (If your company does a lot of interstate commerce, you might want to hire an attorney who can practice in the federal courts as well.)
- What other kinds of small businesses do you represent?
- How long have you been practicing law?
- Who can I call for a reference?

WHEN IT'S A LEGAL MATTER . . . HOW TO WORK BEST WITH YOUR LAWYER

■ Write down the names, addresses, and telephone numbers of all persons involved and all the facts you can recall that pertain to your case. By doing this yourself, you will cut the time your lawyer will have to spend gathering the information.

■ Take all papers relating to the case to the first meeting.

■ Be as concise as possible in all interviews with your lawyer. (Remember, time is money.)

■ Be honest and tell your lawyer all the facts—good and bad. Your lawyer must keep them in strictest confidence and must know everything about the matter in order to best represent you.

■ Have your lawyer analyze the matter and give you the pluses and minuses. Don't expect simple solutions to complex problems.

■ Have your lawyer explain the various steps involved in handling your matter and ask for an estimate of how long it will take. Ask your lawyer to keep you informed of any new developments.

■ Avoid unnecessary telephone calls to your lawyer, but do call when you think it's necessary or if there are new developments.

■ See a lawyer before signing documents or taking legal action. Be sure you understand the ramifications of what you are signing or doing.

■ Remember: No lawyer can guarantee the outcome of any case.

———————————————— ■ ————————————————

SOURCE: New York State Bar Association

33. HOW DO I FIND A GOOD ACCOUNTANT?

Dealing with money is one of the scariest aspects of owning your own business. Figuring out how to make it is one thing, but managing it is quite another.

At first, you can rely on a simple software program like Quicken, Money Matters, or One-Write Plus to keep the books. Quicken, which I started out with, is much like a checkbook register and is very easy to use. Nevertheless, I soon found that keeping the books after a long day of work was sheer hell.

Eventually, if your business grows, you will need to retain an accountant to keep your books straight and to keep *you* straight with the Internal Revenue Service.

The best way to find a good small-business accountant is to ask friends and colleagues for personal recommendations.

Your lawyer or banker may also have some suggestions. You shouldn't have any trouble finding an accountant, even in a small town. There are plenty of them around. The American Institute of Certified Public Accountants has more than 248,000 members, with about 118,000 in public practice.

Your accountant should be one of your closest and most trusted advisers. You'll want to retain someone who is compatible and a good listener, as well as a good number-cruncher. Your accountant should also help introduce you to good business contacts.

Accountants don't just prepare tax returns. They help you with tax planning and can provide overall management assistance. They can also prepare financial reports, provide assistance in securing loans, and design customized accounting systems for your business or personal needs. The firm or person you hire should be able to provide every service you need. For instance, if you need audited financial statements, be sure you hire someone qualified to produce them.

Accountants' fees vary widely. The charges depend on the experience level of the person working for you.

TIPS

Here are some tips on how to get the most value from your CPA from Levine, Cooper, Spiegel & Co. in Los Angeles:

■ Be prepared to discuss your plans and objectives. CPAs are in the best position to advise you and serve your interests if they understand what goals you have set.

■ Explain clearly what you expect and hope from the CPA's services.

■ Keep good records and help your CPA save you money by not using his or her professional time for routine work, such as gathering results.

■ Keep your CPA informed of changes and new directions in your business.

34. SHOULD I HAVE A BOARD OF ADVISERS?

Huge public corporations have them. Tiny nonprofit organizations have them. Most small businesses don't.

What are they?

Boards of advisers or directors.

If small-business owners have any boards at all, they are usually relatives, friends, and maybe an investor. The board usually meets no more than once a year, and it's usually more of a social event than a work session.

If this sounds familiar, read on. Having a bad board is a waste of time, especially when you *need* expert help to run your company. On the other hand, a strong board, made up of respected advisers, gives you perspective, boosts your morale, and can keep you from making terrible mistakes. Good board members are independent, objective thinkers who help solve your tough business problems.

The best advisory board is comprised of people who you not only respect, but who complement your strengths and shore up your weaknesses.

It is important to note the legal differences between advisers and directors. Advisers are unpaid volunteers with no real legal liability. By contrast, a director carries heavy legal and fiduciary responsibilities for your company.

Directors also expect to be paid an annual fee, plus a fee for every meeting they attend. And, most won't serve until you buy an officers' and directors' insurance policy to protect them from personal liability. Advisers, on the other hand, especially small-business advisers, are usually content with a good meal and a well-run, productive meeting.

One bank manager I know hosts a monthly lunch for his informal advisers, who are local community and business leaders. To make them feel close to the bank, he gives everyone personal business cards with the bank's logo. He encourages them to bring in new accounts and serve as members of his marketing team. And he treats them royally every time they set foot in the lobby.

"When entrepreneurs ask, 'Who would do this for me?' I answer, 'Nearly everybody would,' " says Stephen Bennett, a partner in the Los Angeles consulting firm of Schwab, Bennett & Associates. Bennett, who has established boards for nonprofits and large and small companies, says most people are flattered to be asked for their personal opinion.

"In some cases, it's appropriate to put some of your better customers on the advisory board," says Bennett. For instance, if you are in the retail business, you should definitely have consumers on your board.

Bennett's favorite option for a growing business is to set up small ad hoc advisory groups to deal with specific problems within a short period of time.

"Ask them to meet with you only three times for 90 minutes each," advises Bennett. "Then, be very focused, present the problems and the data, identify issues, and ask them to do some homework and come up with recommendations."

Once, when he was advising a company that makes cabinets for new homes, he invited a few local housewives to tour three model homes and tell the builder what features appealed to them. "We had the builders and carpenters there to listen to comments," says Bennett. "We didn't have to pay the women. We bought them lunch."

Bennett also created an ad hoc committee to help his brother Mickey figure out how to boost sales at his northern California Western-wear and feed store. "He couldn't decide if they were selling hay or Levis," notes Bennett, who invited customers, friends, and the family banker to visit the store and make suggestions.

"We had a barbeque in the parking lot and invited everybody

to walk through the store and tell us what they thought of it," Bennett says. Based on their comments, his brother built a separate warehouse on the property to store the feed and grain. Then he decorated the remaining retail areas with saddles and harnesses to maintain the Western theme. Business picked up and Stephen Bennett was paid in clothes and cowboy boots for his consulting time.

Kent Graham, president of the Los Angeles Chapter of the National Association of Corporate Directors and a partner at O'Melveny & Meyers in Los Angeles, suggests bringing in advisers whose skill and experience levels are higher than yours. But if yours is a public corporation that needs a board, be prepared to pay for the expertise. Midsized public companies usually pay directors between $7,500 and $20,000 a year, according to industry studies.

On the other hand, Graham says small, privately held companies should expect to pay their advisers between $5,000 and $10,000 a year. And if your company is privately held, you might be asked to write a letter of indemnification to assure your advisers that you will protect them from legal action.

When selecting your advisers, either formal or informal ones, be sure to check their references. Remember, these folks will be privy to your most confidential business information. You want to be sure they will not betray any confidences or misuse their connections with your company.

Good advisers can help you survive the setbacks and celebrate the successes. My personal advisory board has been meeting regularly since 1990. We are all small-business owners. We support each other, offer constructive criticism, and listen to each other wail when times are tough.

We have wonderful brainstorming sessions. We also refer quite a bit of business to each other because we know we will do the best job possible for each other's clients.

I can't imagine running The Applegate Group without my advisory board. And I know I owe a good deal of my success to their support and invaluable advice.

35. WHO WILL HELP MY BUSINESS FOR FREE?

More small businesses fail due to a lack of information than a lack of money. They also fail when their owners are too stubborn to admit they need help. But take heart: There is absolutely no reason to fret and feel you are alone in facing your troubles.

Free help is available across the country, if you know where to look.

Jack Evans, maker of Comfy-Back Cushions, saved his small business by openly admitting he needed help. You can, too. Here's what happened:

Arnold Schott walked into the cramped offices of the E.J. Evans Co., in Venice, California, eying stacks of Comfy-Back foam cushions piled high on every surface.

"I asked Jack Evans, the owner, if he had a business plan," recalls Schott, a volunteer counselor for the Small Business Administration's Service Corps of Retired Executives (SCORE). "He didn't know what that was."

No wonder the seat cushion company was losing money every month! "Our sales were growing each month, but we were still short of cash because we were underpricing the cushions," confides Evans.

A year and a half after his first meeting with Schott, Evans had a detailed business plan, a new accountant, cost controls, a toll-free 800 number for customers, and several major retail clients. "We have increased sales by five times since we started working with Mr. Schott," says Evans, who openly credits Schott for revitalizing his ailing company. "When he first got here, we had no internal controls, no cash flow information, and we didn't know if we were making or losing money."

Schott modestly accepts Evans's warm praise. "If people would come to us at SCORE, we could prevent a lot of failures," says Schott. "The talents we have are unbelievable."

Schott, in his late seventies, is one of 13,000 volunteer SCORE counselors providing free advice to small-business owners across the United States. In the 1940s, he started Pacific Electricord, a Gardena, California, maker of electric cords and cable, in his garage. By the time he sold the business in 1972, it had 400 employees and $40 million in sales. "I get a great deal of satisfaction out of helping people like Jack," says Schott.

Since its inception in 1964, SCORE has provided counseling and training for nearly 3 million small-business owners. The Small Business Administration supplies office and meeting space for SCORE members, management assistance, and about $2.5 million a year for the association's activities.

Although the help offered is expert and free, only about 20 percent of the nation's small-business owners are aware that SCORE exists, according to a recent SBA survey. In response, SCORE is trying to raise its profile by targeting inexperienced entrepreneurs, women, and minorities.

Just about anyone can make it through the first year or so, but the critical time for a small business is the first three years. Yet many entrepreneurs are reluctant to seek help from the government because they are afraid to disclose sensitive financial information to their counselors. Not to worry: Anything you tell a SCORE counselor remains completely confidential.

Jack Evans said his cushion business limped along for about six years before he contacted SCORE. Evans, a reluctant entrepreneur, worked as a journalist and schoolteacher. When he was younger, he had resisted every effort his parents made to interest him in taking over their modern furniture store in Los Angeles. "I told my father to sell it," admits Evans. "I didn't want it." His parents eventually sold the business, but his mother found retirement boring and now works full-time with her son at the cushion company.

Like many inventions, the Comfy-Back seat cushion was born

out of necessity. Evans was searching for seat cushions to help his father, who has Parkinson's disease, feel more comfortable. When he couldn't find one he liked, he designed one himself and had it made.

At first, Evans sold the rounded cushions through the mail. Later, he hired sales reps who took the product to medical supply stores. By the fall of 1988, Mrs. Evans said she was tired of subsidizing the business. Reluctantly, Evans called the Santa Monica, California, SBA office and asked them to send over a SCORE counselor skilled in manufacturing.

Two weeks later, Schott arrived, and the rest is history.

There are some 400 chapters and 760 counseling locations nationwide. Finding a SCORE counselor is easy: Call either your local SBA office or SBA's toll-free member: (800)827-5722.

36. HOW DO I CREATE A SOLID PARTNERSHIP?

Forging a solid business partnership is hard work. Entrepreneurs tend to be stubborn, single-minded, and uncooperative. Put two or three together and you may often wind up with a recipe for disaster. But if you choose partners who complement your strengths and weaknesses, you can benefit by sharing both the risks and the joys.

Meet the team at Enforcer Products in Georgia.

When Jim Biggs returns the title of president to Wayne Biasetti every two years, there is no ceremonial handing over of the company car keys. "There is no Mercedes," says Biggs, laughing; he also serves as vice-president of sales and marketing for the Cartersville, Georgia, company. "Wayne and I drive identical Chevy trucks. He's got a white one and I've got a gray one."

Biasetti, who founded the growing pesticide and home products company in 1977, decided that sharing power as well as stock with his partners was the best way to keep them happy and productive. Biasetti and Biggs each hold a 40 percent share of the company. Ed Brush, who joined them in 1985, owns the other 20 percent. In order to keep things equal, Biasetti says they took the prestige out of the presidency and rotate the job every two years.

Other than alerting their bankers and attorneys to the change, not much else happens when the power shifts, he says. Employees have no problems adjusting because the partners don't make a big deal about it.

As the company grew, Biasetti says he sought out partners to complement his personal strengths and weaknesses. "I can't imagine a man so diverse in his talents that he could understand chemists and machinery and deal with the balance sheet and the bankers," says Biasetti. "My advice to other entrepreneurs is to get a partner who is good at your weakest thing."

That's good advice, according to Gerald Newmark, a Tarzana, California, management consultant and business owner who specializes in building successful partnerships. Newmark says sharing power is one way to keep a partnership in balance and thriving. Open communication is another essential ingredient. "The most important thing is not to be secretive," says Newmark. "Partners need to have structured time together and regular meetings."

Partners who don't trust and rely on each other are doomed to fail. "Too many partners give lip service to the term *teamwork*," says Newmark. "They think, 'I know what's right so why doesn't my partner understand me?' "

Benjamin Benson, a consultant and family business expert in Boynton Beach, Florida, believes that shared management is effective only if there is a high degree of trust among the owners. "It helps if each owner is relatively equal in ability and responsible for different segments of the business," he writes in *Your Family Business* (See "Books" in Resources guide). "It's also important that the owners have the ability to compromise and reach consensus in decision making."

Back at Enforcer Products, no major decision is made unless all three partners agree. "We have to agree or we all go down the tubes together," says Biasetti, a former chemical plant manager who is responsible for developing most of Enforcer's products.

While Biasetti is busy in the laboratory and production area, Biggs supervises all sales and marketing efforts. Treasurer Ed Brush is responsible for administrative, data processing, and financial issues.

In separate interviews at Enforcer's sprawling headquarters, the partners agreed that the secret of their success was to divide the responsibilities and try not to step on each other's toes. "I'm by no means the smartest one of the three," claims Biasetti. Although he has an MBA, Biasetti admits he is weak on matters of finance. That's why he hired Brush, who used to keep Enforcer's books in his spare time while working for another company. Biggs, who formerly sold mildew remover for another home-care products company, guides a nationwide sales force of about 40 and deals with a network of 50 manufacturers representatives. Biggs and Biasetti met while they were both selling products to hardware stores.

The company recently bought a fleet of bicycles to help employees get around the company's 100,000-square-foot warehouse. In 1991, Enforcer Products projected $50 million in revenues from its 45 home-care and pesticide products.

BUILDING STRONG PARTNERSHIPS

- Find someone whose strengths complement your weaknesses.
- Set up a trial period to see if you can work well together.
- Make no promises or financial commitments until you are sure the chemistry is right.
- Consider rotating positions and titles.
- Communicate regularly to avoid power grabs and misunderstandings.
- Define who will contribute the cash, property, or expertise.
- Specify the percentage of ownership each person will have.
- Prepare a business plan and financial forecast for the life of the partnership.
- Figure out who will provide additional cash if it is needed.
- Be sure the tax profit-and-loss allocations are consistent and fair for all the partners involved.
- Provide a way to remove or buy out partners who fail to meet their obligations.
- Define how, when, and in what order the profits will be distributed to partners.
- Communicate openly and honestly with your partners.

37. HOW CAN A BUSINESS INCUBATOR NURTURE MY BUSINESS?

Surrounded by acres of lush Iowa cornfields, the Golden Circle Business Center is home to 26 growing businesses. Located on the campus of the Des Moines Area Community College in Ankeny, the sprawling, utilitarian complex provides space and support services for entrepreneurs making everything from sausage to electronic elbows.

Last year, the Center's tenants collectively brought in $6 million in sales and employed 80 people, according to executive director Wayne Haines. The Center is also home to Drake University's Small Business Development Center and a Small Business Administration contract procurement center.

Dan Truckenmiller moved his Test Inc. operations from his basement to the Business Center in February 1990. Today, his growing business provides safety training programs and a variety of services for the transportation industry. "Someone at the Chamber of Commerce told me there was an 'incubator' up at the college," Truckenmiller recalls. "I said, 'I don't know what the heck an incubator is.'"

Many small-business owners still don't know how much support an incubator can provide or that there are approximately 400 incubators in 41 states. Each month, about five new incubators open somewhere in the United States. California, Oklahoma, Texas, Indiana, and Mississippi are experiencing the fastest growth rates. A business incubator provides both space and services for fledgling businesses. They can be found in old factories and high-tech office buildings. Some are private, for-profit enterprises, while others are sponsored by economic development centers and colleges. By 1995, there may be double that number, according to Dinah Adkins, executive director of the National Business Incubation Association in Athens, Ohio.

Unlike an office suite with a shared receptionist, a true incubator provides fledgling business owners with affordable space, office support services, and management and financial assistance. Tenants share meeting space and ideas. All this ongoing support definitely contributes to success.

If you tracked a group of small-business start-ups after five years, Adkins says, 80 percent of the companies nurtured in incubators would still be around, compared with an 80 percent failure rate for small businesses in general.

Although most incubators attract a variety of businesses, Adkins has noticed a trend toward specialized incubators set up to serve a particular kind of business. For example, there are incubators specifically for biotechnology companies and a handful established solely for women or minorities.

The National Business Incubation Association publishes a directory of incubators. To find an incubator in your area, write to the association at One President Street, Athens, OH 45701. Phone: (614)593-4331.

Meanwhile, Dan Truckenmiller says he can't think of a better place to run his business. "I absolutely recommend beginning your business in an incubator," says Truckenmiller. "Here, you are not starting a business alone. You can learn lessons from other people who have fallen on their face and don't mind helping you out."

Before he began selling his products and services, his rent was only $100 a month. Now, it's an affordable $450. The rents are pegged to the company's success and increase as products are brought to market. Most companies are asked to move out within three years to make room for new ones.

In addition to allowing tenants to wander down the hall and ask someone for help, the Golden Circle Center offers secretarial services and rents space to business consultants who provide advice to tenants at a modest cost. Start-ups can even find affordable office furniture, because local businesses donate their used furniture to the incubator.

"We've had 57 businesses start in here since 1985," says Haines, the director. "Fifty-one of those are still alive."

A walk through the Center reveals small businesses making eyewear, selling computers, exporting dental supplies to Japan, and making snack foods out of pasta. The National Employment Wire Service, which provides job listings, is also based in the incubator.

As good as it sounds, life in an incubator is not for everyone. An incubator won't work if you are in the retail business and depend on foot traffic. But if location is not key to your business and you think you could benefit from the close support of other entrepreneurs, consider moving into one.

Like a true incubator, the management will gently push you out as soon as your business fully hatches!

38. HOW CAN I OUTSMART A GIANT IN MY INDUSTRY?

Entrepreneurs competing nose-to-nose against the Goliaths in their industries say the only way to succeed is to figure out a truly unique way to sell products. When you can't outspend a big corporation, you have to outsmart it. Here's how two small companies flourished by using creative marketing rather than money to reach potential customers:

The fact that more people around the world use toothbrushes than any other consumer product inspired the founders of Healthgard to develop a new toothbrush-sanitizing solution. Because they couldn't compete head-on with the giants of the oral hygiene market, they started selling Brushgard in health-food stores. Brushgard, a stable form of hydrogen peroxide, comes in a bottle that acts as a toothbrush holder. Each bottle lasts for about 10 days and costs under $1.50.

Healthgard, based in Inglewood, California, and Pro-Dentec of Batesville, Arkansas, share the personal products arena with Colgate-Palmolive, Procter & Gamble, and Bausch & Lomb. But you won't see their ads on television or in magazines. "I was looking for the path of least resistance," Jim Grant, Healthgard's marketing director and an officer of the company, says of the decision to sell Brushgard in 1,800 health-food stores.

He had originally planned to introduce Brushgard to hotel guests concerned about bathroom cleanliness. He changed his mind when he met a woman who worked for a natural food chain. She thought Brushgard's sales pitch—"Fact: Toothbrush bacteria can make you sick!"—would appeal to health-conscious shoppers. So far, the strategy is working. Managers at several health-food stores claim that customer interest in Brushgard is growing and sales are picking up.

Healthgard Chairman Allen Gelbard said a group of his friends dared one another to come up with the most lucrative consumer product. Seeking guidance from a data base at the Massachusetts Institute of Technology, Gelbard discovered that the toothbrush was the most universal consumer item. "Toothbrushes cross over all ethnic barriers," says Gelbard, who previously produced movies and worked in the telecommunications business. Because the toothbrush and toothpaste market was glutted, he worked with dental researchers to create a related product.

While Brushgard is busy cleaning toothbrushes, Pro-Dentec is busy cleaning teeth with Rota-dent, a device that uses a variety of circular brushes to do its job. Pro-Dentec also came up with a creative marketing solution. The company decided to sell Rota-dents directly to dentists after realizing that dental product distributors, who push 2,200 products, would probably not sell their line aggressively. But selling directly to dentists is not easy. "The problem is, most dentists think it's unprofessional to sell things out of their office," says Bill Evans, Pro-Dentec's executive vice-president and marketing director.

To gain credibility in the dental community, Pro-Dentec sponsors about 100 continuing education seminars for dentists and dental hygienists around the country each year. "We are selling Rota-dents one dentist at a time," says Evans. Evans notes that dentists who used to spend most of their time filling cavities are now focusing on helping patients keep their teeth and gums healthy. The change in direction is a result of widespread use of fluoride treatment—a development that has nearly eliminated cavities.

Pro-Dentec brought Rota-dent to the United States under a licensing agreement with a Danish company. Dentists charge $90 to $125 for the sleek, hand-held cleaner. The cost includes at least one lesson on how to use the device. Rota-dent's closest competitor is the Interplak tooth cleaner, which was acquired by Bausch & Lomb in 1988 and is sold through a variety of retail outlets.

At first, Evans says, the Copenhagen-made Rota-dents experienced serious quality control problems. To solve their problems, Pro-Dentec acquired the manufacturing rights and moved the factory to Arkansas.

Approximately 1 million Rota-dents have been sold worldwide, 800,000 in the United States. Pro-Dentec has about 150 employees and its sales force phones dentists every day. If dentists express interest in the product, they are sent audio- or videotapes produced in the company's in-house studios.

Evans recommends that small-business owners develop their own marketing plan before hiring an advertising agency.

"Save your money until you figure out how to sell it first," says Evans, who laughs when he recalls the first time he pitched the Rota-dent to dentists. Hearing that a group of dentists was attending a charity golf tournament at the Lake of the Ozarks Country Club, Evans and a colleague raced out to the golf course. "I sold 200 toothbrushes from a golf cart that day," he recalls.

39. HOW CAN GREAT PRODUCT DESIGN BOOST MY SALES?

For smaller companies, having well-designed products can mean the difference between success and failure; even if you don't have a big marketing budget, the right package and label can boost sales by making your product stand out from the crowd.

"The package itself has to sell your product," says Eileen Harte, a package designer with a studio in Van Nuys, California. "It has to clearly communicate what the product is and be positioned to reach the right consumers." Harte also recommends updating your package and labels at least every five to seven years to keep current with design and color trends.

She helped one small business boost sales without changing anything but the look of an already successful product.

Beloved by grammar-school teachers, the Hoyle Pencil Gripper helps thousands of kids learn the proper way to hold a pencil. Although the company sells about 7 million patented Grippers a year, Hoyle's marketing consultant decided that the product needed a snazzier appearance to appeal to today's kids.

"We silk-screened a series of little bears and dinosaurs on the Grippers," says Jim Schultz, Hoyle's marketing consultant at the time. "Then, we redesigned the displays to feature more friendly, soft, and colorful graphics." When the Fillmore, California, company started making trendy, neon-colored fluorescent Grippers, sales blasted off.

"Those fluorescent Grippers now represent about 60 percent

of our sales," says David Hatton, who bought the 15-employee company last year. "We had to understand the market and realize that kids like bright colors."

Successful small-business owners like Hatton know that making the best product in the world is not enough. In many cases, if your products look dull, people won't buy them.

But too many small-business owners assume that they can't afford to hire professional product and packaging designers to create new products or revamp existing ones.

Hiring a skilled design consultant for a specific project is much cheaper than putting an in-house designer on your payroll. And many product and package designers, who are entrepreneurs themselves, will either charge you by the hour or work for a percentage of future profits if they believe in what you are doing.

Big companies such as Mattel hire outside product designers all the time. Hal Berger and Gary Yamron, partners in Image Design & Marketing in El Segundo, California, work with both big and small companies. "For start-up ventures, we are willing to participate on a royalty basis," says Berger. "Entrepreneurs do need more than a dream, though; they should have at least $500,000 in seed capital."

Berger and Yamron created Nintendo's wildly popular Power Glove video-game controller in eight weeks. They also designed new store displays for Barbie dolls, featuring flashing lights and signs in shades of bright Barbie pink. "Our goal for Mattel was to design something that appeals to young consumers and has great visual impact in the stores," Yamron says. By constantly updating Barbie fashions and accessories, Mattel has catered to generations of girls.

Harte, who designed the bears that decorate the Pencil Grippers, recently created a label for Fresca Foods' Pastabilities fresh pasta.

"We knew what we didn't want to do," says owner Kirk Kuhn, who started making pasta in his kitchen. "Our competitor used a black-and-gold label that looked like death." Fresca's new label incorporates the colors of its unique flavored pastas. So, for example, the squid ink pasta label features black ink. "We were looking for something that would stand out and grab people's attention," Kuhn says.

The message is clear: If your goal is to improve an existing product, make sure your version not only works better, but also looks better. "Business owners should take an existing product and ask consumers what is right and what is wrong about it—then remedy what is wrong," advises Mel Evenson, an award-winning industrial designer who serves as vice-president of new product development for Eldon Rubbermaid.

Evenson believes that a good product designer is a "trend-tracker and a trendsetter who can put you and your products on the leading edge."

HOW TO CHOOSE A DESIGNER

- Save ads and brochures that you like and ask the company for the names of the designers they used.
- Solicit presentations from more than one company.
- When you narrow the field, ask for references and call other clients.
- Insist on a very specific proposal, broken down into phases, so you know exactly what to expect.
- Be sure to meet the actual person handling your account.
- Find out which services will be handled in-house and which will be subcontracted out to others.

40. HOW DO I SET MYSELF APART AS A CONSULTANT?

Being the best consultant in town is not enough. Potential clients like to think they are hiring a recognized specialist in one particular area. Setting yourself apart from competitors in an overcrowded profession often means the difference between success and failure for any kind of consultant.

Jain Malkin, founder of the small San Diego, California-based interior design company bearing her name, said she did not want to be one of thousands of interior designers competing for work in the corporate office world. Interested in health care, she tried to read everything available on designing clinics and hospitals and found a dearth of information. Sensing a business opportunity, Malkin spent weeks visiting health-care facilities. She interviewed patients as they sat in waiting rooms. She asked doctors and technicians what they liked and didn't like about where they worked. She shot thousands of color slides of buildings to document what they looked like inside and out.

"Nobody seemed to be doing very much in health care," says Malkin, who, at 21, opened her own design company to decorate dorms at the University of Wisconsin. "Everyone was kind of amused at what I was doing."

For Malkin, building a successful small business around a personal expertise set her apart from her peers. You can be the best, friendliest, or most aggressive consultant around, experts say, but unless you stand out in some other way, you will still be one of the crowd. "If the individual can be perceived as the authority in a niche market, people will beat a path to their door," says Howard Shenson, an author, consultant to consultants, and publisher of *The Professional Consultant* newsletter.

Shenson suggests finding a market that is not being adequately served and asking potential clients how you can best serve it. "Don't just imagine what people want," advises Shenson. "Interview them and ask what they need."

Make what you offer specific and tangible. "Clients don't buy brilliance, they buy results."

After narrowing the field, Shenson suggests figuring out how you can affordably reach potential clients with your message. Can you rent a mailing list? Do you want to serve readers of a particular publication or members of a specific trade organization?

In addition to direct-marketing techniques, Shenson urges consultants to raise their public profile through speaking, teaching, or becoming active in the leadership of a professional group. In fact, he founded the Academy of Professional Consultants & Advisers to establish standards of professional practice and provide advanced training materials and certification to its members. "What's really important for a professional today is not to be seen as someone who is just selling their service but as someone who is advancing the state of the art in their field," says Shenson, whose office is in Woodland Hills, California.

Malkin, with her staff of 20, has become the recognized leader in the health-care design field. She has written two definitive textbooks and has won many first-place awards in her profession. Her projects have a distinctive, open quality that welcomes patients.

Buoyed by her success in the health-care field, Malkin was tempted to branch out about 10 years ago. She set up a corporate design division, which was financially successful, but strained her staff and diluted her efforts in the field she dominated. "It was definitely a mistake to do it," says Malkin, who closed it within two years. "We were competing for every job with 60 people, compared to three on the health-care side."

Based on her personal experience, she advises small-business owners to stay focused on what they do best. "It's okay to do one thing and do it better than anyone else," says Malkin, whose company has annual revenue of about $1.5 million.

Up the coast in Culver City, California, Ann Mohr also took an unusual tack to carve out a consulting business in a crowded profession. As a young designer working for a large Los Angeles firm, she realized that unless she owned her own business, she would always be overworked and underpaid. But opening another interior design company in Los Angeles's jammed market seemed fruitless.

> Ask your customers and clients to recommend you to their friends and associates. Word-of-mouth referral is the most powerful form of small-business advertising.

Mohr came up with the idea for Phase Six after clients called her back to help repair or maintain the furniture, floor, and wall coverings she designed and installed. Mohr said she felt guilty charging them high design fees for doing what should be considered professional maintenance. So she formed Phase Six, named to conjure up the five phases of interior design. Phase Six has attracted a prestigious client list by maintaining expensive office interiors.

Mohr launched Phase Six by borrowing $3,000 from her mother. She created a brochure describing what the company does and sent it to law firms and large corporate offices around Los Angeles. Her brochure and follow-up letter offer potential clients a complimentary walk-through of their offices, during which she or her associates point out problems and affordable solutions. Once hired, Mohr sends out professional interior designers to detail what needs repair. Then, Phase Six hires a small army of skilled subcontractors to perform the work.

Officer managers who work with Mohr's company said she makes their jobs easier by billing them once a month for solving the problems and then hiring, scheduling, and paying the subcontractors directly. "We represent ourselves as professionals," says Mohr. "We don't want anyone to think we are the cleaning people."

41. HOW DO I FIND GOOD WORK SPACE FOR MY BUSINESS?

If you are like most small-business owners, you started your business on the kitchen table or in a spare bedroom. But once you outgrow the house or the garage, it's time to go out and rent space.

Finding the right location for your business is essential to your success. (See 42. How Can I Make the Most of an Offbeat Location?) So unless you have real estate experience, it's best to find a savvy commercial broker to help you. But many small-business owners are reluctant to deal with commercial real estate brokers because they don't understand how brokers work. For example, you might think you cannot afford a commercial broker. Yet it's the landlord, not the tenant, who pays the broker's commission. Or you may expect poor service from brokers who prefer to deal with major clients. But even the smallest business can benefit from the services of a good commercial or industrial real estate broker—if you are prepared.

Sylvia Fogelman is one small-business owner who thought she couldn't afford to deal with a commercial broker. For five years, she commuted halfway across Los Angeles to an office in Pasadena. Finally, she and her partner, Kit Kurisaki, decided to move their Shur Corp. offices to a more central location.

At first, Fogelman thought she could save money by finding a new office on her own. She looked around for a while and wasted a lot of time. She eventually turned the job over to John Moore, a commercial real estate broker who specializes in serving small businesses.

"By working with John, we got a much better deal because he negotiated the lease for us," Fogelman says. "We also reduced our rent when we moved, because we formerly had a lot of space we didn't need."

Shur, which builds single-family homes in central California, is today happily ensconced in a 1,500-square-foot office a few miles outside of downtown Los Angeles.

Moore, who founded his own firm after working eight years as a partner in one of the largest commercial brokerages in Los Angeles, specializes in helping small-business owners relocate. "If you are not looking for a large space, the attitude among many brokers is that it isn't worth providing the same level of service they provide to bigger companies," he says.

Once you find the right broker, be sure that he or she is looking out for your interests. Moore cautions against dealing with brokers who want to show you only listings held by their own companies.

"If you have any indication of being steered toward certain properties, drop the broker immediately," cautions Moore.

He also suggests you be leery of any broker who does not return your calls within a day—"a broker must be attentive to his clients"—and warns against dealing with brokers who think they know what is best for your business. "The commercial real estate broker should observe the axiom that the client makes the decision," Moore says. "The broker should present a spectrum of alternatives to meet your requirements."

Before you begin asking other business owners for a referral to a good commercial broker, figure out exactly what kind of space you need.

Your office space should fit your business goals, not vice versa, according to Nelson Algaze, an architect and space planner who is a vice-president of P. Patrick Murray, Inc., in Los Angeles. Most small-business owners he deals with seriously underestimate their growth needs. Underestimating can cost big money if you have to move to larger quarters sooner than planned. "There is no average size office," he adds. "The size of your office depends on the functional needs of the business and ego of the people involved. Ego becomes a very important factor, because office size and location is a form of compensation for employees."

Commercial brokers say even the most dedicated broker can easily be frustrated by a small-business owner's lack of direction. No matter how busy you are, it's essential to sit down with your employees and managers and figure out what kind of space you need to accommodate your business.

"Make a list of wish, want, and got-to-have items," advises Tom Miller, a broker associate with Commercial/Industrial Associates in West Los Angeles. "If your business will die if there aren't parking spaces for customers, you'd better have them."

But don't go overboard and spend more than you can afford. Big rent bills kill too many small businesses. "More than one entrepreneur has built himself a Taj Mahal for an office only to realize too late that the Taj Mahal is a tomb," caution M. Freddie Reiss and Theodore Phelps in *Workouts and Turnarounds* (see "Books" in Resources guide).

The kind of work you do dictates where you do it. If you are planning to open a retail store, being on the first floor in a high-traffic area is key to your success. But if you don't have a lot of foot traffic, it's possible to rent office space on the second floor or above and substantially reduce your rent costs.

Figure out how many employees need a place to work and whether you need a reception area, lunchroom, or storage space. Then, pull out a map of your city or town and figure out some good locations for your company. Ask yourself:

Does your office need to be centrally located? Does your business depend on walk-in traffic? Do you need to be near the post office or train station? Do you need freeway or highway access? A big parking lot?

RELOCATION CHECKLIST

■ Complete your business plan, including goals for your business.

■ Discuss your space needs with your employees and managers.

■ Prepare a "wish, want, and got-to-have" list.

- Figure out your parking requirements.
- Determine the best location for your business.
- Drive through the neighborhoods you like and look for buildings that appeal to your tastes.
- Ask colleagues or business associates to recommend a broker who likes to work with small-business owners.
- Provide the broker with all the preceding information.
- Be patient and flexible.

Next, begin driving around the neighborhoods you are interested in, noting FOR LEASE signs on buildings that look appealing. When you find an interesting building, write down the address and phone number on the sign so you can call the listing broker. "Ninety percent of the time," Miller says, "the business of the person who calls me is not suitable for the building they called about, but I usually have 15 other buildings with space available."

Miller says you should be prepared to put down two months' rent as a security deposit, in addition to providing credit references and the names and phone numbers of former landlords.

"Leasing to a start-up business is a very big risk for a landlord because most small businesses fail," he warns. Miller suggests providing prospective landlords with information about your company as well as a financial statement, because landlords want to see "evidence of financial stability, if not financial strength."

Miller, who owns several commercial buildings himself, says most landlords expect the business owner to guarantee the lease payments personally, even if the business is a corporation.

Once you find the space you want, the next step is negotiating the lease agreement. This can be tricky, because a commercial lease typically contains 6 to 10 legal-size pages of very fine print. So before you sign anything, be sure you understand the lease's terms. Ask your broker to walk you through the details and answer your questions.

NEGOTIATING A LEASE

- Determine the market rate for similar space in the area.
- Don't be afraid to ask for free rent.
- Find out exactly what monthly or annual costs will be passed through to you.
- Ask if you must pay any building management fees.
- Find out how many parking spaces are included.
- Determine whether you can sell the lease or sublet the space.
- Find out what kinds of tenant improvements the landlord will provide.
- Make sure there is adequate power to run your equipment.
- Set clear and specific options to renew.
- Have your attorney and accountant review the lease before you sign it.

■

42. HOW CAN I MAKE THE MOST OF AN OFFBEAT LOCATION?

For most small-business owners, rent is the biggest expense. But when you're getting started, you can't afford to move into a luxurious office building or even a modest industrial park. So, creative entrepreneurs around the country are putting their businesses in unexpected locations and encouraging customers to seek them out. "When you choose an unusual location for your business, it adds some character and makes a statement that you are not the average firm," says Michael Geller, executive vice-president of First Property Realty Corp. in Westwood, California.

For years, such creativity-based advertising agencies and restaurants seeking more affordable, offbeat locations have been drawing customers to neighborhoods that they might not usually frequent. Other kinds of client-driven businesses seek unusual locations to save money and set themselves apart. Many downtown businesses are flourishing in areas that once were used only for warehouse space. There are restaurants tucked into warehouses in Houston. Architects are flocking to lofts in downtown Los Angeles. The once run-down area around the courthouse in downtown Des Moines has become a haven for trendy bars and restaurants.

"When the clients arrive here, they are awe-struck," says Patricia Ridgway, founder of Ridgway Associates, a space planning and design firm in downtown Los Angeles. "They are so used to corporate, high-rise space, that they come into this Soho-type district and say, 'Wow, this is really creative; this is really great!' " Ridgway and her 25 employees work in what was once a contemporary art museum above a busy restaurant east of Little Tokyo. In recent years, the area has attracted other creative architects, designers, and artists seeking unique studio space.

Here's my favorite offbeat location. One of the most unlikely location for a riding stable is in the middle of Manhattan, a few blocks from Central Park. But that's where you'll find the Claremont Riding Academy. "Despite the shortcomings of our facility—it's old, small, run-down, and crowded—people are delighted we're here," says Paul Novograd, owner of Claremont Riding Academy, which is next to a vacant lot in a less-than-toney Upper West Side neighborhood.

Beginning at 6 A.M., urban horse lovers arrive by bus, subway, car, and taxi, or on foot, to exercise their horses, take riding lessons, or explore 6 miles of bridle paths in nearby Central Park. The 99-year-old brick carriage house is home to about 100 horses that are specially trained to be calm on bustling city streets. On the list of National Historic Sites, Claremont is slated to undergo a $3-million renovation scheduled to be completed in time for its one-hundredth birthday in 1992.

"Claremont is so accessible, people come here despite the physical limitations," says Novograd, whose family has owned the stable for 60 years. In fact, the popularity of the Upper West Side stable has prompted Novograd and a group of private investors to plan another urban riding center adjacent to Boston's Franklin Park.

"When you are accessible by subway and the only riding stable in town, you have a de facto monopoly," says Novograd.

If you decide to find an offbeat location, make sure the area is zoned to permit what you want to do there.

You will also want to make sure there is adequate parking, security for your customers or clients, and room to grow. (See 41. How Do I Find Good Work Space for My Business?)

MAKING THE MOST OF AN OFFBEAT LOCATION

- Seek out neighborhoods on the brink of redevelopment.
- Talk to other business owners in the area to find out what they like and don't like about the neighborhood.

- Find an adventurous real estate agent who is willing to explore new areas with you.

- Ask architects and designers if they know of space for lease in unusual locations.

- If you find a suitable building in a slightly scary neighborhood, make sure you have enough parking spaces, a safe entry, and provide security, if necessary.

- When you move in, throw a big party to let your customers and clients know you've moved—and include a map in the invitation.

■

43. HOW CAN I SPRUCE UP MY NEIGHBORHOOD?

Even if your business is located in a great place, you may be faced with neighbors who don't seem to care much about keeping their property in good shape. Or maybe you are in an area that seems to be sliding into decay and you want to stop the negative progression.

Changing the character of your neighborhood isn't easy, but business owners nationwide are teaming up to rub out graffiti, clear trash from vacant lots, and otherwise brighten their surroundings.

There's good reason for all this activity. Every dollar invested in fixing up your business district can generate up to $17 in additional income, according to Matt Hussman, a program associate for the National Trust for Historic Preservation in Washington. During the past 10 years, the Trust's Main Street Center has helped more than 650 communities from Boston to Hollister, California, revitalize their commercial areas. "The projects across the country have generated thousands of dollars and created thousands of jobs," says Hussman.

The merchants along West Washington Boulevard in Venice, California, have set a great example for small-business owners around the country. Located a few blocks from the beach in a transitional neighborhood, the merchants banded together recently to spruce up the business district.

The catalyst for action was a move to change the name from West Washington to Abbot Kinney Boulevard, in honor of the founder of Venice, a beach town once home to a system of canals mimicking its Italian namesake.

The problem with the old street name was that it created constant confusion. There are several other West Washington streets in and around Los Angeles, and customers had a terrible time finding the right one. "I've given directions to enough people through the years to be very frustrated," says Carol Tantau Smith, who has been selling jewelry and gifts on the boulevard for about nine years. Tantau Smith led the crusade to change the name. She also pushed the city to plant palm trees in the parkways in front of the businesses.

Although the street is still difficult to find, the general feeling is that business is picking up. On a recent weekday, shoppers filtered in and out of the art galleries, boutiques, coffee bean shop, lighting studios, and trendy restaurants.

"It just feels different," says Tantau Smith. "There is a real energy."

So get out, take a look down your block, and see what you can do to spruce it up.

For information on the Main Street Center, write to:

The National Trust for Historic Preservation
Main Street Center
1785 Massachusetts Avenue, N.W.
Washington, DC 20036

The Center sponsors several redevelopment conferences each year and publishes affordable booklets on how to revitalize your area. Both government agencies and business owners can contract with the Center for help.

HOW TO SPRUCE UP YOUR NEIGHBORHOOD

- Call a meeting of neighboring business owners to gauge interest in fixing up your block.
- If you don't have one, form a merchants' association.
- Talk to other business owners who have spruced up their blocks to gather names of architects and planners who specialize in this kind of work.
- Ask your customers what they think should be done. Do they need more parking? Better lighting?
- Ask local government officials if there is any state or federal grant money available for community rehabilitation.

■

44. HOW CAN A DESKTOP PUBLISHER SAVE ME MONEY?

Even the tiniest business needs an identifiable logo, but many small-business owners can't afford to buy original artwork created by a graphic designer.

But there's no cause for despair. Today's personal computer technology has created a growing desktop publishing industry eager to serve cost-conscious entrepreneurs. Whether your job requires creating a daily restaurant menu, updating price lists, or submitting ads to a newspaper, desktop publishers can save you time and money.

"Computer-generated artwork used to look very tacky, but now with the new technology, it's just as good as something done by a guy sitting there with an Exacto blade and sending copy out to a typesetter," argues Hal Brice, president of Heil-Brice Retail Advertising in San Clemente, California.

Brice, who wanted a fresh look on all the printed materials sent out by his radio and television commercial production company, said he considered logos submitted by three graphic designers before turning to a company specializing in computer graphics. "Within an hour, we went from a rough draft to the finished version," says Brice, who helped create his own logo by faxing versions back and forth.

Critics contend that computer-generated artwork has a harsh, two-dimensional look to it. Traditional graphic designers also point out that a computer program is useless without a creative person telling it what to do. Yet, most desktop publishers formerly worked for ad agencies or on their own as traditional designers.

Designers now working with computers say they fell in love with the new computer technology because the software is fun to use, speeds up the artistic process, and saves clients money. "I don't think pricing in the [design] industry has kept up with technology," says Jeff Turner, president of Marit-Ward in Sherman Oaks, California. "Technology allows us to do things for a fraction of the cost."

Turner, who became interested in desktop publishing when he was working as a product manager for NCR Corp., says companies such as his fill the gap between taking an idea to a local print shop and hiring a traditional full-service advertising agency. Most graphic design companies charge a minimum of $1,500 to create a logo from scratch. By comparison, graphic artists who design at the computer can create a logo for as little as $600.

"The technology is making it possible for small-business owners to get high-quality, economical work," says Roy Antoun, a partner in Eureka & Avalon in Van Nuys, California. Antoun, who produces marketing materials and ads for dozens of large and small businesses, notes that a full-service desktop publisher not only designs logos and graphic material but can create entire marketing and advertising campaigns.

Before going out to find a desktop publisher, though, figure out what kind of message you want to get across to customers. "The business owners should think of who they want to talk to and what they have to sell," advises Antoun. "We want to know if they have $2 million worth of suits to unload or a Valentine's Day special to promote."

Cost is no longer a barrier if you are willing to invest in the computer hardware and software necessary to create graphics and documents and train or hire someone to do the job. Apple Computer created the basic tools for desktop publishing when it introduced the Macintosh personal computer in the mid-1980s. And there are several wonderful desktop publishing software programs available. The pioneering program, Pagemaker, released by Aldus Corp. in 1985, is still selling strong. In fact, Paul Brainerd, founder and chief executive of Seattle-based Aldus, is credited with coining the phrase *desktop publishing*.

"The prices have come down, and the machines are easier and easier to use," says Sandra Churchill, a senior marketing analyst for BIS Strategic Decisions, a division of BIS Group in Norwell, Massachusetts. "The manufacturers' goal is to provide users with the tools to go from initial design to final production."

Once you have the computer and software, additional equipment is required to produce camera-ready artwork or documents. With computer prices plummeting, small-business owners can buy a basic system for under $6,000.

On the other hand, a high-end system can cost up to $20,000 or more, depending on the final production quality you require. And in addition to buying the equipment, you must consider the cost of hiring a graphic designer or training an artistically inclined person on your staff to do the work.

Many graphic artists say that using a desktop publishing system saves time by performing the tedious and repetitive tasks, which frees up their time for more creative design work. But although a desktop publishing system is great for layout, line art, and typesetting, the human touch is still required for illustrations or detailed creative work. And remember, the computer is a tool—it can't teach you good design technique.

If you are not interested in taking the time to learn how to do your own desktop publishing, there are small companies offering their services across the country.

Many are listed in the Yellow Pages under advertising agencies or typesetters, although desktop publishers are pressuring the phone companies to create a separate section for them.

Marketing and public relations consultant David Gering relies on three desktop publishers to help him produce sales material, brochures, and newsletters for his clients. Gering, founder of the Write Source in Canoga Park, California, says he saves time by transmitting information via computer modem to the desktop publishing company. Many desktop publishers can convert copy written on an IBM or IBM-compatible computer to a Macintosh format.

"When you shop around for a desktop publisher, look at their portfolio and ask yourself if you like what you see," advises Gering.

45. HOW CAN MY TELEPHONE HELP BUILD MY BUSINESS?

One of the most productive and affordable tools of small business sits on your desk every day.

It's your telephone.

If you are not using your telephone to the fullest, you're losing money. The telephone can be the most dynamic component of your company's overall customer service and marketing plan.

Here's how one small company put the telephone to work for them:

At Home Health Products Inc.'s Virginia Beach, Virginia, office, four order-takers were often overwhelmed when calls flooded the company's toll-free 800 line. It was especially tough right after the flourishing mail-order natural health-care products company shipped a new catalog to hundreds of thousands of customers across the country.

Instead of hiring more people to take telephone orders in Virginia, founder and president Sam Knoll hooked up with a California company to handle the overflow calls during the day, after hours, and on weekends. By sending out about 3 million catalogs and extending its telephone hours, Knoll's 14-employee company increased its 1991 sales by 40 percent. "We just forward the calls to California when we need to," says Knoll, who plans to invest $20,000 to upgrade and improve the company's overall telephone system.

Companies such as 800-Direct in Canoga Park, California,

which answers calls for Home Health Products, have capitalized on helping other small businesses appreciate the benefits of toll-free 800 numbers. "We present the image that your company is operating 24 hours a day," says Matt Epstein, vice-president in charge of marketing.

In addition to taking computerized orders, companies such as 800-Direct can fulfill orders at their headquarters or relay orders and customer information back to your company via computer modem or fax.

Rich Crocker, president of Inquiry Handling Service in San Fernando, California, also helps businesses field calls and direct customers to their sales outlets. "We handle the peaks and valleys so you don't have to worry about staff problems," says Crocker.

Even if you are not big enough to need 800-lines or fulfillment services, you should make sure your employees have good phone manners. "The telephone is the lifeline of a small business," warns Nancy Friedman, a consultant known as the "Telephone Doctor."

Friedman, who is based in St. Louis, said successful business owners are inevitably those who train their employees to use the telephone properly. She suggests smiling before you pick up the telephone; corny as this sounds, it really makes a difference in your attitude and can improve your telephone manners. Friedman also suggests calling your business when you are out of the office to check on how your customers are being treated by your staff.

Telling your employees exactly how you expect them to deal with customers on the phone should be an essential part of your training program. Having a phone system big enough to handle inbound and outbound calls is also important; you don't like to be left on hold for 10 minutes, so don't subject your customers to poor telephone service.

Once you have established a telephone policy and installed the best system to handle your calls, you can think of adding other telecommunications options:

■ Even the tiniest small business can appear to be big and professional by tapping into the right technology. Computerized voice mail systems can route and answer calls and take detailed messages.
■ New facsimile machines with memory capabilities can be

programmed to send faxes early in the morning or overnight, saving money by operating while the lowest telephone rates are in effect.

■ Telephone companies, including Pacific Bell in California, offer customized 800 numbers for as little as $15 a month, plus installation and per-call charges. With these custom 800 numbers, you can control exactly where customers can call you from, limiting it to one prefix or stretching across state lines with the help of long-distance carriers. AT&T, the pioneer of 800 numbers, also has various new 800 services for small and large companies. You might also consider having different phone numbers to reach different areas of your city. This is especially useful if you run a service business, such as housecleaning, where a customer is more likely to call a local number.

■ If you have a local number that forwards calls from one area to your business, you could increase your reach. Your local telephone company can give you more information on these services.

"Most businesses don't really know how to use the telephone and fax," says Bernard Otis, founder of the Otis Group, a marketing firm based in Woodland Hills, California. Rather than using the telephone to cold-call customers, Otis believes that "true telemarketing is the professional use of the telephone to create a relationship with people."

Many business owners are unaware of how effective a tool a fax machine can be when trying to reach a decision maker. But instead of blindly faxing letters to people, Otis suggests first calling the person's office directly. If the person is unavailable, ask his or her secretary for permission to send a personal fax. Once you have permission, send a letter introducing yourself and explaining exactly which services or products you offer. (If you can't obtain permission to use the fax, don't use it. Send a letter and hope for the best.)

Another tip: "Don't be a pest and call someone five times a day," Otis advises. Being a pest—in person or via telecommunications—is not the way to make a good impression on the people you want to do business with.

TELEPHONE TIPS

■ Ask your customers and employees if they think an 800 number would help boost sales.

■ Review your local and long-distance bills to figure out exactly how much you are spending each month.

■ Shop around for the best discounts and services offered to small-business owners.

■ Sign up for services on a month-to-month basis to retain flexibility.

■ Consider your telephone a prime selling tool.

───────────────── ■ ─────────────────

"Telephone Doctor" Nancy Friedman says: "Think of the telephone as a stage: When the receiver goes up, the curtain goes up."

■ Suggest that your employees smile before they answer the phone.

■ Check your employees' phone manners by calling in anonymously on occasion.

■ Make sure everyone is properly trained to answer calls the way you want them to.

■ Have enough telephone lines and staff members to avoid putting customers on hold.

■ Consider an 800 line for your business.

46. HOW CAN I BUILD MY BUSINESS BY FORGING SMALL-BUSINESS ALLIANCES?

David Nowe, founder of Nowe Video Film, in Newport Beach, California, has built his business by forging alliances with fellow small-business owners.

He learned the concept when he was a partner in a marketing firm that set up an alliance with the accounting firm of Ernst & Young. "The agreement was for us to provide them with training, video services, and to promote the firm in exchange for office space and support services," explains Nowe. "They also offered our services to their clients."

Although the concept made a lot of sense, Nowe felt the accountants were not the best salespeople for the marketing firm's services. So, about three years ago, Nowe launched his own firm—by forming another strategic alliance. He contacted the owner of the video production company where he did his post-production work.

"We sat down and wrote out a contract that called for me to offer my services as writer, producer, and director on a freelance basis," recalls Nowe. In exchange, he agreed to do all his post-production work at that company. The post-production house provided him a desk and business cards so he could meet with their clients. The arrangement worked well for 18 months until they had a falling out.

Nowe moved on and since then has formed several other strategic alliances, including one with a slide production company with

1,500 clients. "We win because the slide company offers my video services to their clients, which increases their revenues," explains Nowe. "They win because whenever we get any slide work, we give the business to them."

Try creating a cross-promotion with another business. When Orion Pictures was promoting the summer release of *Mystery Date*, they sent out postcards offering a $5 discount on any flowers purchased through 800-FLOWERS. "Bring your Mystery Date a beautiful bouquet of flowers," read the ad.

Cross-selling your allies' services, Nowe says, is "a magical way to do business." Here's what he's learned about making strategic alliances work. "Focus on what's in it for the other person," suggests Nowe. "Think, 'What can I offer this person that is going to make this person more successful?' First figure out how are they going to make more money by establishing a relationship with you."

Nowe suggests approaching fellow business owners directly to discuss an alliance. If that's not possible, ask a mutual friend or acquaintance to arrange an introduction.

Now that you know how it works, sit down and make a list of all the companies you know that could help enhance your business. Look at your vendors and suppliers—even customers. Figure out how you could share client lists, mailing lists, or cross-sell your products.

If you spend a few hours on this, you'll see there are some really terrific opportunities. Even better, they don't cost anything to establish.

47. HOW DO I HIRE THE BEST EMPLOYEES?

Every day, thousands of small-business owners are making decisions to hire new employees. The problem is, unless you formerly worked in personnel, you probably don't have much experience in screening and hiring people. But your success is critically linked to the people you choose to hire to work with you. It's scary. Without the very best people, you are sunk.

The biggest mistake made by small-business owners is to hire the first person who walks through the door. The second biggest mistake is to hire friends or relatives just because they need a job.

Be careful—hiring mistakes are incredibly costly! Once you've put someone on the payroll, even if you set up a probationary period, it is extremely difficult to get rid of them.

One secret is to spend a little more time and money to cast a wider net for job applicants. Advertising in your local newspaper—with a well-written ad that defines the job and the necessary skills to do the job—is a good start. Asking your employees for recommendations is a good idea. Just make sure they are referring only qualified friends or relatives. Another tactic is to ask other business owners you know if they have interviewed qualified people they didn't hire for one reason or another. A personal referral means a lot.

Once you've attracted a few applicants, set aside enough time to review their applications and résumés carefully. These are among the most important decisions you have to make. You should not be reading résumés on the run or while talking on the telephone.

Try to set aside at least an hour to meet with each person applying for a management job, or someone who will work directly with you. It will be time well spent. If you are hiring production-line workers or stockroom clerks, you might want to turn over the job of screening applicants to the line supervisor. Still, try to meet and chat with everyone before a job offer is made.

The most important advice I can give you is to *check all references thoroughly*. Applicants with a checkered employment history or something awful to hide are very savvy about falsifying their application forms or résumés.

I would not hire anyone without speaking directly to their former employer to find out exactly what kind of an employee they were and why they left.

Red flags should go up if the former employer or supervisor is unwilling to speak with you and will only verify dates of employment. You may have heard that many employers are skittish about discussing personnel issues because they are afraid of being sued by a former employee if they give a bad reference and the person does not get the job. But be persistent. Someone at the company, whether or not it's a direct supervisor, should be willing to say something. If not, think twice about hiring that person.

Hiring the right people for your business is essential to creating harmony and team spirit. A big company can absorb a few malcontents and clunkers; a small company cannot. A single problem employee can really destroy morale and get in the way of you achieving your goals.

Here's how one small business learned to handle its hiring problems:

Just about every 120 days, Chris Dunham, director of sales training, recruits a new group of trainees for F. D. Titus & Son, a growing medical products distributor in City of Industry, California. Although there are plenty of applicants, Dunham finds hiring good salespeople a continuing challenge. In addition to interviews, he relies on a battery of aptitude tests to help him screen out the duds. "We were using a company that administered a home test and were quite frustrated with the results," says Dunham, who recently hired only 6 of the 70 college graduates he interviewed. "Their test kept showing everyone was suited for sales and we knew they weren't."

Dunham switched to a firm that tests applicants in its office and provides him with a detailed report on the results. He uses the information to confirm his feelings about whether or not the person will succeed. "Hiring the wrong person costs a company 100 times more than the tests do," he says.

"If a small-business owner has employee problems it can put him out of business," agrees Joan Sheridan, a human resources consultant in Woodland Hills, California.

Business owners may be surprised to learn that a battery of aptitude tests can cost less than $300 and a basic background check can run under $100 in most parts of the country. The kind of test you administer depends on what kind of person you are looking for to fill a particular job.

Scores of companies, usually run by personnel administrators or industrial psychologists, offer intelligence tests, aptitude tests, achievement tests, and personality tests. Some companies even offer job simulation tests, which create a real-life situation for applicants. For example, a potential stockbroker or insurance salesperson would be asked to sit in an office and make phone calls to mock customers. But the customers are actually psychologists who review how the applicant behaves under pressure.

"When given properly, tests help determine a person's mental abilities, organization skills, people skills, and level of motivation," says Harold Weinstein, senior vice-president of Caliper Corp. in Princeton, New Jersey.

Once you've narrowed down the best candidates for a job, it is essential to verify the information presented on their résumés carefully. Overlooking details can often lead to a hiring disaster, according to Robert Hobert, a Minneapolis industrial psychologist who runs a testing firm. For instance, "In St. Cloud, Minnesota, there is a university and a penitentiary," says Hobert. "When people tell employers here they spent time up at St. Cloud, you had better ask if it was in the prison or the school."

About 16 percent of the résumés reviewed by Assessment Systems in New York City contain false information, according to company president Bernard Reynolds. The firm's Proudfoot Reports subsidiary has been doing employment background checks since

1900. "If you do nothing else, you certainly want to verify that the background the applicant is presenting to you is real," advises Reynolds. "If you are paying $40,000 to someone who has an engineering degree, you want to make sure they have it."

In today's litigious world, business owners have to be especially careful about whom they hire because they can be held liable if an employee injures someone or causes harm to a customer. Failing to check the driving record of your truck drivers can be a disaster if a driver hurts someone and you learn too late that he or she has a history of drunk driving convictions.

Can you improve your hiring procedures with a new application form and new guidelines for interviewing people? Surprisingly, the answer is, "It depends." You'll need to be careful about the kinds of questions you ask applicants. State and federal laws prohibit asking for information that might be used against someone in a discriminatory fashion.

Many small-business owners may be unaware that you are not supposed to ask about a person's age, sex, birthplace, religion, national origin, race, or physical disabilities. Asking if someone has an arrest record or if they served in the military is also prohibited. You can ask if someone has been convicted of a felony and whether they acquired any skills in the military, and you can ask to see a report from the Department of Motor Vehicles if the job involves driving. Most state departments of fair employment and housing publish helpful guidelines for business owners.

If you decide to run a background check on an applicant, you must obtain written permission on a release form signed by the applicant. Reputable employment-screening firms provide the forms for you. It wouldn't hurt to ask a competent business attorney who is familiar with privacy laws to review the form as well.

Even the best tests and screening procedures won't help you hire better people if you don't attract a large group of qualified applicants. Personnel experts encourage business owners to place help wanted ads in local newspapers, trade magazines, and newsletters to attract the largest possible pool of applicants.

TIPS FOR BETTER HIRING

- Draft a clear job description before you advertise for a new employee.
- List the qualifications and skills the person needs to do the job.
- Figure out what kind of person will fit in with other employees.
- Ask your state fair employment or job development office for a list of preemployment inquiry guidelines.
- Invest the money in a professional background check or assign someone on your staff to collect information from schools, court records, and other public sources.
- Before hiring a testing company, compare prices, services, and ask for references.
- Carefully check references before hiring anyone.

48. CAN AN EXECUTIVE SEARCH FIRM HELP MY BUSINESS?

When Steve Olson, former president of Signet Scientific, wanted to improve the quality of new managers joining his small instrumentation company, he insisted that every prospective employee be interviewed and rated by five supervisors. Although this helped screen out some potential problem employees, it was very time-consuming. Olson eventually turned to a small executive recruiting firm for help.

"I think it's been money well spent," says Olson. "When you have 250 people in an organization and you make a mistake, it doesn't make much difference," he says. "But, when you have *five* people in a company, the impact can be significant."

Most entrepreneurs resist working with recruiters because they fear losing control over the hiring process or believe they can't afford the fees. To a small-business owner, spending $30,000 to locate a $100,000-a-year executive vice-president may seem expensive, but search consultants say the fee should be viewed as an investment in the future. "Start-ups can't afford the wrong players," argues Jay Berger, a principal in the Pasadena search firm of Morris, Berger. "They need the right people to put together the dream."

Berger says most business owners hire on the basis of a gut feeling. "But if the person doesn't have the right skills, the chemistry will wear thin."

Kris Morris, his partner, says it is even more important to get help with your hiring in a sluggish economic climate. Why? "With so many corporate downsizings, mergers, and takeovers, the smaller businesses are seeing an increased number of over-the-transom résumés," says Morris. "On the one hand, there seems to be an abundance of wealth and resources, but it also means you have to pay even closer attention to the quality of candidates you interview."

Although there are a lot of very good people who are out looking for work, Morris says there are also many problematic people you *don't* want working for you. "The temptation is to say, 'Oh gosh, look at all these great people,' but you really need to spend more time reading between the lines." An executive search firm can help.

Many people are confused about the kinds of services an executive search firm provides. Unlike employment agencies, which charge fees to job seekers, search firms are paid by companies looking for middle- and upper-level employees. Although some firms charge flat fees for a search, most consultants charge between 25 and 33 percent of the salary being offered the prospective employee. They also bill the client for travel and out-of-pocket expenses, including telephone calls, postage, and entertainment.

There are more than 1,200 search firms nationwide, so finding the right one can be daunting. As usual, I suggest asking colleagues and business associates for a personal referral.

The first thing a competent search firm should do is learn as much as it can about your company and style of doing business. Next, they should help you create a clear job description for the position you are trying to fill. Then, they should interview all the people who will work with or for the new employee to find out what kind of person will fit into the mix. At some point in the relationship, they should also meet with your management team and design a human resources strategy, including exactly what types of people are needed to help you meet your goals.

"What evolves is a partnership," explains Gary Kaplan, who specializes in searches for the entertainment and communications industry. "A search consultant becomes part of the company." Kaplan, whose Pasadena firm bears his name, says his job is to identify the best and brightest employees for his clients. Before hiring a search firm, Kaplan suggests, ask for a list of other clients and references. This is important because as a matter of policy, search firms are not supposed to raid their own clients when they are looking for job candidates. What this means is that a large firm with hundreds of clients may find its hands tied because employees of all those firms are considered off-limits.

Once the consultant has all the information from you, he or she launches a nationwide search, usually seeking out people working in similar jobs for competing firms. After they review résumés— important because up to 25 percent of job applicants lie about some part of their background—and screen the people over the phone, they will interview the finalists in person. After the interviews, you will receive a written report on the finalists.

The top finalists will be asked to meet with you, at your expense.

HIRING A SEARCH FIRM

If you are thinking about hiring a search firm, here are suggestions from business owners and consultants:

■ Find people you feel comfortable confiding in and working with. This is important because the search firm will represent you and your company to prospective employees.

■ Find out exactly how much the search firm will charge for services. Insist on a careful explanation of charges and expenses so there will be no surprises.

■ Ask who actually will do the search work for your firm. In many larger firms, the principals are out signing up new clients, leaving less experienced associates to find the candidates.

■ Find out if the company has worked for companies your size and in your field. Many search firms specialize in serving certain professions or industries.

■ Ask for a list of clients and call them for information. Ask if the search firm was responsive. Find out if they brought in good candidates and how long it took to fill each job.

49. HOW CAN I MAKE MEETINGS WITH MY EMPLOYEES MORE EFFECTIVE?

In the beginning, when you are trying to sell your small-business concept to your family, investors, or the public, you become a great communicator. You talk nonstop about your dreams and how you plan to achieve them. You explain your concept so many times that you could do it in your sleep.

But once the doors are open, many entrepreneurs stop communicating. Big mistake! If you don't continue to share the dream and encourage the people who work with you to participate in running the business, you are losing out on a tremendous amount of brain power.

"Two-way communication with your front-line staff is important for many reasons," says Thomas Timmons, a turnaround expert and founder of Business Directions in Mission Viejo, California. "It enables you to share your visions for the business with them. It allows your staff to tell you what they believe is working and what is not. They can also tell you what they hear and see from your customers. All of this information is vital for business success."

Timmons recalled his work with a business owner who was about to lose his formerly successful business. The owner blamed his crisis in part on strained labor relations.

He took Timmons on a tour of his plant. Timmons noticed the owner only said hello to 2 out of more than 200 employees. When Timmons asked him why he didn't speak to his workers, the owner replied: "I don't need to talk to those people. I have managers to do that."

Timmons knew exactly why this man was losing his business: He didn't think he needed to communicate with his employees.

No smart entrepreneur is "too busy" to set up a structured time to meet with his or her managers and employees.

True, meetings are often synonymous with wasted time. A 1989 study of 2,000 business leaders by Hofstra University and Harrison Conference Centers revealed that unproductive meetings cost American business about $37 billion a year, according to Thomas A. Kayser, author of *Mining Group Gold* (see "Books" in Resources guide). In fact, Kayser, who is the manager of organization effectiveness for Xerox Corp., figured out that the meetings held by Xerox's 24,000-person development and manufacturing group were costing about $78.9 million a year, based on salaries and other factors.

So if meetings cost so much time and money, why have them?

"Group sessions are the lifeblood of organizations," according to Kayser. "Whether we like it or not, sitting down face to face with a group of people is often the right way—the *only* way—to process information and achieve goals."

In most small businesses, you—the owner—must run the meeting. Your job is not only to make full use of the time the group spends together, but to encourage everyone to participate.

Kayser suggests answering these five questions before scheduling your next meeting:

1. What are the purpose and desired outcome?
2. Is a group session necessary?
3. Who should attend the session?
4. What is the composition of the group and what can be learned about its potential chemistry?
5. What is the agenda content and topic flow?

Once you get into a meeting, your job is to keep what Kayser calls "idea killers" to a minimum. Here are some common ones:

"That will never work."
"We've always done it this way."
"We're not ready for that yet."

"Don't be ridiculous!"

"It's a good idea, but . . ."

If you hear any of these, intervene and suggest people listen more carefully to what the person is suggesting before cutting them off.

Big corporations are notorious for "meeting" people to death. You certainly don't need to have more than one meeting per day in a small company. But you do need to meet. "No matter how small your business is, you still need to hold meetings," confirms Judith Learner, president of Effective Communications in Beverly Hills.

While most meetings deal with day-to-day or short-term problems, Learner says, it is extremely important to share your long-term vision with your employees. These planning meetings can be very productive if you ask the right questions. "Ask everyone, 'Where do you see us in a year and in two years?' " she suggests. "Projections are just as important as paying the bills every month."

But how do you make time for meetings when there is almost no time during the day to get the work done? Learner offers the following 10 tips to help you run a great meeting:

1. *Set a goal.* Determine the kind of meeting you need to reach that goal, whether it's brainstorming, decision making, or information gathering.

2. *Put it in writing.* Include a purpose, limited to three objectives, on your premeeting memo.

3. *Invite key players.* Ask only those you really need.

4. *Start on time.* Begin on the dot and don't backtrack for latecomers (they'll get the message to be prompt). End the meeting on time, too.

5. *Take detailed notes.* Ask one person to keep notes so you can double-check information later and speed through your agenda.

6. *Stay on track.* If the group goes off on a tangent, table the discussion until later.

7. *Make it quick.* An hour or less is sufficient for most meetings.

8. *Establish who's the decision maker.* Are you looking for a group decision or will you have the final say? Employees need to know.

9. *Don't attend.* If the meeting can be run without you, delegate. You can get work done and so can your staff.

10. *Listen up!* Only bad bosses hold meetings to hear themselves speak, so don't pontificate. Your goal is to exchange ideas, reach a consensus, and go back to work.

Use these tips and your reputation as a great discussion leader will flourish.

50. WHY DO I NEED EMPLOYEE AND POLICY MANUALS?

One of the biggest problems faced by small-business owners is maintaining open communication with employees. Even in a tiny business, where you work elbow to elbow with your staff, communication problems can arise. A well-written policy manual can not only solve communications problems, but keep you out of legal hot water and help your supervisors do a better job managing the troops.

Here's how one small-business owner used a manual to save time and money:

When new or temporary employees arrive at Vector Inc., they are often puzzled about what the company does and what they are supposed to do. "Most people who come to work for us have never heard about what we do, which is provide vocational rehabilitation for injured workers and serve as expert witnesses," says Marcia Andersen, co-owner of the small Westminster, California, company. To eliminate confusion and save time, Andersen hired Linda Reitman, a consultant and technical writer, to develop a job manual describing exactly how Vector's front-office operation should work.

"The feedback on the manual has been very positive," says Andersen. "New employees tell us they don't know how they would have gotten through the first week on the job without the manual." By using the manual, Andersen says, she can train new employees in a few days, rather than a few weeks, saving her both time and money.

Personnel consultants say even the smallest business should have written policies and procedures to avoid confusion. There are several different types of manuals, each covering a specific aspect of your operation:

- *Employee handbooks* outline company policies on everything from dress codes to maternity leave.
- *Operations manuals* outline company operations from crisis management to customer relations.
- *Job handbooks*, such as the one written for Vector, clearly outline the duties and responsibilities of each position.

Job handbooks are not only used to train new or temporary employees, but can help "cross-train" employees to cover for each other during vacations or other absences.

And once you spend the time writing a policy handbook, or hire experts to write it for you, don't just sit it on a shelf—use it! "One of the quickest ways for you to get in trouble with an employee is to put out a policy handbook and then not follow it," warns Edgar Ellman, a veteran personnel consultant with offices in downtown Chicago.

Each year, Ellman writes about 200 policy handbooks for large and small companies, from wholesale distributors to banks. He usually works by mail, charging about $750 to complete a customized handbook. To collect the necessary information, Ellman asks business owners or managers to fill out and return a detailed, 17-page questionnaire. Ellman writes the handbook based on the information provided about the company and existing personnel policies. Before completion, he sends a draft back to the company for editing and review. In the interest of an accessibly written guide, Ellman strongly recommends against hiring an attorney to *write* your policy handbook; he does, however, urge clients to make sure their attorney *reviews* the handbook and, if necessary, to add information about applicable state and local regulations.

You want your handbook to be as clear as possible because it may play a key role in court if an employee sues you for wrongful termination or any other labor dispute. According to Ellman, many courts around the country have ruled that a policy handbook often serves as a contract between employee and employer.

"We live in such a litigious society that any employer who doesn't have an employee handbook is just asking for trouble," says Reitman, founder of The Writer's Bloc in Costa Mesa, California. "A good manual is going to save an employer a lot of time and money because it documents everything an employee needs to know and establishes a company's policies and procedures."

Job manuals can also help managers review job performance by setting certain standards. "A good manual makes a manager's job easier by contributing to a more accurate performance appraisal," she adds.

Above all, be sure your handbook is accurate and easy to understand. You may also want to have it translated into other languages for employees who are not proficient in English.

Personnel consultant Edgar Ellman says a policy handbook has two major goals: to inform all employees about company policies and regulations and to give supervisors support when they have to enforce those regulations.

Your policy handbook should address a variety of issues including:

- Hours to be worked
- Benefit programs
- Salary reviews
- Holidays
- Leaves of absence
- Overtime pay
- Vacations
- Severance pay
- Performance reviews
- Pension plans
- Causes for discipline
- Handling of complaints and grievances

51. HOW CAN I ENCOURAGE MY EMPLOYEES TO DRESS FOR SUCCESS?

You might not think the way your employees look could hurt your business. But it can and it does.

Don't feel guilty if you are reluctant to discuss this problem. The subject is so touchy that "Dave M.," a Maryland business owner, refused to sign his last name when he wrote me a letter asking for advice. In Dave's case, one of his best customers was upset by the way his female salespeople were dressed.

"Apparently, his staff remarked to him that the split skirt my salesperson was wearing was not very flattering," writes Dave. "He personally saw her and added that the outfit was not very professional. . . . I am used to making business decisions every day. Yet, I think you can note my discomfort in dealing with this issue."

Although good managers feel comfortable criticizing an employee's tardiness, work habits, or sales material, criticizing an employee's clothes or personal grooming causes consternation. And with good reason: If you are not tactful, you may damage a good working relationship.

"Even if you have a problem with one employee, it is important not to single anyone out," advises John T. Molloy, author of *Dress for Success*. Molloy has been invited to speak at big meetings just to get the message across to one vice-president. "Try to hold a group meeting to discuss appropriate attire," suggests Molloy. "And be sure to inform every new person you hire about how you expect them to dress."

Business owners should be concerned about how their employees dress, because appearance can affect profits, Molloy contends. "A poor first impression loses more sales than anything else," says Molloy. "A large percentage of sales die as soon as a person walks in the door."

When in doubt, Molloy advises business owners to encourage conservative, nonfaddish dress. "If people are dressed conservatively, people will buy from you," says Molloy, pointing out that although critics frowned on IBM's insistence that employees dress conservatively, "IBM laughed all the way to the bank."

Regardless of fashion trends, men at IBM are expected to wear dark suits, white shirts, and somber ties. Says one IBM executive: "We wear basic undertaker clothes, but with a lot of red 'power' ties." IBM's female employees favor conservative suits and dresses.

Fashion editors say that although shorter skirts are acceptable for business wear, employees should dress to please their bosses and their industry colleagues. "I don't think it is unfair for a business owner to expect his employees to project a certain look," says Cathy Horyn, fashion editor of the *Washington Post*. "It takes a very enlightened owner to discuss fashion, but in some cases they might use an office memo to spell out what is appropriate."

Horyn encourages business owners to keep up with fashion trends when setting rules. "A lot of women look incredibly dowdy if they cling to that midcalf skirt length," notes Horyn. "It says to people you are not in touch with things." But if skirts are too short, she adds, "it's ridiculous and becomes a distraction."

Horyn and Lynne Cusack, a freelance writer who specializes in fashion, suggest small-business owners invite a representative from a local fashion boutique or department store to conduct a workshop on a business dress for their employees. This way, the problem is defused because the advice comes from a third party and not from you personally.

Cusack also suggests complimenting employees when they dress appropriately and expressing dismay immediately when they don't dress to your liking.

"Be consistent and set a standard of dress at the top," advises Cusack.

Gregg Pawlik, with Jon Douglas Co., a Los Angeles real estate agency, confronts the question of proper business dress by being open about his fashion likes and dislikes. His pet peeve is colored or patterned hose, and he asks the women who work for him not to wear them. "But it's very difficult for a male manager or business owner to say something to his female employees because women feel the way they dress is a statement," Pawlik admits. "I tell people you can dress like a rock star in the evening, but that's not a proper image during the day."

Jay Berger, a principal in a Pasadena, California, executive recruiting firm, says he frequently counsels job candidates about how to dress for the particular company they want to work for. But instead of criticizing the way a person is dressed, he tells them the company encourages a more conservative look among its employees.

"I've had to tell my own employees to class up their act," says Berger, who, on one sizzling summer day, had to tell a secretary wearing a low-cut blouse with nothing underneath that she was not properly dressed for the office.

Kathy Taggares, the owner of a successful food business, has one employee who shows up for work every day in some kind of costume. Some days, she's wearing a sailor's uniform or police hat. Other days, she wears thrift shop finery with 20 bracelets on each arm and six or seven earrings in each ear.

Maybe *your* workplace fashion problems aren't so bad, after all.

DRESSING FOR SUCCESS

Encouraging your employees to clean up their act can be a challenge. Here are some tips on how to do it:

- Set a good example by dressing professionally yourself.
- Be clear about how you want employees to dress for work.
- Ask other business owners in your industry or profession how they handle fashion problems.
- Suggest that your employees dress to please your customers.
- Compliment employees who look great and express your dismay immediately when they don't.

- When you have to criticize someone's appearance, be diplomatic and do not mix it in with other work issues.
- Be informed about fashion trends so you are not labeled as a stick-in-the-mud.

52. HOW DO I BUILD EMPLOYEE MORALE AND ENTHUSIASM?

"Owning a business is great, except for the people." I've heard this said many times by frustrated small-business owners. With a shrinking skilled labor force, keeping good employees around your business is becoming critical. But how do you do this? If you can't pay top dollar and can't offer incredible benefits, the next best thing is to make your business a truly enjoyable place to work. You might not go to the lengths Norman Howe has to generate enthusiasm, but you can learn something from his unusual approach:

When L. Norman Howe's employees say they are willing to walk across hot coals for him, they mean it. A session with a fire walker is one way Howe has built trust and team spirit for L. Norman Howe & Associates, his Pasadena, California, marketing and consulting firm.

Howe was formerly a marketing director for the Kal Kan pet food company. He knew he was not long for corporate life when he began resisting the rigid rules set up by M&M Mars for Kal Kan when it acquired the company in the late 1960s. When Howe learned that even Kal Kan's president had to punch a time card, he said, "Whoa, this doesn't feel right. I'm not going to go any place in this organization."

Convinced that he could make money *and* have fun, he set out to provide marketing and promotional services primarily to the food industry. Called F&P Inc. (which stands for Fun & Profit), the company was incorporated in 1977, Howe also consults with companies trying to boost productivity and employee morale.

Howe believes his people-centered approach to business can be adapted to any small business with owners who care about getting the most from their employees. F&P's corporate symbol is a teddy bear because, Howe says, "We are a warm and fuzzy company."

But not everyone is ready for F&P's innovative style of management. And some company policies surprise people. According to the employee handbook, F&P employees agree to:

- Keep my word, not lie to anyone . . . including myself.
- Be a partner, not a helper, in reaching company goals.
- Take responsibility for and acknowledge broken agreements.
- Be clear, in writing, about my personal goals, and ask for what I need from my associates to accomplish them.

Your employee manual probably doesn't include most of these rules, but maybe it should. (A complete list appears at the end of this section.)

F&P staffers work in teams, setting clear goals and being rewarded for both team and individual efforts with bonuses and other perks. Employees participate in frequent encounter groups to hone their communication skills. They take turns leading staff meetings to improve their leadership abilities. Howe also challenges his troops with exercises, including the session with a fire walker who taught them how to walk across hot coals without burning their feet. "If we get together just to push the rock up the hill, it is a pretty boring way to spend our lives," says Howe, who embraces Eastern philosophies. "The workplace can provide an opportunity to have fun." In fact, when he formed F&P, he ran the business from his house, conducting much of it around the swimming pool.

Today, approximately 30 people work with Howe in what used to be a mortuary. Through creative remodeling, he has transformed the rambling brick building into a comfortable workplace. It even has a cozy dining room where the staff eats lunch as a group every day.

F&P's main business is cooking up promotions and marketing research for grocery giants such as Ralphs and Shoprite. Since 1980,

F&P's Coupons of Hope promotion has raised millions for the City of Hope medical center. The coupon books are supported by hundreds of manufacturers and virtually every supermarket chain in California and in other states. In 1985, *Advertising Age* magazine named the promotion one of the best of the year.

Howe also works with companies seeking to improve productivity. For instance, Howe served as a consultant to RBT & Associates, a Cerritos food brokerage with offices in San Francisco and Phoenix. The company was created by the merger of four brokerages. This meant the new company was faced with four different corporate cultures and conflicts needing resolution, according to Vic Trutanich, RBT's president. "We felt we needed to go outside for a fresh approach," Trutanich says.

Howe interviewed each of his 200 employees, both individually and in groups, he says. Based on his evaluations, Howe suggested new ways to organize RBT's operations. Trutanich said Howe's suggestions directly contributed to RBT's sales growing 30 to 40 percent in the past few years.

Howe said most of his clients are unaware of how he pushes himself and his staff toward personal growth. But he believes that his approach improves the quality of the work that F&P does for clients. Although most small-business owners may feel that their operations do not lend themselves to Howe's concepts, he believes a few simple changes can significantly boost employee morale and productivity.

One thing any business could do is ask employees to write up a weekly "to do" list every Monday morning. At F&P, the lists are shared, not only to increase communication but to provide an opportunity for teams to be formed to complete the work.

To increase communication with customers and vendors, Howe asks every employee to make a list of all the people they deal with outside the company. The list can be narrowed down to a few key people to save time, if necessary. "These people are a company's emotional stockholders," says Howe. At F&P, the 1,000-plus name list includes everyone from UPS drivers to top food-company executives. Three times a year, F&P sends each person a letter thanking them for their business and reminding them that F&P is ready to serve again. This is a technique that can help any business grow, Howe says.

Howe also suggests a way to cut the amount of time spent in meetings. "Starting with a meeting agenda is wrong," says Howe. "You first need to identify the purpose of the meeting and decide why you are meeting. Then, deal with what needs to be done and how you intend to make it happen."

F&P has three types of meetings:

■ "A" meetings have a definite ending time that will be adhered to, no matter what.
■ "B" meetings have an approximate ending time.
■ "C" meetings have no stated ending time and will go on until the agenda is complete.

By establishing what kind of meeting you want to have, up front, you can really save time and cut the anxiety produced by never-ending meetings.

Howe says this approach not only dramatically reduces the hours spent in meetings but makes the ones you have much more effective.

F&P ASSOCIATES AGREEMENTS

I agree to . . .

1. Keep my word and not lie to anyone . . . including myself.
2. Support each F&P associate in keeping these agreements.
3. Take responsibility for and acknowledge broken agreements.
4. Be a partner, not a helper, in reaching company goals.
5. Be clear, in writing, about my personal business goals and ask for what I need from my associates to accomplish them.
6. Plan and prioritize my activities daily.
7. Intend to get desired results, not reasons "why not" from everything I do.
8. Keep the office neat and my personal workspace organized.
9. Communicate strong feelings ("positive" or "negative") responsibly to the person(s) involved.
10. Come from the position of solution, not problem.
11. Look and act like what I do makes a difference.

12. Create and communicate satisfaction and aliveness from what I do.

Reprinted by permission, F&P Inc.

F&P BUSINESS-TO-BUSINESS AGREEMENTS

1. It is our intention to have our association result in fun and profit for both parties.

2. We hold our relationship to be a partnership to produce an agreed-upon result.

3. As partners, we are equally responsible for solving the problems and producing the result.

4. As partners, we will answer all questions you may ask about any aspect of our business that might affect the results we want.

5. We will keep our word to you absolutely . . . and if we slip, we will acknowledge our miss.

6. We will keep you informed on matters that could affect the results we have agreed upon.

7. We will give and receive constructive feedback without apologies or excuses.

8. We will not complain about your products or services to others . . . or state negative perceptions if we have not first communicated them to you.

9. We will support the growth of your business in any appropriate manner.

These are the promises we make
to all our associates, suppliers, and clients.
We request their reciprocity.

Reprinted by permission, F&P Inc.

53. HOW DO I DEAL WITH HANDICAPPED WORKERS AND THE AMERICANS WITH DISABILITIES ACT?

The Americans with Disabilities Act (ADA) breaks down barriers to employment for millions of disabled citizens. And it affects small-business owners because nearly two-thirds of all disabled workers are employed by small companies.

Although many small-business owners think they are exempt from its provisions, they are not. As a small-business owner, you not only have to make your workplace more accessible to both customers and employees in wheelchairs, but make employment opportunities available.

Before you panic at the cost, think about this: How many jobs in your business are done by people sitting at desks all day? Would it matter if those people were in wheelchairs, as long as they were qualified to do the job? Would it really take so much to install some ramps and widen a doorway or two if you could find a dependable, skilled employee who happened to be unable to walk? Couldn't your telephone sales reps be blind if they knew how to type on a special computer?

Bringing disabled workers into your business is just one aspect of employing the disabled. Many small-business owners across the country rely on "sheltered workshop" employees to assemble products, stuff envelopes, fold brochures, and fill containers.

A sheltered workshop provides a supervised setting for disabled workers to learn new skills. These workshops are located all across the country and offer very affordable help for you, whether it involves finishing an emergency project or filling your regular orders.

Read on for more information about the financial and moral benefits of working with the disabled.

Jim Roberts, founder of Gourmet Entertainment in Los Angeles, was frustrated. A maker of delicate alignment gauges for satellite television dishes, Roberts had trouble finding workers both patient and skilled enough to assemble his intricate products.

When a friend suggested he try hiring blind workers at the Foundation for the Junior Blind in Los Angeles, Roberts decided to give them a try. "The workers assembled about 1,300 tools with a zero error rate," he says. "It was a very complicated and sophisticated job."

Business owners like Roberts are increasingly turning to handicapped workers to do their assembly, packing, stuffing, folding, and collating projects. As soon as they finished with Roberts's alignment gauges, the Foundation workers began stuffing thousands of red net Christmas stockings with hard candies.

Although the Association for Retarded Citizens has a policy of encouraging American business owners to hire mentally retarded workers directly, as they do any other employees, there are still thousands of sheltered workshops operating in cities and towns around the United States.

"We consider the sheltered workshop a developmental step," says Dr. Sharon Davis, director of research and programs for the Arlington, Texas–based association. "Our ultimate goal is to have people in competitive employment."

Davis says many business owners don't realize there are state and federal funds available for what is called supported employment. The support takes several forms, but one popular option is to have a job coach accompany a handicapped worker to help teach him or her the skills needed to succeed. Sometimes the coaches stay for a few weeks; other times, they remain with the worker for longer periods of time.

There are also federal on-the-job training funds available to reimburse business owners who hire handicapped workers. "Employers are reimbursed for 50 percent of the wages for the first 160 hours of employment and 25 percent of the second 160 hours," says Davis.

The stipend offsets the cost of the additional time needed to train a handicapped worker, but Davis says once employees learn the skills required, they are expected to work just as fast and efficiently as their fellow workers.

The Association estimates that 75 percent of the country's mentally retarded adults are unemployed, yet many of them could find and maintain jobs with the right kind of support. "Once they have been given the chance, handicapped workers do really well," says Santa Bonaparte, family and membership support coordinator for the Association for Retarded Citizens' northern Virginia chapter.

She says there are at least a dozen workshops operating in the Washington metro area, some through public programs and others organized by private, nonprofit groups. The goal is for workshop graduates to go out into the community and work for all kinds of companies. "We love to have business owners welcome them into their businesses," says Bonaparte. "When they do, both the employers and the employees are happy."

Carole Jouroyan, director of the Glendale Association for the Retarded, claims her workers at the Self-Aid Workshop in Glendale, California, offer a perfect resource for small-business owners. "We can train people to do just about anything with the right kind of supervision," says Jouroyan. "Our disabled workers love to work and take a great deal of pride in their work."

In her workshop, the workers do a lot of folding, collating, and stuffing for local printers. They package nuts and bolts in heat-sealed bags and assemble elevator parts. To set a price for the job, the workshop coordinator performs a time study on the particular tasks required. The price is based on the time study and the prevailing wage. Most workshop employees earn the minimum wage or a little more.

But business owners can still save money because they are not paying the overhead or benefits for the workers.

The Americans with Disabilities Act, signed into law in July 1990, requires practically all businesses to make their facilities accessible to customers and employees with disabilities. It also requires businesses with 14 or more employees to accommodate disabled employees, not only with physical improvements such as ramps, readers, or interpreters, but possibly by hiring attendants or job coaches as well.

The law is so broad that five government agencies are preparing regulations. For more detailed information, see the resource guide that follows.

These resources can help small-business owners find ways to make their companies more accessible to the disabled:

"What Business Must Know About the Americans with Disabilities Act," a U.S. Chamber of Commerce publication covering all aspects of the law. It is available from Publications Fulfillment, U.S. Chamber of Commerce, 1615 H Street, N.W., Washington, DC 20062. Credit card orders can be phoned to (800)638-7582 (in Maryland: (800)352-1450). Specify Publication No. 0230. The price is $20 per copy for U.S. Chamber members, $33 for nonmembers.

The President's Committee on Employment of People with Disabilities offers technical help and management consulting on the subject. Write to the committee at Suite 636, 1111 20th Street, N.W., Washington, DC 20236.

The Job Accommodation Network's Committee on Employment of People with Disabilities offers free consulting for employers who face specific challenges in accommodating disabled individuals in the workplace. Technical experts counsel small firms. Call JAN'S hot line at (800)JAN-7234. In West Virginia, call (800)526-4698 or (304)293-7186.

The Architectural and Transportation Barriers Compliance Board offers copies of the access standards it developed for the law. Call (800)USA-ABLE.

The Office on the Americans with Disabilities Act, which is part of the U.S. Department of Justice, operates an information line concerning the disabilities law.

Courtesy: *Nation's Business magazine.*

HIRING THE HANDICAPPED

■ According to the Association for Retarded Citizens, mentally retarded workers reward their employers with loyalty and diligence. They do not have more accidents than normal workers or require extra employee benefits.

■ Small-business owners who are having trouble finding entry-level employees should look at this group as a source of potential talent.

■ To qualify for federal job training funds, an employer must offer year-round employment and be nonsectarian. Employers must also intend to employ the person after the training period ends, but they have the right to terminate them.

■ Employers must pay the trainee at least minimum wage and hire the trainee for at least 20 hours a week.

■ A trainee cannot be supervised by a member of his or her immediate family or be hired if a layoff status exists for the same or equivalent job at the company.

For further information, call the ARC National Employment and Training Program, (800)433-5255, or write: ARC, P.O. Box 6109, Arlington, TX 76005.

54. HOW DO I FIRE A PROBLEM EMPLOYEE WITHOUT GETTING SUED?

No one likes to admit they made a mistake in hiring, but sometimes you just can't determine what a person is really like until you work with them for a while. And no matter how careful you are in screening potential employees, you will probably have to fire someone someday.

These days, it's essential to know the right way to fire a person because doing it wrong can land you in court. In recent years, angry employees have taken to suing former employers for "wrongful termination." And, much to the chagrin of business owners, state and federal courts not infrequently side with the employees, not employers. This is why you must be both very careful and very fair in documenting the reasons for termination.

I asked human resources expert Joan Sheridan to explain the right way to terminate an employee. She covers the subject in detail in her excellent book, *Creating and Updating Your Company's Personnel Functions*.

Once you realize you have a problem employee, begin carefully documenting what Sheridan calls "progressive discipline." A progressive discipline plan must be specific and follow a path of progressive penalties. It must be fair and consistent, must not discriminate, and must be clear and understandable. The most important thing, according to Sheridan, is to be sure you *follow the plan*.

Well-documented verbal and written counselings are part of a progressive discipline plan. The number of counselings and corrective measures depends on what the employee is doing wrong. How you handle problem employees and what disciplinary action you will take should be carefully spelled out in your employee handbook to avoid confusion. (See 50. Why Do I Need Employee and Policy Manuals?)

Whenever possible, every counseling session should be documented and signed by the employee, the supervisor, and a witness, Sheridan says. If the employee refuses to sign the counseling report, you can note the fact on the bottom of the form and put it in the personnel file. After every counseling session, set a time limit to review the employee's behavior and determine if any improvement has been made.

If the problems persist and you want to put the person on probation, make sure the employee knows that failing to correct the problem within the set probationary time will lead to termination. "Never extend a probationary period," advises Sheridan.

If you need to investigate an incident involving your problem employee, you can suspend them without pay for a limited time. Before you suspend an employee, however, write down all the details leading to the suspension and make sure it is signed by the employee and the supervisor and has been approved by senior management.

What if you have tried counseling, probation, and even suspension, but you just can't have this person around anymore? Remember, firing someone is a very serious step. Be sure you have reviewed all other possibilities, including a transfer to another department or position. And make sure your decision does not involve discrimination or favoritism.

"When all else fails, and you must terminate the employee, take the time to conduct an exit interview," advises Sheridan. The exit interview will provide you with information to help you understand what caused the problem. You might also get a sense of whether or not the employee intends to file a lawsuit against you.

At the exit interview, give the person a final paycheck and, if they qualify, talk to them about the right to continuing their benefits coverage. Also explain what happens to their company stock, pension plan, and so on. Sheridan suggests collecting everything that belongs to the company—company car keys, beepers, credit cards, etc.—and giving the person a receipt for these items so no questions will arise later on.

Two more tips:

Don't walk the fired person to the door. A business owner who did this was sued by the distraught employee. A judge ruled that ushering the fired employee out the door was indeed humiliating and caused emotional trauma. The employer was ordered to pay damages.

Be careful, too, in what you say to potential employers who ask you for references. By law, you should only verify their employment and the dates they worked for you. As tempting as it is to go into the gory details of what they did wrong and why you fired them, restrain yourself.

55. HOW CAN TEMPORARY WORKERS HELP MY BUSINESS?

When you are growing fast, but not fast enough to bring on full-time people, hiring temporary help can be the perfect solution. In fact, on most workdays, about 1 million temporary workers are on the job across America.

Many business owners think temps should only be hired when someone is away on vacation or takes time off for a family emergency. But many savvy businesses rely on temporary workers to handle special projects, fill new orders, or take up the slack until permanent workers can be found.

Today's temps are highly skilled professionals who can not only answer your phone and type letters, but do your accounting, run complex computer programs, or assemble your products.

"The obvious advantage to using a temp is that you don't pay payroll taxes and you don't have to worry about benefits, insurance, or Social Security," says Marc Spilo, president of Charles Spilo Co., a national beauty supply distribution company in downtown Los Angeles, who frequently engages temporary workers to supplement his 40 regular employees. "You can keep your staff fairly lean and mean in these times, but still get the work done without a tremendous overhead," Spilo says.

A word of caution: Although the employer doesn't have to pay benefits directly, that cost is built in (as is the record keeping and government reporting) and so the hourly rates charged by temporary services are higher than for ordinary employees. In Los Angeles, for example, a temporary mail-room clerk costs about $10 an hour and a highly skilled legal typist $20 an hour. But wouldn't you rather pay for these services when you need them, as opposed to paying people for down times?

"No business has 52 identical weeks a year," says John Fanning, president of Uniforce Temporary Services, based in New Hyde Park, New York. "The beauty of using a temporary worker is you can turn on a dime."

As the economy has tightened, business owners are becoming much more cautious about hiring new, permanent workers. And by using a temporary worker, you not only can evaluate that particular person's skills, but use the time to decide whether or not you really need to create a new position.

There's more good news: In recent years, more temporary service companies have recruited temps with technical and mechanical skills. For instance, General Industrial Technologies Inc., based in Valley Stream, New York, specializes in placing technical workers in a variety of businesses across the country. Jeff Pickett, West Coast sales manager for General Industrial Technologies, says he has also received requests for temporary workers from companies making parachutes, radar-jamming devices, calculators, and military clothing.

Patty De Dominic, president of PDQ Personnel Services in Los Angeles, says software manufacturers are keeping her temps very busy. "When times are lean, companies look for computer solutions to their manpower problems," says De Dominic.

The National Association of Temporary Services in Alexandria, Virginia, offers a free booklet called "How to Buy Temporary Help Services." For a copy send a self-addressed, stamped envelope to NATS, 119 South St. Asaph Street, Alexandria, VA 22314.

Many aerospace and engineering firms, forced to lay off skilled workers, have encouraged their former employees to sign up with temporary service companies. This way they can bring them back on a short-term basis.

Bonnie Nash, president of Irvine-based Thomas Temporaries,

said temporary workers are an excellent resource for new business owners who are not ready to take on the responsibility of full-time employees.

HOW TO BRING ABOARD A TEMPORARY WORKER

- Don't be afraid to ask what you will be charged for a temporary worker. Reputable firms will quote you a rate within a dollar or so. Hourly rates are based on the worker's skills, with the highest wages paid to temps in Los Angeles and New York City.
- Determine exactly what you need the temp to do.
- Estimate the length of the project or time you will need the worker.
- Make sure you have a place for temps to work and the proper equipment when they arrive.
- Know exactly what hours you want them to work and where they should park their cars.
- Designate one person to supervise temps.
- Ask fellow business owners to recommend their favorite temporary service companies.
- Ask for references and call companies in a similar industry to see whether they were pleased with the workers provided.
- Ask the companies how they test and screen their workers.
- Ask for an estimate of the total cost of bringing the worker aboard.
- Determine whether the company will guarantee your satisfaction and replace a worker who isn't meeting your expectations.
- Try to call a day or two before you need someone, although most companies can fill requests on short notice.

56. WHAT DO I NEED TO KNOW ABOUT USING INDEPENDENT CONTRACTORS?

When you first start your business, you usually can't afford to hire full- or even part-time employees. Most small-business owners, including myself, rely on a network of independent contractors to help out until the business grows enough to support a payroll.

But be very, very careful about using independent contractors. The Internal Revenue Service is going after small-business owners around the country for alleged abuses in this area.

"Independent contractors pose a real problem for small-business owners even if they have a written agreement with people they contract with," says Nancy Iredale, a tax litigation specialist in Los Angeles. "If those folks apply for unemployment and disability benefits some years later, the state goes after employers for the money and says, 'Fork it over.' "

Iredale, who helps clients deal with the IRS, says the agency is trying to clarify its policies. Meanwhile the agency has pledged to stamp out the illegal use of independent contractors.

"For a while there, everybody and their brother was converting employees to independent contractors," says Rob Giannangeli, spokesman for the Los Angeles district of the IRS. He says while small-business owners might not want the hassle of keeping payroll records and paying taxes, they should be very careful.

The IRS uses 20 criteria to distinguish between an employee and an independent contractor. The essence is whether or not you control where and when the person works and whether you provide direction on how to do the job.

The safest kind of independent contractor to hire is a painter who owns his or her own business, submits a bid for the job, buys the paint, paints your walls, and presents a bill. In contrast, if you hire someone for a few hours a week to move boxes around your warehouse and tell them where to put the boxes—watch out. It costs more, but you may want to hire temporary workers through a bona fide agency. These folks are employees of the agency, which is responsible for keeping track of their taxes and benefits. (See 55. How Can Temporary Workers Help My Business?) You might also hire workers at a sheltered workshop, which provides training and jobs for handicapped people.

For more information on independent contractors, visit your local IRS office for a booklet on the subject, or consult your CPA.

57. SHOULD I CONSIDER LEASING MY EMPLOYEES?

You know you can lease a car or a fax machine, but did you know you can also lease your employees?

Today there are approximately one million people working for about 1,700 leasing or co-employment firms. These workers, in fields ranging from medicine to food service, are employed by the leasing firm, but work for thousands of large and small businesses around the country.

To small-business owners bogged down with government paperwork and payroll hassles, leasing provides an attractive way to eliminate headaches. The leasing firm not only takes care of all payroll and tax filings, but the leasing firm can frequently offer employees better benefits than you could.

"The small- and medium-sized business owner is caught in a terrible, terrible squeeze between trying to run a business and trying to meet all the government requirements," according to Marvin Selter, founder and chairman of National Staff Network in Van Nuys, California.

Selter, who is considered a pioneer in the leasing industry, says clients who lease their employees usually sign only two checks a month—one to cover the payroll costs and one to pay for his company's services.

Employee leasing emerged in the early 1970s and gained popularity after changes in the 1982 tax laws created potential tax savings for companies that leased workers. The 1986 tax reforms eliminated most of the tax savings, but the industry flourished anyway.

Unlike temporary workers who change jobs frequently and receive limited benefits, leased employees are long-term workers who receive a full range of benefits, including, in many cases, a pension plan. In most cases, the benefits are more affordable because the leasing company is covering hundreds or thousands of workers at a substantial discount from what the average small-business owner would pay for the same benefits.

As the legal employer, the leasing company not only provides benefits, but interviews and hires workers, keeps track of vacation and sick days, issues payroll checks, and fills out all the necessary government forms. The leasing company can also help workers laid off by one company find another job with another of the clients it serves.

Many leasing firms can also provide attractive rates, charging an administrative fee of 2.5–3 percent.

With leasing, you can fire your own valued employees one day and immediately lease them back. That's what Win-Tex Products in Dallas did a few years ago. "After the move, nothing really changed except the benefit package was dramatically improved," according to Dwayne Lovell, chief financial officer. "We had our insurance agent try to put together a similar package and he couldn't even touch it," says Lovell.

Leased labor has been very popular with the government, which leases thousands of workers each year. Thousands of nurses, doctors, and medical technicians also work for leasing companies.

Gordon Brown, president of Your Staff in Woodland Hills, California, has about 5,000 employees working in 500 California companies. "The trend in the 1990s is 'out sourcing,' which means finding others to run your mailroom and your computers," says Brown. "We fit into the trend. The more difficult the government makes it to be an employer, the more need there is for a company like ours."

Once you decide to convert your employees, it takes about two to three weeks to complete the process. "We could do it in one day, but we want to spend some time educating the employees about how it will work," says Brown.

Although it is initially somewhat upsetting and confusing to switch employers while continuing to work at the same job, most leased employees say they soon adjust to the change. They like getting a better benefit package. They also like the fact that if the company they are working for has financial troubles, they can be considered for another position at a different firm served by the same leasing company that employs them.

"Employees don't really care who they get their check from, but they do care about their benefits," says T. Joe Willey, president of the Aegis Group, in San Bernadino, California. Willey, who has written several books on employee leasing, also develops software for leasing companies.

"I think small-business owners are attracted to the freedom leasing offers them," says Willey. "If you don't have to deal with government regulations and finding health insurance, it is really a blessing."

FINDING THE RIGHT LEASING FIRM

Shop around for the right employee leasing company by asking these questions:

■ How long has this company been in business? Will your company provide bank references to verify financial stability?

■ Are your employee benefits offered by major insurance companies?

■ How long does it take for your insurance companies to pay off claims?

■ Will the fringe benefits be tailored to meet our company's needs?

■ Will the company provide references for me to check?

■ Do we have to sign a long-term contract? Can I cancel with only 30 days' notice?

■ Will they furnish quarterly statements showing that payroll taxes, pension fund contributions, and insurance premiums have been paid?

For a free fact sheet on employee leasing or a referral to a leasing firm in your area, write to: The National Staff Leasing Association, 1735 North Lynn Street, suite 950, Arlington, VA 22209-2022. Phone: (703)524-3636.

58. HOW CAN GOOD TRAINING PAY ME BACK IN PROFITS?

A few years ago, Valerie Shaw was recruiting students for a technical school. Today, she recruits trainees for the Shoe Healer, her own high-tech shoe repair shop at Sunset and Vine in Hollywood, California. "The number one problem in my industry is finding good people who will stay," says Shaw, whose father is a veteran shine man in San Diego.

"The short-term needs of businesses are so great that many can't pay attention to longer-term needs like training," says John Hurley, president of the Alexandria, Virginia–based American Society for Training and Development. Hurley, who heads the corporate training department at Chase Manhattan Bank in New York City, says American businesses and corporations invest about $475 billion a year in capital improvements, yet spend only $30 billion yearly on training and education programs.

Although most big companies budget for some in-house training, small-business owners have to be more creative. Hurley suggests asking the bigger companies you do business with to help train your workers. Many large public companies, including Ford, Motorola, Xerox, and IBM, spend millions of dollars training workers at all levels and attribute their growth and profits to investing in their employees.

Another route is state-financed training. In 1991, 46 states offered some type of state-funded, industry-specific training programs. In 1990, California's Employment Training Panel paid companies

$62.8 million to help business owners train or retrain 35,000 workers who were previously collecting unemployment benefits or needed new skills to maintain a competitive edge. Seventy-nine percent of the participating businesses have fewer than 250 employees. The only catch: You won't receive the money from the state until after you train and hire the workers.

The federal Job Training Partnership Act also provides about $4 billion a year to train economically disadvantaged workers. About 11,000 business representatives serve on the private industry councils set up across the country to allocate the federal funds.

In her quest to find energetic and loyal employees, Valerie Shaw has hired former gang members and felons, as well as skilled cobblers she affectionately calls "the cowboys." Shaw and her master cobblers are using state employment training funds to stretch her dollars.

Shaw obtained her training funds with the help of Nanci Prince, executive director of the Central Park Five Council, a nonprofit organization in Los Angeles. As part of her job, Prince helps clients prepare grant applications for a modest fee. If the grant is denied, she refunds the money. If the grant comes through, they pay her an additional sum.

To qualify for state training funds, business owners must contribute to the state's unemployment insurance program and have the ability to train people at their place of business. They must also be willing to hire a third of the workers who complete the training program and help find jobs for the others, Prince says.

For workers who can earn at least $8 an hour, employers can qualify for about $3,000 in training funds. Businesses that can provide training for jobs paying $10 or more an hour can qualify for about $5,000.

For more information on programs in your state, contact the state employment department.

The American Society for Training and Development is at 1630 Duke Street, Alexandria, VA 22313. Phone: (703)683-8100. The Society publishes a variety of brochures and information on training programs for big and small businesses.

59. HOW CAN I PREVENT EMPLOYEE THEFT FROM KILLING MY PROFITS?

One Arizona small-business owner I interviewed is still stinging from being ripped off not once but *twice* by two different office managers. "It's sad to say, but you are better off taking the attitude that everyone you hire is a potential thief," says the business owner, who agreed to discuss his woes but was too embarrassed about his $36,000 loss to see his name in print.

The young woman he hired to manage his office stole about $20,000 from his manufacturing business. She did it after persuading him to convert his bookkeeping system from a handwritten ledger to a computerized accounting program that she alone could run. Over several years, she diverted funds into her own account and destroyed computer records to cover it up.

Vowing never to be a victim of employee theft again, the owner hired a woman he described as "a real Mary Poppins type." Well, "Mary Poppins" stole about $16,000 before he found out she was on probation for stealing from a previous employer. She had hidden her identity by using her maiden name, so nothing came up during his check into her background.

Each year, American businesses lose about $40 billion to employee theft, according to the U.S. Chamber of Commerce. And investigators who specialize in business crime say that up to 75 percent of the thefts go undetected by management. Don't think your employees are too loyal to steal from you. A recent survey revealed that a third of employees interviewed would steal from their employers if they thought they could get away with it. Another survey showed 38 percent of those interviewed had already stolen something.

"Employee theft has a tendency to be contagious and cancerous," says John Case, president of John D. Case and Associates in San Diego, California. "Theft results from a breakdown of procedures and a poor management attitude." Case, who counsels business owners around the country and abroad, adds that the most lethal form of theft involves collusion between an employee and an outsider. "The employee is able to circumvent procedures and the outsider can transport the goods off the property."

Every business owner, no matter how busy, should take time to watch for danger signs, including any unexplained shortage of inventory or a sudden drop in profits.

Make frequent, unannounced visits to your warehouse or storage area to look for merchandise that is out of place or in partially filled boxes, which may mean things are missing. You should also randomly check deliveries to make sure everything you paid for is really delivered. And, make sure your delivery people are taking out exactly what they are supposed to each day. A very common crime against a small business is to take along a few extra boxes of whatever it is you're selling. The delivery person then makes a stop, delivers it to a friend, and sells it on the side for extra cash.

Another tip: Photocopies frequently replacing original invoices and other documents could mean trouble. And an employee who handles cash or accounts receivable and refuses to take a vacation or accept a promotion to another department is also worth investigating. Crooks often refuse to leave their jobs because their deeds might be uncovered by someone filling in for them.

Private investigators encourage business owners to listen to employee gossip, because eventually rumors will surface about illegal activities. "A number of employees usually know what's going on," warns Case, "but they don't like to snitch."

He also suggests talking openly with employees about the impact of theft and emphasizing that a dishonest employee not only steals from the company but jeopardizes the jobs of his or her fellow workers by weakening the business.

Investigators agree that preventive action, including careful screening of applicants, is cheaper and easier than trying to trap a thief later on.

"By the time a business owner figures out someone is stealing, the company may not have any money left," says Daniel Jones, president of D. Y. Jones & Associates in Glendale, California. "The best thing a business owner can do is not hire bad people to begin with."

Jones has developed several techniques for detecting résumé fraud. He encourages employers to tell applicants that they plan to conduct a thorough background check and ask if there is anything they would like to share or add to the form. The next step is to ask for the name and phone number of their former supervisor. When you call, ask to speak to the supervisor directly rather than to the company personnel director. If you can, talk to former co-workers or a receptionist to get a real sense of what the person was like as an employee.

Take the time to check municipal court records to see if the person has been sued or has filed for a business license or a fictitious business name. If a résumé shows long periods of self-employment, ask for the names and numbers of vendors or clients. Then call them to find out exactly what kind of services the applicant provided. Complete the check by calling several neighbors (criss-cross telephone directories provide the phone number if you have an address) and ask how long the person has lived in the neighborhood.

Jones also suggests asking the applicant to provide a Department of Motor Vehicles report so you can review his or her driving record. You are liable for the damage your employees cause to others, so you don't want to have a person with a drinking problem or poor driving record behind the wheel of your company truck.

A few more red flags:

If an employee suddenly shows up with a new expensive wardrobe or new car, I would ask where all the new cash came from. The odds of winning a lottery are slim, and not too many rich uncles really die and leave a comfortable inheritance to their relatives.

If you suspect someone is stealing from you, be careful not to make wild accusations. Before calling in the local police or a private investigator, try to collect as much evidence as you can. Be prepared, though: The police may not be too interested in helping you.

They are usually too busy to put much time into solving small-business crimes. It might be worth your trouble to hire a private investigator who can put together a case and turn it over to the district attorney or appropriate authorities.

Too many small-business owners refuse to prosecute thieves because they don't want the publicity—or they don't want to spend the money on lawyers. This is a mistake. If you don't stop someone who steals from you, they will certainly go on to steal from others.

One lumberyard owner filed charges against three clerks who were looting the cash register every day. He posted all the legal documents and sentencing reports on the company bulletin board as a deterrent to others. He also learned, in a very expensive way, that he had created the problem by not training the clerks how to use a sophisticated cash register. Because they couldn't figure out how to work it, they didn't use it at all! So, it was easy to pocket most of the cash every day.

It's important to set a good example for your employees. If they see you or your family carrying out boxes of product, they will think it's okay for them to do the same. If you fill your pockets with pens and paper clips from the company storeroom, your employees will, too.

Make sure everyone knows what you expect of them and that the rules and policies are clear so there is no confusion. It is also a good idea to have regular staff meetings to air gripes and problems before they affect morale. If your workers feel cheated, underpaid, or overworked, you're asking for trouble.

Here are some additional resources:

John Case's booklet, "How to Identify Dishonesty Within Your Business," lists 97 early-warning signs of internal theft. It costs $5.45 and is available from John Case & Associates, 3510 Park Boulevard, San Diego, CA 92103.

The Chubb Group of Insurance Companies and Ernst & Young offer a free booklet, "White Collar Crime: Loss Prevention Through Internal Control." Write to the Chubb Group, Warren, NJ 07060.

"White Collar Crime 101 Prevention Handbook" by Jane Y. Kusic is available from the author for $8.95. Kusic covers the gamut of fraud schemes, including ones perpetrated on business owners. Write to Kusic at 8300 Boone Boulevard, suite 500, Vienna, VA 22182. Virginia residents should add sales tax.

WAYS TO THWART EMPLOYEE THEFT

■ Try not to allow the same person to handle money coming into and going out from your business.

■ Ask your insurance agent to visit your business and check it out before buying a substantial theft insurance policy.

■ Ask a bonding company to bond your employees if possible.

■ To catch problems early, ask your accountant to conduct quarterly audits of your books.

■ Have the bank send all canceled checks directly to you for review.

■ Check the phone bills for frequent employee calls to unrecognized businesses or locations.

■ Closely monitor the petty cash fund.

■ Question any excessive number of voids, credits, or damage claims.

■ Be suspicious of any employee who has a sudden change in financial status or starts buying expensive clothes, gifts, or cars.

60. HOW DO I MAINTAIN A SAFE WORKPLACE?

David Coots, foundry manager for Valley Brass, Inc., in El Monte, California, was so proud of his new safety equipment for workers who pour molten lead that he actually welcomed health and safety inspectors into the sprinkler plant. Since then, however, his attempts to meet the requirements of California's strict health and safety laws have taxed his time and patience.

"You have to be an environmentalist, hygienist, or lawyer to understand what they want," laments Coots.

California led the nation in requiring all businesses to have a written injury and illness prevention plan, and other states and the federal government are quickly following suit. No matter what kind of business you are in, you will be forced to deal with workplace safety issues.

"The public does not want to put up with any unnecessary hazards in any aspects of their lives and especially not at work," says Majorie Drucker, founder of Drucker Health & Safety Management, Inc., in Manhattan Beach, California. Drucker, who formerly worked for the U.S. Environmental Protection Agency, also says that business owners who tackle their health and safety problems head-on will see positive bottom-line results. "Businesses can reap substantial benefits, including reduced insurance claims and premiums, improved productivity among workers and ultimately higher profits," she says.

A whole new segment of the safety industry is cropping up to help California business owners comply with Senate Bill 198. Effective on July 1, 1991, the law emphasizes worker training and requires companies to set up internal safety inspections and safety committees. Consultants who specialize in workplace safety are reaping the benefits by helping large- and small-business owners comply. One Orange County video production company, realizing there was a need to fill, produced a line of corporate-sponsored videotapes addressing workplace safety issues for various industries. And because California has a multicultural workforce, many business owners must not only produce their safety materials in English, but in other languages as well.

When you're just starting out in business, it's easy to ignore safety concerns. But beware: State and federal laws are very clear and impose stiff penalties for noncompliance. The good news is that safety issues do not have to bog you down if you take a little time every week to deal with them.

Start out by finding out exactly what your state requires. Most states have government safety consultants who will visit your business and help you figure out what you need to do to comply.

If you give your business the following safety checkup, you'll be on your way.

You might also write to Krames Communications for a free sampling of their health and safety booklets. The address is 1100 Grundy Lane, San Bruno, CA 94066-3030.

Their employee education materials can be incorporated into your customized safety program.

A SAFETY CHECKUP

- Create a safety committee to tour the company to check for hazards in every department.
- Make plans to correct the hazards before an accident occurs.
- Develop ways to comply with all state and local health and safety regulations.
- Investigate and record all workplace accidents.
- Explore the need for protective clothing and equipment.
- Make sure you have a fully stocked first-aid kit near each work area.
- Post the address and phone number of the nearest hospital or clinic.
- Offer your workers classes in first-aid and cardiopulmonary resuscitation (CPR).
- Keep track of how many work days were missed due to accidents or injuries.
- Schedule regular safety meetings.
- Prepare a written safety plan and circulate it to all employees.
- Offer incentives for improved safety records, such as prizes or bonuses for accident-free months.

61. HOW DO I FIND AFFORDABLE HEALTH INSURANCE FOR MY BUSINESS?

Ariel Zakwin, founder of 45-year-old California Jewelsmiths, Inc., began to worry when his health insurance premiums doubled in the space of a month. And when the rate for his 15 employees topped $6,000, he said enough is enough.

Like many small-business owners, Zakwin shopped around in his quest to reduce his insurance burden. Last spring, his workshop jewelers decided to buy their own policies, leaving five employees, including Zakwin's daughters, Wendy and Gigi, in need of coverage. Trying to find coverage for a tiny group is hard enough, but Zakwin faced an added challenge: Gigi Zakwin has interstitial cystitis, a painful and chronic bladder inflammation that requires her to be under a doctor's care.

The Zakwins turned to James Lawson, an independent insurance broker in Beverly Hills, who persuaded Blue Cross of California to write the Zakwins a policy under the insurer's small group access plan.

"When you get down to five or six employees it becomes real tricky," says Lawson, who specializes in finding coverage for closely held businesses. But having seen Gigi at work, he knew her condition was not disabling. "When you know somebody personally, it helps quite a bit in dealing with the insurance carriers."

Gigi Zakwin says Lawson's persistence paid off. Although they pay about $1,700 a month for health insurance, the premium hasn't gone up as fast, and the Zakwins hope to keep the policy in effect for a long time.

Insurance industry experts say the small-business health insurance crisis continues but may be improving.

"We have hit the worst and it will get better," predicts Mark Weinberg, executive vice-president of Blue Cross of California's consumer services group, adding that insurance companies created the current crisis for small-business owners by focusing on providing coverage for larger, healthier groups of workers at the expense of the smaller companies.

"Industry-wide, 35 percent of all applications for small-business health insurance are turned down and that is even when the business owners have money in hand," Weinberg says. But he and others say insurers are slowly realizing they have a responsibility to cover small businesses and must change their attitudes. They have also been under increased pressure by elected officials and groups like National Small Business United to provide affordable coverage.

As a result, some insurers have slowed rate hikes, and at least two major companies have dropped the practice of declaring certain industry groups ineligible for coverage. Some companies blacklisted law firms, for example, on the grounds that their employees would be more likely to sue.

Even with some 1,700 insurance companies doing business in the United States, however, finding the right coverage for your company takes research and persistence.

"My advice to the small-business owner is to deal with an independent agent or broker," says Robert Bland, president of Quotesmith, a Palatine, Illinois, company that tracks rates offered by health insurance companies across the country as well as other kinds of insurance carriers. Independent agents can shop around and find the best rates because they don't represent a particular company.

"It's a jungle out there and people don't realize that there are huge price differences between companies for the same insurance coverage," Bland says. And many small-business owners are angry because they sign up with a company that offers an attractive initial rate, only to find their rates skyrocketing six months later. To make matters worse, in 1990 and 1991, health insurance companies raised their rates between 25 and 30 percent to cope with the rising cost of health care.

There's no reason for despair, however. With time and persistence, you will eventually find suitable coverage. One good way to find affordable insurance is to join an organization such as Washington, D.C.,–based National Small Business United, which has a relationship with Mutual of Omaha, or the National Association of the Self-Employed. (See Resources guide for details.)

Ask other small-business owners you know to recommend a good independent insurance agent.

HOW TO FIND AFFORDABLE HEALTH INSURANCE

Finding health insurance for your business does not have to be a major headache. The time you spend looking for affordable coverage will be well spent.

■ Ask friends or fellow business owners to recommend a reputable, independent insurance broker.

■ Ask your employees how much they will be willing to contribute toward their own health insurance coverage.

■ Get quotes from several different companies with both $250 and $500 deductibles.

■ Try to deal with insurance companies based in your state so they will be licensed and monitored by state officials.

■ Choose an insurance company that's been awarded an A or A-plus rating from the A.M. Best Co. rating service.

■ Establish a wellness program for your business and encourage people to stop smoking, lose weight, and take better care of themselves.

62. SHOULD I ESTABLISH A PENSION PLAN?

When you are young and starting a business, pension plans seem very far away. But the federal Social Security system is teetering on the brink of insolvency, and if you don't start putting money away for yourself now, you won't have anything to live on later.

By 2020, 49 million Americans are expected to reach age 65. Someone had better be thinking about taking care of all those people and their financial needs. And that someone is us—America's owners of small businesses.

Although there is no legal requirement to offer pension benefits beyond paying the required Social Security taxes, many small-business owners view their pension plan as an incentive to recruit and retain loyal employees. But setting up a pension plan is not something you can do yourself. This is one area where you should definitely work with an expert. A maze of federal regulations governs pension programs, and you will not be able to navigate alone.

You might think your business is too small to worry about a pension plan. But even if you have only six employees, you can do wonders without spending a fortune.

Willi Winzelberg is one small-business owner who planned well for his retirement in 1991. For years, he set aside about $30,000 a year for himself and his employees at Authorized Camera Service, in Sherman Oaks, California. "It may seem like a lot of money to put in yearly, but it's nothing compared to the benefits you get out of it," says Winzelberg, who was able to give his partner $67,000 when he retired from the business in 1987. Winzelberg works with his accountant and pension administrator, Sam Gilbert, to manage the plan.

But not every business owner is as forward-thinking as Winzelberg. And, as the economy faltered, a shocking number of businesses cashed out their pension funds because they couldn't afford them any more.

"In the past three years, 46 percent of small businesses terminated their pension plans," says Gilbert, who is president of United Plan Administrators, in Westlake Village, California. "However, it is vitally important that small-business owners [re]establish retirement plans, because this country will soon experience major problems with government retirement programs, mainly the Social Security system."

Now, pension programs are not cheap, and they do not take the place of Social Security taxes. (In 1991, employers had to pay 7.65 percent of each employee's salary into Social Security.) But a major advantage of starting a pension program is that every dollar you put away is tax deductible as a business expense. And all interest earned is tax-deferred until the money is withdrawn. Still, "The attitude has to be that pension programs are employee benefit plans, not tax dodges," says Donna Hopson, president of Hopson Pension Services, Inc., in Tustin, California.

Where to invest the pension money is left up to you and your financial adviser. Most small-business owners invest the money in government bonds, certificates of deposit, or other conservative instruments. However, many businesses put their pension money in the stock market, hoping to earn a higher rate of return. Do whatever allows you to sleep better at night.

Small-business owners have a variety of options to consider when setting up a pension plan. Tax laws are ever-changing, so consult your accountant and other professional advisers for up-to-date details about the following options:

■ A *profit-sharing plan* allows you to set aside up to 15 percent of each employee's annual compensation. Under this type of plan, the percentages can change each year depending on the company's fortunes. Employees do not contribute anything to a profit-sharing plan.

- If you select a *money purchase pension plan*, you may set aside up to 25 percent of a person's salary, but the percentage must stay the same every year.

- A *defined-benefit plan* requires you to pay the retiree an amount defined by a formula based on years of service and salary. Both employers and employees may contribute to this kind of plan.

- A *401(k) plan* is another popular option, named after a section of the U.S. tax code. These plans enable both the employer and the employee to contribute money tax-free. Most employers match the employee's contribution in some way, but it is not required.

- A *target-benefit plan* is a hybrid between defined-benefit and money purchase plans. This plan works well to give older employees a higher percentage of employer's contribution.

- A *simplified employee pension plan* (SEPP) requires that even part-time employees who have received a minimum amount of money must be included in the plan. The contributions are made to individual retirement accounts in the name of the participants. Employees like it because they are 100 percent vested right away and can take the money with them when they go. Most employers don't like SEPP because of this provision, according to Hopson.

■

I strongly advise you to retain a pension plan administrator to manage the plan. It may cost several thousand dollars a year, but it will be money well spent if you choose the right manager.

"We drum into our clients' heads that this is your retirement—don't lose it, don't gamble," says Hopson. "Be careful, it's not Monopoly money."

63. SHOULD I CONSIDER BUYING DISABILITY INSURANCE FOR MYSELF?

No one likes to think about getting sick or being injured, but when you are running a business and are responsible for your family and the welfare of others, you must think about these things.

Buying disability insurance is one way to secure the future of your family and your business. But insurance is fairly expensive, and most people don't understand how it works.

Here's how disability insurance helped one small-business owner hang on to his business after his worst nightmare came true:

On a rain-slicked road, Bob Page's car was hit head-on by a drunk driver. The drunk driver died. Page survived, but suffered 15 broken bones and a bruised heart. For five months after his release from the hospital, Page was in a wheelchair, depending on his parents, friends, and employees to keep Replacements Ltd. going. Fortunately, his Greensboro, North Carolina, company, which supplies customers with obsolete china, crystal, and silver patterns, survived his personal disaster and has flourished.

"I had personal disability insurance that paid about $1,000 a month," says Page. "My salary continued because I owned the company, and I was lucky to have people around to help me run the business."

But not all small-business owners are as lucky as Page. Insurance executives estimate that only 30 to 40 percent of the nation's small-business owners have disability insurance. This is a chilling estimate when you consider that at age 37—the prime age for an entrepreneur—the probability of becoming disabled is $3\frac{1}{2}$ times higher than the probability of death.

Hard-driving, passionate entrepreneurs are especially reluctant to think about what would happen to their business if they were disabled, and persuading them to buy personal disability insurance is tough, according to insurance agents and executives. Yet a busy entrepreneur risks losing everything if he or she is unable to work—and is not properly insured.

"There are two forms of death," says John Swenson, who specializes in disability issues at New York Life Insurance Co. in New York City. "One form is where the insured dies and the family is left to work things out. The other, more agonizing death is when the individual becomes disabled and there is no income."

Virtually all personal disability policies offer the same kinds of benefits. They generally pay a monthly benefit that is slightly less than what you would earn if you were healthy and working. This gap is intentional: Insurers want you to have an incentive to get well and return to work.

The kind of policy you qualify for depends on what you do for a living. Professionals, such as attorneys and architects, have the easiest time buying disability insurance. Automobile and real estate salespeople, subject to the ups and downs of the economy, have a tougher time. People in risky professions, such as private detectives, construction workers, and actors may have to look a long time for a policy.

"The underwriter looks at the likelihood of a person being disabled and how long they will stay on disability," says Harris Kagan, a New York Life agent in Santa Monica, California. "An agent needs to know how much money you need to protect your mortgage, debts, wife, husband, and children." Disability insurance underwriters also consider the number of employees you have, the length of time you have been in business, and the claims history in your industry.

You can save money on the premium if you're willing to wait 60 to 90 days after the disabling event for the benefits to kick in. The purpose of this "elimination period" is to remove some of the incentives for the insured to begin collecting benefits. "The longer a person has to go without receiving income from their normal job, the less incentive they may have to claim a disability," says Danny

Lerner, a partner at Commercial Benefits, a Woodland Hills, California, firm specializing in individual and business insurance planning.

Normally, disability benefits are tax-free. But if your company pays for the premium and takes a tax deduction, your benefits will be taxed. To avoid this, most insurance planners suggest you pay for the policy with personal funds.

It is also important to make sure your policy covers your specific occupation, not just *any* occupation. This means if you are president of a tool manufacturing company and you suffer a heart attack that prevents you from doing your old job, you can collect your benefits even if you take up a less-taxing, lower-paying occupation later on. And although it's cheaper to buy a policy that provides benefits to age 65, Lerner recommends paying a bit extra for a policy with lifetime benefits.

Meanwhile, Bob Page is fully recovered and has increased his personal disability coverage to $5,000 a month. He also purchased disability coverage for his workers.

WHEN BUYING DISABILITY INSURANCE . . .

■ Figure out how much you need to cover all your personal monthly expenses.

■ Obtain estimates from several insurance carriers.

■ Check the financial stability of the company you buy a policy from.

■ Although it costs more, try to buy a policy with lifetime benefits.

■ Consider buying business interruption insurance to further protect your business from collapsing if something happens to you.

64. HOW CAN I BOOST SALES FOR MY BUSINESS?

Nothing is more frustrating than having a product you know is great, but just doesn't move out the door. It all comes down to sales.

For these sales tips, I turned to someone whose advice I really trust: my grandfather, George B. Coan. Coan is a veteran retailer with more than 50 years experience in the men's clothing business. At 85-plus, he is also the snappiest dresser I know. Coan has been in the retail business since he was a kid selling clothes in his father's store. He worked his way up from a junior clerk at Howard Clothes in New York City to a senior executive. By the time he retired the first time, his responsibility was personnel matters and he'd become a troubleshooter skilled at negotiating with unions.

Bored at home, he went back into the retail business in his seventies, opening a small sportswear shop in North Miami Beach, Florida, a shop he closed to manage his condominium association for a few years. Retired again, he had time to offer this hot sales tip:

"Multiple selling means the difference between success and failure for a small business," says Coan, who implemented a system still utilized by major retailers today.

For decades, the tradition in retailing was for sales clerks to write up the sales tickets at desks stationed around the main sales floor. As a young store manager, Coan realized this system thwarted efforts to sell shirts, ties, and accessories to go along with the new suits. His solution: Ditch the desks and move all the sales-ticket writing into the men's furnishings department, where the accessories were beautifully displayed. This meant every sale was written up in plain view of all the shirts and ties that went so well with the suits and jackets being purchased by the customers.

"This way, you could pull out a tie and show the customer how great it looks with the suit he is buying," notes Coan. "Nothing high-pressure. You are just showing the customer what else you have to offer." Eventually, furnishings accounted for 30 percent of Howard's total sales in his stores, Coan says. And today, you'll see many fine retail stores place their cash registers behind glass display cases to encourage those last-minute, impulse purchases. This works because people are busy, and they prefer to do all their shopping in one place if they can.

Coan also recommends that small-business retailers encourage rather than discourage layaway sales. Why? It not only builds goodwill, but can create a nice little nest egg. Although you might need to refund the deposits if the customer changes his mind, you should deposit the money into a separate bank account and collect interest on it. Even if you return the principal, the interest is yours. Sometimes, if the item is in great demand, you can require a nonrefundable deposit. You can set a time limit, and if the item isn't paid for, the money is yours.

> Here's another hot sales tip: Dream up all kinds of off-season sales to generate excitement and offer your customers great deals.

Coan came up with this approach in 1931 when he was managing a store in Brooklyn, New York. On July 5, he asked his window trimmer to set up a display of winter coats. The window trimmer, preparing new displays for fall clothes, thought Coan was crazy. "Do it," said Coan. "I'll take full responsibility for the consequences."

Once the overcoats were in the window, Coan instructed all his salespeople to drape an overcoat over their arm and show the customer how nice it looked over the suit they were trying on.

At the time, a $5 deposit held the overcoat until a week after Labor Day. The coats were selling briskly, although it was sizzling outside.

A few weeks after the promotion began, the store's general manager stopped by, looked at the window full of overcoats, and called Coan outside. "What's all this about?" he asked, pointing to the window full of overcoats while standing in the sweltering summer heat.

"We're having a preseason sale," said Coan calmly. He admitted it was not an original idea and took the general manager to see that their competitor also had overcoats in the window.

"Is it working?" asked the manager on the way back to Coan's store.

Coan didn't answer. Instead, he led him upstairs to a third-floor storage room, where coats on layaway were stored. "I had 200 topcoats, raincoats, and overcoats lined up like soldiers," recalls Coan.

No one questioned his off-season sales again.

Another essential sales tip: Make sure you have the right salespeople dealing with your customers. "The people on the sales floor will make you or break you," asserts Coan.

Make sure they *never* tell your customers they bought the same item. Here's why:

One day a very handsome man walked in to Coan's store with his wife. They wanted to see a suit that was in the window.

The salesman who was assigned to wait on him was portly, slovenly, and unshaven, with cigar ashes spilled down his front. But he was personable enough and found the suit the man wanted to try on. The customer, a well-built man of 6'1", 195 pounds, looked great in the suit.

The beaming wife spoke up: "I like the way it looks on you," she said with a smile.

"I love that suit, too," blurted out the short, dumpy salesman. "In fact, I bought the same suit last week!"

The customer blanched. He took off the coat and handed it back to the salesman.

"Mister, I don't want to look like *you*," he said as he walked out with his wife in tow.

SALES TIPS

■ Make sure your salespeople are well trained and well acquainted with your particular products.

■ Hire people who fit the image you want to present to customers.

■ Always know what your competition is up to. Read their ads, visit their stores, and buy their merchandise to see how their salesclerks treat customers.

■ Figure out ways to set your store apart from the competition. Better prices are not enough today. Offer better service, longer hours, more selection, free alterations, or free delivery.

65. HOW CAN MY SALES TECHNIQUES SET ME APART FROM THE COMPETITION?

One of the most outrageous entrepreneurs I've ever met is Rudy Cervantes. Cervantes is a living legend in the novelty-tie business. I met him because he was absolutely convinced his story belonged in my "Succeeding in Small Business" column.

He left several messages on my answering machine, imploring me to call him back. Then, one day he called and said we had to meet right away because it was an "emergency."

"What kind of emergency?" I asked, busy with two other news stories that day.

"You'll see when you get here—just come quickly," Rudy implored, giving an address that turned out to be the Los Angeles Convention Center. Peeved, perplexed, yet curious, I raced down to the Convention Center and found him sitting in his booth at a menswear trade show.

"I knew you'd come," he said, grinning. "I have a good story to tell and I'm the best salesman you'll ever meet." I sat and listened and learned. His story shows how you, too, can set yourself apart from your competition.

Although he also sells a standard line of men's neckwear, Cervantes's passion and profits stem from novelty ties. His crowded showroom is filled with Bicentennial ties, Olympics ties, Mickey Mouse ties, "Joe Cool" Snoopy ties, and Dodgers ties. And after more than 30 years in sales, Cervantes, founder and president of Cervantes Neckwear Inc. in downtown Los Angeles, has perfected an aggressive and witty sales approach. "You have to have ideas," says Cervantes. "You can't just walk in and show them ties or whatever it is you make. And you don't need to have an appointment. Just drop in, because a potential customer is always interested in something different."

His favorite trick is to send celebrities novelty ties. He also likes to present potential customers with color mock-ups to show them exactly what their ties would look like. Persistence is Rudy's middle name. After five years of sales calls, he finally got an order from the Magic Mountain amusement park in Valencia, California, for Bugs Bunny ties.

He chose Mickey Mouse to decorate his earliest novelty ties because "I worshipped Mickey Mouse—I grew up with him."

Cervantes remembers when his accountant called him a *nut* for paying $5,000 for the licensing rights to make Mickey Mouse ties. Today, those Mickey ties are still best-sellers. "Next to Disneyland, I think I sell more of Rudy's Mickey Mouse ties than anyone," says Barbara Williams, owner of a fashion accessories shop in the Los Angeles Farmer's Market. "In the novelty-tie field, I don't think anyone can touch him," says Williams, who has known Cervantes for more than 30 years.

No matter what business you are in, tailoring a sample of your product to your customer can be extremely effective. Putting your customer's logo on the package, if appropriate, or otherwise customizing the product to meet their needs, helps sell the finished product. For instance, Cervantes sold McDonald's executives on buying thousands of corporate logo ties after he showed them what he had done for other large companies.

"When I call on a customer, I am well prepared," explains Cervantes. He says any salesperson must take the time to analyze the customer's needs and offer the right product at the right price. "Sometimes, I tell the customer, 'My ties are not for you,'" he says. "Why show something they can't afford and make them feel bad?"

Cervantes has sent ties to all kinds of celebrities, from Los Angeles Mayor Tom Bradley to Elvis Presley. He has sent ties to Presidents Gerald Ford and Ronald Reagan and has their thank-you notes and photographs to prove it.

He still laughs about the way he got me to interview him. "See, I *am* the best salesman there is!" he says.

66. HOW CAN I BRING IN NEW CUSTOMERS?

Here's how one successful small-business owner attracts customers. His method might not be for you, but we can all learn from Al.

Al's Sun Valley Tire & Automotive Center has been open since 1956. He believes a secret of his success is making people laugh so they remember to bring him their cars when they need repairs or a new set of tires.

Five days a week, several hours a day, Al stands on the corner of Sunland and Penrose wearing a rubber mask. Sometimes, he's Bart Simpson. Other times, he's a lion or a chicken or a scary-looking, bald pinhead.

Al waves, struts, dances, and shimmies. He runs up to cars, grabs kids' hands through open car windows, and pats them on the heads as their startled parents watch.

"We've always done crazy things," says Al, who prefers not to reveal his last name. "We once had a wooden horse that we wheeled out there. Then, we had girls in bathing suits for a while."

Al says wearing masks is a great tension-reliever. Not just for the uptight people rushing by him, but for himself. And the attention he creates on the corner pays off in increased sales and loyal customers. "When people have to make a decision, they'll say, 'I'll go where that looney guy stands out in the street.'"

His antics attracted me into his garage. When our car needed a tune-up and a brake job, we pulled into Al's Sun Valley Tire. It was astonishingly clean and well-organized. The waiting area is tidy and decorated with folksy sayings and jokes; the employees are attentive, efficient, and friendly. "We are a fun place and try to convey a fun image," says Al. "We are also cheaper than Disneyland."

One morning he was working on the marquee out front. "Happy Birthday, Ruben!"

For about 20 years, Al kept the shop open seven days a week. When business was strong, he cut back to six and a half days. Now, he's open only five days. "Our customers are 80 percent returns and referrals," says Al. "Only 20 percent are first timers or drifters."

He still balances tires for $1.95. No catches or hidden charges. "There is more to life than just a dollar," says Al as he pulls on his lion mask and heads out to his corner.

Create a flier to promote a special discount, two-for-one sale, or free offer. Ask the owners of local dry cleaners, hair salons, and restaurants to distribute them in exchange for bigger discounts on your products or services. Why? These businesses generate lots of foot traffic and can build word-of-mouth referrals for you.

---

67. HOW DO I EXPAND MY SALES TO ETHNIC GROUPS?

If you haven't already noticed, America has become a truly multi-cultural country. Thousands of Asian-Americans, Latin Americans, and people from every other continent are living and working in nearly every city and town across the country. Although many recent arrivals prefer to wear, eat, and drink familiar products, they still need to buy a wide variety of consumer and business products and services *you* sell.

If you are not trying to sell your products or services to a variety of ethnic groups, you are missing out on new sales to loyal customers.

How do you reach out to them?

The secret is to tailor your advertising and marketing campaign to a specific group without offending their customs or beliefs. To take one simple case: using the wrong color can be a disaster. For instance, Japanese people who are in mourning wear white, not black. So, if your ads feature a happy family dressed in white clothes, they won't be effective with Japanese-American consumers.

Merely translating your materials from English into another language can also be a big mistake because every language has its particular nuances and subtle meanings.

One of the biggest bloopers in cross-cultural marketing was made by Chevrolet a few years ago when the company tried to sell the popular Nova model in Mexico. They began advertising the car, but no one seemed to want it. It was easy to see why the Nova was a flop. In Spanish, "No va" means "no go." How's that for the worst possible name for a car selling in Mexico!(?)

If your business is in an ethnically diverse neighborhood, be sure to carry products familiar to your customer. The Sun Valley Discount Center, a swap meet in a predominantly Hispanic neighborhood, imports Coca-Cola from Mexico to please its customers.

Your best bet is to hire a native speaker to rewrite your materials into the language.

With a little bit of research and some help from people who specialize in cross-cultural marketing, you can expand your horizons without leaving this country.

Two young San Francisco advertising executives offer some great advice on dealing with Asian-Americans—and you can easily apply their observations to other ethnic groups.

Small-business owners who don't try to reach Asian-Americans are missing out on a chance to deal with the fastest-growing, most educated, and most affluent ethnic group in the United States, according to the owners of East-West Advertising in San Francisco.

"It's a market up for grabs for businesses run by visionaries," says Rafael Ungson, creative director for East-West. Asian-Pacific Americans, who represent about 7.3 million people, or 3 percent of the U.S. population, outnumber blacks in 10 states and Latinos in 3 states, according to the 1990 census. California, New York, Hawaii, and Texas top the list of states with the most Asian-American residents. Illinois, New Jersey, Washington, Virginia, and Florida also experienced an explosion in Asian-American population growth between 1980 and 1990, according to census figures.

"The problem is, nobody wants to be the guinea pig in approaching a new market," says Len Fong, East-West's director of client services. "But by being first, you will gain a loyalty that will pay off for years."

Fong and other advertising executives say too many mainstream companies make the mistake of merely translating or repackaging existing ads to reach Asian-American consumers. In recent years, major advertisers have offended Asian consumers, rather than attracted them.

Playboy magazine, famous for its rabbit-eared logo, once ran full-page newspaper ads wishing their Chinese-American readers a happy "Year of the Rabbit." Unfortunately, the Chinese characters were out of order and made no sense. And in 1988, Coors published an ad in the defunct *Rice* magazine featuring a nude Polynesian woman draped in the folds of a ceremonial dragon. The ad was intended to honor the Chinese Year of the Dragon. Instead, it shocked and offended *Rice*'s readers.

"Some ads are done in very bad taste, but others happen out of ignorance—like the *Playboy* ad," says David Chen, a principal in Muse Cordero Chen, a multi-ethnic advertising agency in Los Angeles.

Instead of trying to translate or subtitle your existing ads to reach Asian-American buyers, Chen advises business owners to establish a general marketing concept and then figure out which aspects might appeal to Asian consumers. Themes such as family togetherness, security, and respect for elders cross many cultural lines.

One of his agency's most effective Asian marketing campaigns was a public service ad designed to promote Asian participation in the U.S. census. "We used an abacus, a counting device, and arranged the beads on the abacus to represent an American flag," Chen says. Although the copy appeared in several languages, the image of the abacus-as-flag remained as the unifying element.

Chen and other advertising executives say that American business owners are finally realizing the great untapped buying power of Asian consumers.

Suppose you would like to pursue the Asian-American market or sell to another ethnic group but don't have a clue where to start?

If you can afford to hire a specialty advertising agency, the money will be well spent. If you can't, help is available from the advertising department of the local newspapers and radio or television stations serving the people you want to reach. Most large cities have radio and cable-television stations devoted to serving the ethnic American markets.

If you devise your own sales campaign, it is essential to learn everything you can about the particular group you want to reach.

Remember, even the smallest businesses can work hard to please their ethnic customers. For a good example, note the lengths the food vendors at the Sun Valley Discount Center go to (see box on page 228).

Why? Because the shoppers like to drink from the small green glass bottles so familiar to them back home.

> Be sure to carry clothing sizes and styles that fit your area. A men's clothing store in a Chinese neighborhood couldn't figure out why it was dying until it realized that the sizes it carried were way too big for its potential customers.

REACHING THE ETHNIC MARKET

■ Learn as much as you can about your potential customer's traditions and beliefs.

■ Avoid translating English slogans into foreign languages. Hire someone who knows the language to express your message properly.

■ Create positive images that are meaningful to the consumers you want to serve.

■ Sponsor a cultural event or celebration honoring the consumers you want to reach.

■ Show great respect in your advertising for everyone's holidays, ceremonies, and values.

68. HOW CAN FREE SAMPLES BOOST MY SALES?

Between January and September, 1991, Roger Melanson, president of Great American Software Inc., gave away at least 3,500 copies of his small-business-oriented accounting programs.

"When I gave it to people they thought there was no diskette in the box or it was an old version," says Melanson, who quickly assured recipients that the free computer software was indeed brand-new and ready to use.

Giving away software to business owners and accountants had two purposes. It not only increased awareness of Money Matters and the company's other programs, but Melanson believes the goodwill generated by the giveaways definitely contributed to a 40 percent increase in sales, which hit $8.6 million in 1991.

"If you give out samples of your product and your product is good, a satisfied user will tell five to ten people about it," says Melanson, a former accountant who cofounded the Nashua, New Hampshire, company.

No matter what you do, giving potential customers a sample is a terrific way to attract attention and make a positive impression. "*Free* is a very powerful word," says Nina Segovia, director of development for PROMAX Field Force in Irvine, California.

Segovia, a marketing specialist who has been giving away free samples of food on behalf of her clients for years, says giving something away for free "means the company is willing to put some money behind its product, that it has a great deal of confidence in the product." In recent years, Segovia helped promote the sale of Citrus Hill orange juice by giving free canvas tote bags to shoppers who bought two cartons of juice. PROMAX recently sent representatives into grocery stores to offer hungry shoppers free samples of cooked rice mixed with Contadina tomato sauce. In addition to the free food, Contadina sponsored raffles to give away $200 cash or four tickets to Disneyland. Segovia has also given away hot dog-shaped magnets for Oscar Mayer and cooked artichokes in supermarkets to encourage shoppers to taste them.

Free samples definitely boost food sales because one taste is worth a thousand words. For example, when Manhattan Beach plum pudding maker Patti Garrity gears up for the holiday season, you will find her distributing free samples at Bristol Farms and other gourmet food stores. Garrity says the samples are her best sales tool, because once people taste the pudding, they want to buy it.

Big food companies such as Kellogg's have been giving away free samples for years. "The key is to give your sample to the audience you want to reach," says Karen MacLeod, a product spokesperson for Kellogg's in Battle Creek, Michigan.

In 1991, Kellogg's gave away thousands of Nutri-Grain cereal bars to consumers to encourage them to buy the cereal-coated fruit bars as a snack or quick breakfast food. In addition to in-store samples, Kellogg's sends out thousands of miniature boxes of cereal to consumers at home and passes out samples at trade shows and conventions.

Great American's Melanson began giving away software before he spoke to user groups, because not everyone was familiar with his software products. He also passes out hundreds of copies at trade shows. At one San Francisco trade show, accountants lined up three and four deep at the Great American booth to pick up their free software packages.

The only request Melanson makes is to ask recipients to fill out a registration card so he can keep track of them. Money Matters, which retails for about $60, is his most popular giveaway.

If your product doesn't lend itself to tasting or is too big to hand out, why not offer a free trial to qualified customers? Try shipping it out with no strings attached to prospective customers.

In many cases, they will appreciate the opportunity to try your product and like it well enough to buy it.

If your product or service isn't suited to offering a free sample, consider publishing a free booklet of information or helpful tips for your customers. Be sure your company name, logo, address, and telephone number appear on everything you pass out.

You might also try offering your services as a way to generate new business. For example, if you own a retail clothing business, send out a flier inviting your customers to come in for a free fashion consultation. This should definitely draw them into the store to see what you have to sell, even if they don't buy anything right away.

69. HOW DO I IMPROVE MY CUSTOMER SERVICE?

When a salesclerk ignores you or refuses to accept a return of merchandise, how many people do you tell about your bad experience?

Customer-service experts say the average unhappy customer complains to about a half-dozen friends, neighbors, and colleagues about poor service. Imagine, then, the impact that 10 unhappy customers could have on your future earnings! "Any business lives by word of mouth, and for a small business that can't afford other kinds of promotion, word of mouth is a life-and-death factor," says William Davidow, coauthor of *Total Customer Service* (see "Books" in Resources guide).

Davidow, a Menlo Park, California, venture capitalist, says small-business owners should ask their best customers to describe exactly what kind of service they expect. Then ask the customers if they recommend your company to others. And, if not, why not?

In recent years, too many companies have focused on bottom-line profits and beating the competition, leaving customers to fend for themselves. But American consumers, impressed by the high quality and good service provided by many Japanese, Korean, and European companies, are now demanding better service.

Even such giants as IBM are paying heed: To provide greater convenience for his rural customers, an IBM sales representative in North Carolina set up a portable showroom—the "Solution Mobile"—by filling a mobile home with computer equipment and visiting customers at their homes and businesses.

But no matter what size your business is, you should take a close look at how you treat customers and clients. "Customer service expectations have to be set by the top management of a company," contends Ellen Forman, president of Courtesy Counts. Forman's Potomac, Maryland, company reports on employee performance and attitude by sending representatives to visit stores across the country.

Forman, who founded the company in 1981, says the message from the business owner has to be loud, clear, and consistent. "The president might say, 'Customer service is the most important thing for us, so do it,'" says Forman. "But the next person down the line might say, 'Count the inventory' and the next, 'Clean up the store.'"

Elaine Locksley, founder of the Locksley Group in Pacific Palisades, California, claims that customer service gives companies a measurable edge over the competition. Locksley sends shoppers into large and small businesses to monitor their service and provide customer-service training programs, if necessary.

Locksley developed her customer-service techniques while working 20 years in the savings and loan industry. Hiring mystery shoppers of all ages to visit stores, banks, and other businesses, she presents the owners with a detailed report and expects the information to be shared with employees.

Kay Hollenbeck, a "mystery shopper" and manager at the Locksley Group, says one of the fastest ways to lose business is for a salesclerk to be talking on the telephone, see a customer standing there, and then turn his or her back on the customer. Another sure turn-off is for a salesperson to start helping a customer and then get distracted and never return. Hollenbeck has had both things happen to her.

Even the best training programs and promises of cash rewards won't be effective unless your employees feel a sense of ownership and pride in the business, according to Locksley. Everyone who works for you should be given the power to make decisions needed to please your customers.

"We were concerned that even with all the thousands of dollars spent on our training program, when the boss is gone, the standards drop," says Jack Ryan, whose parents Bob and Jean Ryan opened their first women's apparel store in 1954. They have three Jean

Ryan stores employing about 30 full- and part-time employees in Orange County, California. "We are living in a service-oriented society," says Ryan. "With too many competitors you have to offer better service."

Locksley's shoppers visit Ryan's stores at different times of the day and week. Frequently, they make a purchase or return an item. "We try to use her service as a positive tool," says Ryan.

John Irving, senior vice-president at Premier Bank in Northridge, California, pays about $450 a month for Locksley's services. For that amount of money, Locksley reports on three visits and three phone calls to Premier's three bank branches. Irving asserts that the money is well spent because, "An outside opinion has a tremendous value."

Once you figure out what customers expect and where you are falling short, quickly establish ways to improve your service. But, Davidow says, written policies and programs won't work if you don't have the infrastructure in place to help your employees. For example, having legions of employees trained to answer the phone properly won't matter if you don't have enough phone lines to serve customers.

> Three times a year, send a thank-you letter to every customer, vendor, or supplier. This reminds them you are still in business and may result in new orders.

If you can't afford to pay professional shoppers to monitor the service you provide, ask a few friends or relatives who are not known to your employees to check on the service. Knowing what goes on when you are not around is vital to the success of your business—this is especially true because customer-service experts estimate that it costs about 10 times more to bring in one new customer than to keep an old one.

The worst thing you can do is make it difficult for people to do business with you. Many small-business owners are taking the lead from Nordstrom, the Seattle-based department store chain that cheerfully takes back anything. No questions. No hassles.

They have even been known to take back merchandise purchased elsewhere.

Shopping at Nordstrom is a pleasure. A pianist fills the store with upbeat music. The store is brightly lit and a dizzying assortment of merchandise is piled high. The salesclerks are friendly, gracious, and make you feel welcome.

There is no reason you can't give your customers the same warm feeling and keep them coming back.

George Coan, a veteran retailer, says there are good customers and bad customers. *Good* customers will tell you when something bothers them or if they are unhappy with your products or services. *Bad* customers get upset, but *don't* say anything and never come back.

This means, you should hope all your customers are *good* customers who will express their anger if your employees do not treat them right. So, when you do hear complaints, act on them immediately.

Ten Steps to Improving Customer Service

1. Ask your best customers to tell you honestly what kind of service they expect from your company.

2. Establish clear and simple service policies to match customers' expectations.

3. Give authority to people at every level so they feel empowered to provide good service.

4. Eliminate all red tape involved in merchandise returns.

5. Set clear customer-service goals for your employees and make sure everyone understands them.

6. Provide specific training and information so employees know exactly what to do in every situation.

7. Make employees accountable for their actions.

8. Write specific job descriptions for every employee and offer incentives for promotion so people don't feel stuck in a dead-end job.

9. Publicly reward and recognize good service.

10. If you can't hire an outside consultant, ask your friends or neighbors to visit your business and report on the service they received.

■

70. HOW DO I KEEP SELLING IN A SLACK ECONOMY?

Marketing consultants say you should revise your business strategy every six months or so. And for a good reason: Companies that remain flexible and open to new marketing ideas have a better chance of surviving, if not flourishing, in a slack economy.

Your focus should be on encouraging existing customers to spend more on your particular goods and services.

"Keep your focus on increasing the amount of every sales transaction rather than going after large numbers of new customers," advises Jay Abraham, a veteran marketing consultant who counsels large and small companies. "If you offer every customer a better deal, like a larger quantity or a package of items or services in addition to the one the customer is buying, 30 to 40 percent will say yes," says Abraham, whose office is in Palos Verdes, California.

If you contact every customer within 10 to 20 days after they've bought something from you, many will buy something else. Abraham also suggests hooking up with other small-business owners who sell similar, but noncompetitive products. For example, if you sell shoes, ask the owner of a reputable clothing store to refer customers to your business, and offer to return the favor.

Lawrence Kohn, president of Kohn Communications in Century City, California, organizes what he calls cooperative marketing groups. His aim is to bring together noncompeting but compatible business owners or managers. He teaches them how to share client and customer lists, improve their telemarketing skills, and refer clients to each other. "The groups meet once a month," says Kohn. "Each person accepts an assignment and then there is peer pressure to complete it."

From a career counselor in Des Moines, Iowa:
When someone asks you for your business card, give them two. Ask them to keep one and pass along the extra one to a friend or business associate.

One real estate-oriented group might have a building contractor, a real estate agent, a title company manager, and a real estate attorney. Together they cook up a variety of ways to increase business for each other. They also offer each other moral support and professional expertise, two important things in uncertain economic times.

If you must trim expenses, reduce your use of print or television ads or run them in smaller newspapers and on cable tv stations. You can also save money by running ads in the zoned editions of major newspapers. This allows you to target your market to the area surrounding your business, or reach a neighborhood more likely to need your services or products than the one you are in.

When you do advertise, Abraham suggests making your ad stand out with a punchy headline promising a desirable deal. Make sure your ad tells people exactly why your product or service is better than anyone else's. Be sure to offer a money-back guarantee to eliminate the risk of buying anything from you. An effective ad also tells people exactly how to order or respond.

Bob Bly, a copywriter and marketing consultant based in New Milford, New Jersey, says your goal should be to "wrap a warm blanket" around all your valued customers or clients. Bly, who specializes in business-to-business marketing advice, encourages business owners to emphasize credibility and build a reputation as a company customers can depend on for excellent products and services.

Positioning yourself as a leader in your industry, even if you are still a feisty underdog, is another excellent way to build respect and boost sales. For example, for a client who specializes in direct mail marketing, Bly wrote a booklet explaining the different types of direct mailing services available. The company sent out the advice-packed booklet to customers and prospective customers. Bly also sent it to 100 reporters and editors. One mention of the booklet in a newspaper article generated about 1,000 inquiries. Bly knows some of those inquiries will result in new business for his client.

Here's a terrible marketing idea. An insurance agent I know sent a form letter asking me for the names and addresses of 10 people. He also wanted copies of my blank letterhead. Why? He wanted to send letters out on my stationery which touted his services to my friends and colleagues.

The nerve of this guy!

In a soft economy, you'll see your customers become more price-sensitive and willing to shop around. To hang on to them, consider reducing your prices by 15 to 20 percent. "But don't instantly lower your prices to rock-bottom," Bly cautions. "You may never be able to raise them again."

Instead of being depressed when things are slow, Bly suggests, business owners should do the things they put off during busy periods. Why not clean out files, make technical improvements in products or services, revise your sales letters, or redesign or create a slide presentation?

Since some income is better than no income, he also recommends clients take on smaller projects that they would normally refuse. For instance, if you are a carpenter who specializes in room additions, but no one is buying rooms, call your clients and offer to do smaller jobs and "handyman" projects until the larger remodeling jobs reappear.

"The most important thing about a slow period is not to be depressed by it," says Bly. "If you are depressed, prospects can sense your desperation and fear, and it has a negative effect on your dealings with them."

HOT MARKETING TIPS FOR COOL ECONOMIC TIMES

- Follow up by telephone after mailing brochures or advertisements to customers or prospective customers. Research shows you can significantly boost sales if you follow every written contact by a telephone call.
- Eliminate the risk buyers feel by improving your money-back guarantees, warranties, or service commitments.
- Establish joint promotions with other companies to share the cost of marketing your products or services.
- Offer additional products or services at a reduced price to boost your income.
- Be optimistic and share your entrepreneurial spirit with customers, suppliers, and vendors. Depression over the economy is contagious and counterproductive.

To order a copy of Bly's 16-page booklet on recession-fighting marketing strategies, write to him at 174 Holland Avenue, New Milford, NJ 07646. The price for Special Report 109 is $5.

DIVERSIFYING YOUR BUSINESS

- Revise your business plan to prepare for an economic slowdown.
- Look at new or different uses for your equipment, vehicles, buildings, etc.
- Ask your customers what new services or products you could provide to them.
- Cut costs by farming out projects to other small businesses.
- Discuss new business possibilities with your vendors or suppliers.
- Consider what other consumers could use your products.

71. HOW CAN I PROMOTE MY BUSINESS WITHOUT SPENDING A LOT OF MONEY?

How many of the pens, notepads, calendars, or letter openers cluttering up your office were given to you by people who want to do business with you? The lesson is clear: Most business owners will keep a free gift if it's remotely practical and useful. That's why you should be giving something away, too.

Small-business owners contribute mightily to the $4.5 billion spent each year on a spectacular range of business giveaways, according to Marvin Spike, president of the Advertising Specialty Institute in Langhorne, Pennsylvania. "Even the smallest business with a marketing plan can be competitive in its area with the right kind of specialty advertising," says Spike. "And we find specialty advertising particularly effective in soft markets when 'something for nothing' becomes more appreciated and respected."

But giving out a flimsy key chain or cheap magnet is not a good strategy, according to Jay Conrad Levinson, author of a series of books about "guerrilla" sales and marketing. "You will make as many enemies as friends if you give them junk," Levinson says. "People like free things, but it's important to match the giveaway to the people you are marketing to."

Small-business owners have traditionally given customers pencils, pens, calendars, and key chains. But today, the selection of affordable business gifts is staggering. Items range from personalized packages of chewing gum to crystal clocks and neon-hued sunglasses. You can emblazon your company's name on playing cards, digital watches, plastic Frisbees, nylon "fanny packs," or "sipper" cups popular with athletes.

> Work with a graphic artist to design a snappy flier for your business or product. Because printing costs diminish with volume, print a lot. Then, after mailing them to current and potential customers, include one with every order or bill you send out.

In recent years the hot item was the fanny pack, a bag worn around the waist or hips. But trends change and if you want to be on the leading edge, you'll need to talk to several advertising speciality salespeople for advice. Checking a business-to-business telephone directory under "advertising specialties" or asking other business owners where they buy products are usually the best ways to find distributors.

Instead of spending dollars on expensive ads, spend money putting your company logo and telephone number on something useful. The beauty of giveaways is that they don't perish and can be passed out on a moment's notice.

If you have even $100 to spend, you can put your company name on bumper stickers, decals, buttons, plastic license plate frames, or baseball caps.

> One savvy Los Angeles Cadillac dealer has its name embedded in the rear window brake light. Every time the driver steps on the brakes, he unwittingly provides a plug for Dixon Cadillac.

Because you want customers or potential customers to think of your business first, the key is to give away something that is both useful and visible. Magnets, paperclip holders, paperweights, and letter openers are likely to sit on someone's desk as constant reminders of your company. Ceramic coasters are also a very elegant way to keep your name in front of a decision maker.

Donna Benson is a clever graphic artist living in Ames, Iowa. Benson designed a direct mail piece with a punch-out Rolodex card. Instead of just throwing the card away, recipients are encouraged to punch it out and add it to their Rolodex file for future reference.

Clair Schutte, owner of Schutte's Pool & Spa service company in Sepulveda, California, has spent more than $1,200 in the past year on ceramic coffee mugs and T-shirts with his company logo. He gave his helpers company shirts to wear to assure neighbors that they are going into people's backyards for a legitimate purpose. He also ordered blue-and-gray mugs for his best customers so they will keep his name and phone number handy. "It's worth every cent," says Schutte, who spends about $1,000 a month to advertise in the Yellow Pages and the Pennysaver. "I think it's a very wise investment."

Businesses serving big corporations or executives may want to buy leather business-card holders, marble paperweights, or sophisticated, personalized calculators.

"Specialty advertising is attractive because the cost of other forms of advertising is prohibitive for most small-business owners in a big city," says Susan Margol, of Smith & Margol in Los Angeles. In recent years she developed a "Charlie the Tuna" bank for Starkist and all kinds of free gifts to go with purchases of Neutrogena.

If giving small gifts doesn't appeal to you, try sending Thanksgiving cards to beat the Christmas crush. The Leanin' Tree in Boulder, Colorado, has a special line of business-to-business greeting cards featuring original paintings by mostly Western artists.

"We think business card usage is increasing because businesses are recognizing the importance of personal contact in this day and age of computerization and impersonalization," says Ed Trumble, who founded the company about 40 years ago.

Twenty years ago, Trumble says, it was not uncommon for the typical American family to send 200 Christmas cards a season. Now, because of 29-cent stamps, changing social habits, and just plain laziness, fewer cards are being sent. The good news is that with fewer holiday cards in the mail, the card you send will really stand out and be appreciated.

Free is the most powerful word in the English language. I know it for a fact. When I offer my free Small Business Owner's Resource Guide through my column, the requests pour in by the hundreds.

Giving something away, even a modest gift, coupon, or discount, is a great way to warm up potential customers.

SMART TIPS FOR BUSINESS GIFT-GIVING

- Review your marketing plan to see if specialty advertising fits in.
- Choose gift items to reflect the interests of your customers, suppliers, and vendors.
- Don't give away junk. Making a poor impression is worse than making no impression.
- Make sure your logo is attractive and easy to read.
- Be sure to include your company's full name, address, and phone number someplace on every item.
- Order early to take advantage of discounts and avoid the holiday rush.

72. HOW CAN GOOD PUBLIC RELATIONS HELP MY BUSINESS?

Many small-business owners say they *know* that good public relations is important to their success, but are unclear about exactly what public relations is.

"Public relations is communication management," says Helen Vollmer, founder of Vollmer Public Relations in Houston, Texas. "It is not just publicity, although that certainly is part of it. Public relations tactics address specific publics on a very narrow, targeted basis to achieve specific objectives."

Howard Bragman, founder of Bragman and Company in Beverly Hills, agrees that there is much misunderstanding about what public relations is and isn't. "Public relations has been referred to as free advertising," says Bragman. "It's not."

Advertising must look and sound like advertising. Public relations-generated stories, by contrast, appear in the news portions of newspapers, radio, and television shows, where they are likely to be taken quite seriously. "You cannot pay a television station or newspaper to get coverage in these slots," says Bragman.

What is the advantage of news coverage versus paid advertising? "Public relations stories carry the implied third-party endorsement of the publication which has the story," notes Bragman. "While you may purchase an ad from the *Los Angeles Times* **saying** you have great products, that's often not as valuable as a story that appears in the *Los Angeles Times* **reporting** that you have great products."

TIPS

Read the business section of your local newspaper to figure out which reporter is assigned to cover the industry you are in. Don't be afraid to send the reporter a personal letter, introducing yourself as a possible source for a future story. Reporters always need new people to talk to. This approach is very effective because you are not pitching a story, you're just making yourself known to the writer.

■

Bragman, who is my personal public relations counselor, says it is important to be realistic when figuring out whether your company has any newsworthy qualities. "If you owned a typical neighborhood dry-cleaning establishment, chances are the media wouldn't be interested in your company," comments Bragman. "If, however, you created a revolutionary new process that would dry clean your customers' clothes while they're wearing them, you might be ripe for extensive media coverage."

So, if you've decided you want to seek outside public relations counsel, how do you go about finding a good agency?

It is important to understand how a public relations agency works. Public relations firms are set up much like law firms with partners, associates, and billable hours. You are expected to pay all out-of-pocket expenses, including travel expenses, mailing costs, and facsimile costs.

Firms typically charge in these ways:

■ *Retainer fee*—Generally a monthly fee that covers all the work for a set period of time.
■ *Project fee*—A specified fee for a project completed over a set period of time.
■ *Hourly billing*—Billing clients for time actually spent. The hourly fee depends on who is doing the work.

> Expect to spend a few thousand dollars a month, even for the tiniest one- or two-person agency. You can try to negotiate, but many firms will not adjust their fees.
>
> "Don't beat your agency down to the lowest cost possible," advises Bragman. "If they're not being paid fairly, it will show in their work."

Once you decide you want to find an outside firm, ask other business owners for recommendations. If you know any media people, ask them which public relations people they respect and enjoy working with. Remember, your goal is to convince reporters and editors to cover your story, so you don't want to hire a public relations firm with a bad reputation.

Decide who at your company will be responsible for dealing with public relations, besides yourself; that person will handle day-to-day liaison work. Still, it is very important that you, the owner, be involved in the creative process, even if it means added work. This is *your* business, and P.R. should reflect that.

Then write to at least three firms, describing your business and explaining that you are soliciting proposals for representation.

Once a few agencies respond to your letters, set aside several hours to listen to their presentations. If you don't have the needed equipment for a presentation, such as a television monitor, VCR, slide projector, or overhead projector, be sure to ask the agency to provide their own.

Begin the interview by telling them a little about your company and your goals. Then, let the agency folks talk. They'll bring samples of their work. Look at the materials they've prepared for other small businesses. Listen to the senior management team. Find out which person will be assigned to your account.

Is that person arrogant or friendly?

How is the chemistry between you and that person?

Can you imagine working closely with that person and sharing your business secrets with him or her?

> If you are looking for free publicity, check out the *Catalog of Free Publicity*. Call (800)722-6641.

Although it is increasingly common for companies to ask prospective agencies to write up a public relations program on speculation, Bragman recommends against it. The best agencies don't want to write a program on speculation. Why? Because the most effective program is written with your help, not by an agency in a vacuum, Bragman says.

Instead, Bragman says, trust your gut instincts and choose the agency with the people you feel most comfortable with.

Once you've hired an agency, send letters to the ones you didn't choose, thanking them for their time.

Ask the winning firm to draft a contract or letter of agreement. It's okay to make a four- to six-month agreement, if you are reluctant to make a yearlong commitment.

Most contracts have an "out" clause, which permits you to fire the company on a 30- to 90-day notice. And expect to see an indemnification clause, which means you are legally responsible for the approved materials the agency sends out on your behalf. This clause is common and appropriate, says Bragman.

> Helen Vollmer shares these additional secrets of good public relations:

■ Know your audience. Segment your customers into specific, identifiable groups, such as Hispanic married professionals with a household income of $40,000 or more.

■ Don't fall into the trap of just telling prospects how good your product is—you must *sell* them on what it will do for them. What's the benefit to a given audience: Will it make them prettier, richer, smarter?

■ Keep your employees in the loop. The best PR a company has is through its employees. Internal communication is the beginning of an effective PR plan for any company. A loyal, proud staffer will not only do his job better if he knows the company's goals and philosophy, he'll spread the word through vendors, friends, and family in a multiplying effect.

■ Develop a mission statement—a written document that tells what the company stands for and how it will achieve its goals.

■ The chief executive or president's job is to "polish the chalice" or to protect the image of the company. The smart business owner understands that the image of the company rests in his or her hands and to delegate this responsibility to others is ineffective at best.

■ Public relations takes time. Management must commit time and resources to the PR program.

■ Be pro-active. Don't wait for disaster to strike. Smart management makes sure that even before operations start, the community is informed and there is an open-door policy.

■ Operate with complete candor. Be honest with everyone. "No comment" is seen as an admission of guilt, but "I don't know, but I'll find out," is viewed as a willingness to move forward together.

■ Before hiring any firm, check references by talking with other business owners. (See 89. How Do I Handle a Business Catastrophe?)

73. HOW CAN ADVERTISING HELP MY BUSINESS?

Unless you've worked for an ad agency, you probably don't know much about the world of advertising. That's why, although I am a big advocate of the do-it-yourself approach, I recommend you deal with experts in this area. The main reason is that advertising is very, very costly and one blunder can set you back for good.

When they think of advertising, for instance, most small-business owners immediately think of the Yellow Pages. But while Yellow Page advertising works very well for many kinds of businesses, it can be very expensive and totally inappropriate for others.

Ric Militi, founder of The Ad Group in Los Angeles, says one of his clients, a rental car company, was spending $250,000 a year on Yellow Page ads and was not convinced the ads were drawing the customers. "We sat down and reviewed all the ads, with the goal of reducing the budget to about $40,000," says Militi.

Part of what Militi and other advertising experts do is tell you what *not* to spend your advertising dollars on. They keep up with what's hot in advertising and know how to translate what works for big business into what can work for your business.

For instance, when Lexus introduced their cars, they sent out a mailing offering consumers a free videotape to show them their cars. The response was absolutely overwhelming. Now, you may not be a major car company, but offering a free videotape showing your products in action may be just what you need to jumpstart your sales. With the cost of videotape production dropping and the fact that millions of people own VCRs, even the tiniest businesses can take advantage of the technology.

Militi and other ad executives say every small-business owner should first figure out who you want to reach, then figure out the best way to reach them. If your particular target market does not watch television, even the most expensive TV ad campaign will be a disaster. And if your customers are avid radio listeners, why spend your dollars on newspaper ads?

The secret of successful advertising is to consciously target your campaign to the people you feel would buy your products if they knew about them.

Small-business owners have the tremendous advantage of dealing one-on-one with customers every day. We can easily ask our customers how they found out about the store, where they heard about our products, and what made them decide to buy from us.

People love to be asked their opinion, so ask away. Or invite a group of customers to review and discuss your products and services so you can learn what they like and don't like about your company.

In the beginning, most small businesses rely on business cards, fliers, and word of mouth to reach potential customers. When sales pick up and you feel you can handle more customers, your next step depends on what you are selling and how much money you can spend to spread the word.

If you have a retail store, an ad in the local newspaper or the zoned edition of a major newspaper may be enough to draw more foot traffic. If you are selling business products, you might want to advertise during the drive-time hours on a local radio station, in the local business journal, or chamber of commerce newsletter.

If your product is visually appealing or needs to be demonstrated, advertising on a local cable television station provides an affordable way to reach a broader audience. Note, however, that you'll want to make sure you spend the money to produce a professional-looking commercial, because nothing looks worse than a tacky commercial airing adjacent to a slick national cable broadcast.

Many small businesses, especially those selling cosmetic lines or promoting seminars and books, have tapped into the profits generated by "infomercials." With an infomercial, you have total control over the creative content of the show, and all the commercials tout your products. Most infomercials also feature a toll-free 800 number so viewers are enticed to call and order your products immediately.

If you want to air an infomercial, work with a production company to develop a show around your products. The production company will buy the time from the station, produce the show, and share the profits on the products sold.

There are companies all across the country that produce and distribute infomercials. Any good advertising agency can help you find one to see if this form of advertising would work for you.

Sometimes a combination of radio and newspaper advertising makes the strongest impression on potential customers. Ron Kaatz, a veteran advertising consultant and professor at Northwestern University's Medill School of Journalism in Evanston, Illinois, recalls that the owner of a Chicago area computer store was surprised after he launched a combined radio and newspaper ad campaign. The surprise was that customers thought they were watching the ads on television!

But maybe advertising is not the best way to reach customers. "If what you do or sell is unique, you might launch a public relations effort to attract media attention instead," says Kaatz. (See 72. How Can Good Public Relations Help My Business?)

Kaatz's book, *Advertising and Marketing Checklists*, is an excellent source of information for small-business owners interested in developing an advertising strategy. The book, priced at $17.95, and published by NTC Business Books in Lincolnwood, Illinois, has 77 valuable checklists to help you shape your advertising strategy.

Another book I recommend is *The Advertising Handbook* by Dell Dennison and Linda Tobey. The $8.95 book is published by Self-Counsel Press, 1704 North State Street, Bellingham, WA 98225. It provides a broad yet detailed overview of advertising and explains how to develop a strategy to fit your business.

Read these books and then find a small advertising agency that will give you a low-cost consultation before you spend a penny on advertising.

To find a good agency, ask your colleagues for recommendations. Before you meet with an agency, collect other business ads that you like and don't like so you can focus your tastes.

Remember, the money you spend on advertising can never be recaptured if the ads fail. Advertising is expensive, but necessary, and should never be taken lightly.

74. HOW CAN DOING SOMETHING GOOD HELP MY BUSINESS?

In the 37 years Judith Raphael and her family have owned California High Grade Furniture Corp., they have watched their downtown Los Angeles neighborhood go from "worse to worst." Vandalism, graffiti, litter, gang violence, and drug dealers beat down the area to the point where customers were afraid to visit. At one point, the city resorted to erecting barricades to stop people in cars from cruising the streets to buy crack and other drugs. Merchants complained to the police, but there was not much the cops could do.

Finally, in 1990, Raphael had had enough. "I looked around me and said, 'We were here before this place went to pot' and told myself, 'Somebody ought to do something about it!' "

That somebody turned out to be her.

Determined to keep the neighborhood from further deterioration, Raphael asked her city council representative to send out letters to 250 local merchants, inviting them to attend a meeting. Enough merchants showed up to get started. They decided to meet on a regular basis to air their complaints and share possible solutions. In July 1990, the merchants and residents of the neighborhood formed the Business and Residents Community Association. Since then, BRCA has organized regular street cleanups and kicked off a fund-raising campaign to open a community center to keep the kids off the streets.

In September 1991, with the blessing of City Hall, Raphael took eight former gang members to Sacramento to meet their legislators. For most of them, it was their first trip out of the neighborhood—a real revelation. When they returned, they were eager to work for the community.

Recruiting kids while they are still in school is one of Raphael's top priorities. "We came to the conclusion it would be better if we started from the bottom up and provided something for the young people *before* they got into the gangs," says Raphael.

By joining hands with the mayor's office and the school district, BRCA is placing the kids in community service jobs, encouraging them to take pride in the neighborhood, and teaching them how to earn a living.

If she could do it, Raphael says, merchants anywhere can band together and take back some control over their neighborhood. But, she cautions, the hours are long—Raphael often spends 40 hours a week on community activities, leaving her husband to run the business—and the rewards far between. "The results don't show overnight," says Raphael. "It's a long-range investment."

Starting a neighborhood association may not be your thing, but there are all kinds of ways doing *good* can help your business. Doing something good will not only boost your morale and the spirits of your employees, but is an excellent way to draw attention to your business and garner a few paragraphs in the local newspaper.

How about organizing a food collection drive? All you need is a barrel in front of your store or in your office and a place to donate the food. You can promote your collection drive with fliers and offer customers a discount or a small gift if they bring in something to donate.

Why not sponsor a five-kilometer walk or run for your favorite charity? Or organize a bake sale, or work with a social service agency to sponsor a few homeless families until they can get on their feet? If you make something, why not donate some of it to a homeless shelter, day-care center, or other social service agency? The donations won't cost you much and the gesture will generate tremendous goodwill.

How about giving away gift certificates to outstanding local students? Sponsoring an essay contest? Organizing a sidewalk cleanup drive or graffiti paint-out? Recycling aluminum cans and donating the proceeds to your favorite local charity?

There are so many *good* things you can do that don't cost any money. You will not only feel better after you do them, but your customers will appreciate your intentions and patronize your business.

Write and tell me about the kinds of good things you've done for your community. I'm collecting ideas from small-business owners around the country. My address is: P.O. Box 637, Sun Valley, CA 91353-0637.

75. HOW CAN I USE BARTER TO BOOST SALES AND SAVE CASH?

Every year, thousands of small-business owners barter about $1 billion worth of goods and services through 300 American trade exchanges.

Commercial trade exchange executives say barter has increased in popularity in the past decade, and they are bracing for a new wave of clients because a drooping economy makes trading more attractive than buying.

Bartering has been around since one cave man swapped his neighbor something he had for something he needed.

It once had something of a shady reputation as a less than legal way to do business. But in the early 1980s, the Internal Revenue Service recognized barter as a legitimate way to do deals as long as "trade dollars" are treated exactly like real dollars for all tax purposes. It is especially attractive for small-business owners who don't have a lot of money to spend on the things they need to run their business on a daily basis.

For instance, when Barry Wood, founder of Botanical Decorators in Clarksville, Maryland, picks up the phone to call his broker, it's not to play the stock market. "Barter transactions make up about 5 percent of my business," says Wood, who has traded for printing, advertising, painting, electrical, and concrete work since 1978. Wood has even asked his broker at Barter Systems in Silver Spring, Maryland, to track down a computer repair service and a hot tub for a customer of his retail nursery and landscape company.

"Our employees are on a dental plan through barter, and that's how we put on our Christmas party," says Wood. "I'm really hot on the barter system—I think it's great."

Depending on where you live and how big your business is, expect to pay a membership fee ranging from $100 to $1,000 to join an exchange. Most exchanges also charge a 10 percent transaction fee on every deal. A bona fide exchange will provide members with monthly account statements and a year-end 1099-B form that tells the government how many trade dollars changed hands. Bartering exchanges also publish directories and newsletters that promote members' companies, and they employ brokers who seek out the merchandise or services their members need.

The benefit of joining an exchange is that you don't have to trade your products or services directly for someone else's. You build up credit and can trade it for anything offered by another exchange member.

"Our biggest problem is a lack of awareness about how barter works," says Susan Groenwald, who serves as president of the Chicago Barter Corp. and president of the International Reciprocal Trade Association in Alexandria, Virginia. The international association represents about 10,000 businesses in the United States, England, New Zealand, and Australia, among other nations.

Sondra Ames, whose husband, Michael, founded Orange County, California–based Trade American Card almost 20 years ago, bartered with her obstetrician for the delivery of her daughter, Allyson. Because the doctor and a local pet-store owner both belonged to her exchange, the doctor got some Alaskan malamute puppies in exchange for services rendered to Ames and her baby.

"The biggest advantage is getting things without spending business dollars for them," says Don Gibas, owner of Gibas Golf Products in Huntington Beach, California. Gibas, who belongs to two barter exchanges, uses barter for his business and personal life. He has bartered for hotel rooms in Las Vegas to attend a trade show and used trade dollars to pay for wallpaper and paint for his home.

Exchange representatives say membership can increase sales by 5 percent by bringing in business customers it would not have otherwise found. "Barter cannot save a company that is going under, but it can lead it away from its competition," says Ronald Daversa, vice-president of marketing for Barter Systems, which serves about

1,000 members in the Washington metropolitan area. "If more companies knew about it, they would participate."

Bob Lichtle, president of Lichtle Flat Roof Co. in Detroit, belongs to two trade exchanges and does about $100,000 worth of bartering a year. "When I join an exchange, their six to eight brokers become my salespeople," says Lichtle, who bartered for materials to build a new home in Sterling Heights, Michigan.

Through the years, he has bartered for his company's advertising, accounting services, printing, equipment rentals, and propane. He sometimes pays his workers in trade dollars, which they can spend at a barter store set up much like a K mart. He recently bartered for several rooms' worth of furniture and $2,500 worth of scuba-diving equipment.

"You can get anything," says Lichtle. "I love it, and it brings in business I never would have had."

MAKING BARTER WORK FOR YOU

Barter works especially well for companies with excess inventory or manufacturing capacity. Professionals can also fill in their schedules with barter clients. Some tips:

- Don't pay more for an item through barter than if you paid cash.
- Be willing to wait a bit longer to receive goods or services.
- Join a legitimate trade exchange that reports transactions to the IRS.
- Encourage trade brokers to promote your company to other members.
- Keep a good balance between barter and cash transactions so you don't jeopardize your cash flow.
- Don't accept more bartering deals than you can handle.

76. HOW DO I MAKE A DEAL WITH A MAJOR CORPORATION?

Sometimes buying a business spun off from a big corporation is the best way to get started yourself. With corporations cutting and contracting every day, there are enormous opportunities to acquire an existing business from an unhappy corporate parent.

Here's how one savvy small-business owner turned a corporate disaster into a fabulous success:

Kathy Taggares, born in the tiny, potato-growing town of Othello, Washington, had been in the food business most of her life. Tired of working for someone else, she started asking everyone she knew if there was a good food-processing business on the market. She looked at all kinds of businesses, from a trout farm to a peanut factory, but nothing seemed right for her.

In 1987, she heard from a business broker that Marriott was about to jettison its ailing Bob's Big Boy salad dressing operation. Intrigued by the nostalgia surrounding Bob's Big Boy hamburger restaurants, especially for southern California baby-boomers, she approached the giant Marriott Corporation with an offer to buy Bob's Kitchens, a faltering subsidiary located in Glendale, California. "I'm not sure the Marriott executives knew how minimal my resources were and I wasn't about to tell them," recalls Taggares. "But I figured, it's up to them. They could throw me out, but what else could they do?"

Instead of throwing her out, Marriott agreed to sell her the flagging operation, accepting a combination of cash, a collateralized loan, and the payment of the balance through future product royalties. "I basically bought a $6-million company with $200,000 in cash," says Taggares, who admits bluffing her way through the negotiations to appear more financially solvent than she was.

But she is a good actress. When the deal was signed, she raced back to Washington to sell her life insurance policy, her condominium, and all her jewelry. She barely met the deadline, but managed to raise the needed cash in a few weeks. In June 1987, she was handed the keys to the factory and immediately changed the name to K.T.'s Kitchens—using her initials.

Being a woman in the food business is hard enough. But when she bought Bob's Kitchen, Taggares faced several major obstacles. Not only was the factory sluggish and the workers dispirited, but the predominantly male Latino workers had a tough time dealing with a new female boss after being supervised by the white male middle managers of Marriott.

Taggares still can't speak much Spanish, but she manages to communicate with a mixture of Spanish, English, and sign language. She takes a special interest in her workers and their families. For several years, she cared for "Shorty," a mentally retarded man who was her perpetual sidekick until he died.

And when one of her favorite employees was dying of cancer, she spent many evenings sitting at his bedside. She also helped his family hire an attorney and file a medical malpractice suit. Since the workers are there 24 hours a day, it's not unusual to find Taggares striding through the factory at 10 P.M., making one last round through the production areas.

K.T.'s has the exclusive right to make all the Bob's Big Boy salad dressings for the Marriott-owned Big Boy restaurants, but Marriott, which has a couple hundred Bob's restaurants, primarily on the East and West Coasts, is in the process of converting them to Allie's, a trendier family-style restaurant.

Taggares is a little worried about the loss of the familiar Big Boy restaurants, but she isn't frantic. Her marketing research has shown that the people who eat at Bob's restaurants are not the same ones who buy Bob's salad dressings. "I think our primary users grew up with Bob's and now they don't necessarily frequent the restaurants, but they have this wonderful memory of dipping their French fries in Bob's bleu cheese dressing," says Taggares, who once sponsored a Bob's Big Boy look-alike contest to generate publicity for her dressings.

About 20 percent of the dressing she makes is sold to Bob's, other restaurant chains, and food service outlets. The remaining 80 percent is sold at the retail level and is available in virtually every supermarket, big and small, in southern California. At nearly $2 a bottle, Bob's dressing is aimed at the high end of the refrigerated salad-dressing market. It is costly, she says, because it contains only natural ingredients, and some flavors feature imported cheeses from France.

Most days, K.T.'s Kitchens manufactures about 10,000 gallons of Bob's salad dressings, filling 150 jars a minute on a modern conveyer-belt system. The company, which employs about 200, is divided into two parts: One side of the factory makes the salad dressings, the other makes refrigerated pizzas for several labels.

Using the first year's profits from her salad-dressing business, Taggares purchased a Monterey Park pizza crust company and moved it into her factory. (Buying the pizza crust company is another story. The day she signed the sales contract, the baker had a heart attack. See why I say small-business owners *are* the business?) Once she had learned how to make a good crust, she decided to make whole pizzas to serve the booming, low-cost pizza market. Her pizza is packed under the Poni and K.T.'s brands as well as several other private labels, including one very expensive brand.

Taggares, whose lean frame can support a diet consisting mainly of corn chips dipped in Bob's ranch dressing and her own pizza, says the pizza business is growing much faster than the salad dressing business. In 1991, combined pizza and salad dressing sales reached $20 million.

K.T.'s has a very lean management team. The company is run by Taggares and her general manager, Joan Paris, a longtime friend and colleague who has worked with Taggares at various food companies for more than 15 years. The two women said they finally won their employees' respect by proving that they really knew everything about the food-processing business. "I've done every single one of these jobs," says Taggares, who studied dance in New York as a teenager and still looks and dresses like a dancer.

"I like being the boss, and I thrive on chaos and commotion," admits Taggares. Her greatest frustration is dealing with the constant mechanical and refrigerator breakdowns that plague any food-processing factory.

The breakdowns add to the pressure of meeting tight deadlines because she makes everything to order for customers. And her customers and vendors apparently love this tough negotiator. On a recent birthday, her office was filled with 17 bouquets. Despite the daily aggravations, Taggares remains passionate about her work and her mission: to provide high-quality, affordable food products.

In 1991, she was cash-rich when many companies were ailing. She took advantage of the recession by renegotiating her trucking contracts and buying all the equipment she needed for outrageously low prices. She is always looking for compatible new products, with an eye toward items sold in the refrigerated section of the grocery store. Taggares plans to expand by acquiring a food business or two.

"I make a lot of cold calls to business owners," says Taggares. "Some are terribly flattered and others think we are trying to buy one of their children."

77. HOW DO I BECOME AN OFFICIAL MINORITY CONTRACTOR?

Convinced that access to big companies was essential to the success of his travel agency, Chuck Covington jumped through all the hoops necessary to get his agency certified as an "official" minority-owned business.

"If it weren't for the minority supplier councils and the exposure they give us to corporate America . . . I would never get to the people who make the decisions," says Covington, who owns Belleville, Michigan–based People's Travel with his wife, Tina. After filling out piles of forms, answering scores of questions, and opening his books and records for inspection, People's Travel was certified by Pepsi-Cola, Ford, and several local minority supplier councils.

Covington, who is black, also qualified for certification by the University of Michigan and the U.S. General Services Administration. "Business depends on who you know, and people don't like to do business with strangers," says Covington, who is no longer a stranger to his biggest clients.

Although many minority business owners moan about the certification process, most say it's worth the time and trouble to participate. Most government agencies and public utilities are required by law to do a portion of their business with women and minorities, and many other companies and corporations make similar commitments. Each agency and company has a different certification process, but most require information on company ownership, financial backing, company history, and qualifications.

One coveted form of minority certification is offered through the U.S. Small Business Administration's Section 8(a) program. Through the program, the SBA acts as the prime contractor and enters into all kinds of subcontracts with qualified minority-owned firms.

About 3,650 companies nationwide are active in the 8(a) program, which handled 3,968 contracts in fiscal 1990. Under the program, minority-owned businesses received about $4 billion worth of U.S. government contracts in fiscal 1990, according to SBA spokeswoman Juanita Weaver.

> If you are a member of a minority group, you can learn more about how to apply for the 8(a) program at your local SBA office.

While the 8(a) program channels government money to small businesses, most major American corporations also make some effort to buy goods and services from minority-owned businesses. "Minorities buy our products; therefore they should be part of the system," says John Haines, director of minority supplier development for General Motors in Detroit.

Haines, who coordinates purchasing for all of GM, relies on a computer data base to keep track of 1,350 minority-owned companies identified by the automaker's minority-supplier program.

In 1990, GM purchased $1.1 billion worth of goods and services from minority-owned companies—more than any other U.S. corporation, according to Haines. "The (certification) system is working—evidenced by the number of companies being identified as minority-owned and controlled," says Haines.

Helen Marquez, who owns a Remedy Temp franchise in Vienna, Virginia, has been certified as a minority-owned business by about six local agencies and several companies. "It's not enough for them to look at my deep, dark brown eyes and verify that I am your basic Mexican kid on the block," says Marquez with a laugh. She admits being surprised at the extent of the questioning and background checks done by some organizations, especially the transit authority in Washington, D.C.

Marquez emphasizes that obtaining certification means nothing if your company can't competitively provide the goods or services needed. "None of this rigmarole guarantees you anything," says Marquez. "Everything still depends on your prices and the quality of your work."

How do you become certified?

If you are a member of a minority group, own 51 percent or more of a business, and are involved in day-to-day operations, contact one of the 45 minority supplier councils across the country. If you are certified by one council, certification is reciprocal.

Write or call the National Minority Supplier Development Council, 15 West 39th Street, 9th floor, New York, NY 10018. Phone: (212)944-2430.

Minority- or women-owned businesses nationwide that are interested in doing business with 16 California public utilities should contact The Clearinghouse at (800)869-7385.

78. HOW DO I PREVENT COLLECTION PROBLEMS?

Debt collection.

The very words have an ominous sound. Yet, most small businesses are plagued with uncollected bills, which can devastate an otherwise healthy business. And even the boldest entrepreneur may have trouble demanding money from customers because he or she is afraid of alienating them.

But collecting money from customers or clients need not be so awful—*if* you develop a collection strategy.

Reid L. Steinfeld, an attorney who specializes in collections at the Encino, California, law firm of Weissman & Weissman, has become a strong proponent of preventive medicine when it comes to debt collection.

Steinfeld says the first step is to insist every new customer fill out a detailed credit application unless he or she plans to pay cash on delivery. By demanding certain information up front, serious problems can be avoided later. "At the beginning of a relationship, everyone loves each other," Steinfeld says. This is the time for you to collect all the financial and personal information needed—before you extend credit.

You can draft your own credit application or buy a standard form at a stationery store and adapt it to fit your company's needs.

The purpose of the form is to find out:

- With whom has the company had prior business dealings?

Insist on a list of contacts, addresses, and phone numbers, and be sure to verify references.

■ Where does the company have its bank accounts? What are the branch addresses and account numbers?

■ Does the customer or company own any property? Where is the property and is it mortgaged?

■ Can the debt be secured with a tangible asset such as the equipment you are selling the company, or some other item of value?

■ Is the business owner willing to provide a personal guarantee for the money owed, even if the company is incorporated?

This is the most important thing:

Before extending one dollar of credit, *verify* everything on the application.

Start by calling the companies listed on the application, and ask how the company seeking credit pays its bills. Check the owner's or company's credit rating through TRW or Dun & Bradstreet. Have the secretary of state's office run a UCC (Uniform Commercial Code) search to determine whether the company has any secured creditors. This will affect how and when your company would be paid off if the other business fails.

Steinfeld also suggests adding a line or two on the credit application stating that any litigation stemming from the transaction must be filed in the city where *your* business is, rather than where the customer has his or her business. This will make life easier if you end up having to sue the company to recover your money.

To avoid disputes about whether goods were received, Steinfeld recommends following up each order with a brief confirmation letter detailing the products or services you provided.

What if you checked the customer's references, called his bank, and assured yourself that he is a good credit risk—and he still ends up owing you money?

"It becomes a race," says Steinfeld, who represents collection agencies. "The longer you wait, the harder it is to collect." If you have not been paid during the normal 30-, 60-, or 90-day payment period, first write a letter requesting the money you are owed. Then have your credit manager or other responsible person call the debtor.

In Steinfeld's experience, debtors will either refuse to take your calls or launch into a long list of excuses about why they cannot pay you. If they make excuses, Steinfeld suggests saying, "I'm not interested in excuses."

Tell the debtor you sold him something in good faith and that you expect to be paid promptly. Tell him you have a business to run and your own payroll to meet. "You have to be firm and positive," says Steinfeld. If the debtor is unwilling to work out a payment schedule, you may be forced to go to court.

At this point, most business owners turn to their attorneys for help. If the debt is under $25,000, a business owner can usually take action in a municipal court. If the debt exceeds $25,000, the claim can be filed in superior court. "You must take a strong legal position because debtors are much more sophisticated and know how to play the game better than ever," says Steinfeld.

If it is time to play hardball, your attorney can help you obtain a prejudgment writ of attachment. A judge will issue such an order if he or she is convinced that you have a valid claim against the debtor. This type of court order permits you to freeze a company's assets and prevent any disposition until there is a hearing on the dispute. "The threat of attachment is very powerful," notes Steinfeld; many debtors pay up immediately after receiving legal notice that you are going to court to attach their assets. "In our experience, the debtor either files for bankruptcy, calls to make a deal, or hasn't got the money and doesn't care anymore," says Steinfeld.

He also reminds business owners that any three creditors can force a business into involuntary bankruptcy, but that can be an expensive proposition because of the legal fees involved. "It's always best to try to make a deal—because you can lose in court," advises Steinfeld.

THINGS TO KNOW BEFORE GRANTING CREDIT

- Is the customer an individual, partnership, or corporation?
- What are the names and addresses of all partners or owners?
- How long has the business been around?

■ What is the name of their bank? Account numbers? Loans outstanding?

■ Ask for a detailed financial statement. Refusal to provide one is an immediate red flag.

■ Ask for the name of three business references and call them up to check on the customer's bill-paying history.

79. HOW CAN I PROTECT MY BUSINESS IF MY CUSTOMERS FAIL?

If you are losing sleep worrying about customers who owe you money, there is a solution—and it's better than sleeping pills. Business credit insurance, or "sleep insurance," as brokers call it, may be just what you need to rest easier.

European companies have long relied on credit insurance to protect their profits, but U.S. businesses are just waking up to the benefits. Historically, credit insurance companies have deliberately kept a low profile, catering mainly to carpet and furniture manufacturers, apparel makers, and lumber mills. But today, brokers who specialize in this type of insurance are marketing the concept to all kinds of businesses willing to pay for protection against unpaid bills. "A lot of little companies go out of business because someone doesn't pay their bill," says Jerry Glickman, an agent for American Credit Indemnity (ACI) Co. in Los Angeles.

Credit insurance is really catastrophe insurance—protection against a huge loss. Ideal candidates are businesses that have at least $2 million a year in revenue and are heavily dependent on a few customers for most of their sales. Businesses with a broader customer base tend to have their risk exposure spread more evenly and may not need such insurance.

Insurance is just one strategy for guarding against credit problems. Experts say you should also learn to diagnose your company's credit health. If your accounts receivables are falling behind, get on top of the situation quickly. Remember that extending credit means you are investing your money in your customers, so don't be afraid to ask new customers for financial statements and check out the credit references they provide.

In 1990, the country's major credit insurance companies wrote about $100 million in premiums, covering about $60 billion in business transactions, according to James Gammino, senior vice-president of marketing for Baltimore-based ACI. Because the economy is still wobbly, Gammino says, more small- and medium-size companies are applying for coverage.

Although credit insurance is not designed to boost cash flow—it takes about 90 days to collect on a policy—this type of insurance has other benefits. For instance, bankers love it. Why? Because when they lend you money, their interest is protected. Bankers say your delinquent customers are also more likely to pay if they know an insurance company is watching them and reviewing their credit histories.

John Thomas, president of Griffin Printing & Lithograph Co. in Glendale, California, bought credit insurance when he revamped his credit and collections department a few years ago. The insurance and weekly assistance from a credit consultant are helping him sleep better. "One area that was always foreign to us was credit and collections," says Thomas, who commutes between Griffin's Glendale and Sacramento printing plants. "After some bad debt losses caught us by surprise, we felt prevention was the only answer."

At his banker's suggestion, Thomas hired consultant Eric Shaw, founder of New York Credit in Marina del Rey, California, to serve as his part-time credit manager. Shaw works one day a week at Griffin, running credit checks on customers, prodding others into paying, and keeping on top of accounts receivable.

"We really needed an objective source to help make the credit decisions," Thomas says. "If somebody dangled a big order in front of us but it was a downright unacceptable risk, we just looked at the positive side, saying, 'Look, it's a big order.' Now we're aware it's also a potential loss."

Shaw, who works with dozens of small businesses, believes credit insurance is essential if you think your biggest customers could put you out of business. "When you have big-dollar invoices from a few customers, you want to insure them," Shaw says.

Lola Sacks, an independent credit insurance broker for LNS Insurance Services in Los Angeles, says the premiums generally run about one-half of 1 percent of sales for a small to midsize firm. Larger firms can often negotiate more attractive rates.

Sacks became interested in credit insurance when she saw how it saved a former employer from going under. She was working for a rapidly growing toy company that was overextended and starved for cash. The credit insurance policy saved the company from collapse when a big customer failed to pay a $160,000 bill.

So where can you buy this kind of insurance coverage?

Surprisingly few companies sell credit insurance. Sacks says six companies serve the U.S. market. Baltimore-based American Credit Indemnity Co., which is owned by Dun & Bradstreet, has a 100-year history in the business. Continental Insurance is based in Piscataway, New Jersey. Fidelity & Deposit Co. is also headquartered in Baltimore.

A.I. Global, a division of American International Underwriters, has offices in New York and specializes in serving companies with sales of $100 million or more. Pan Financial U.S., Inc., is also based in New York.

Citibank's Citicorp International Trade Indemnity Co. specializes in insuring exports, but Sacks says the company plans to move into the domestic arena.

80. HOW DO I MANAGE MY COMPANY'S TRAVEL EXPENSES?

With about 180 stores in 24 states, Fast Frame president and founder John Scott is on the road—or in the air—much of the time. Fast Frame's travel expenses run more than $250,000 a year, a substantial amount of money for a company with about $23 million in sales in fiscal 1991 and expectations of $33 million in sales in 1992. But because being on the spot to support new franchisees is critical to his company's success, Scott views travel expenses as an investment in the future.

For most business owners, spending travel money is easy. Keeping track of it is another story. "Checking employee expense reports is probably my least favorite job—it's a real pain in the backside," says Scott, who started the Agoura Hills, California–based company in England before exporting his concept of quick, professional picture framing to the United States in 1987. Like most small-business owners who travel, Scott says he is constantly seeking ways to simplify the arduous task of booking business trips and keeping track of money spent away from the office.

Keeping careful records of travel expenses is especially important as travel costs climb. "Travel costs have been rising dramatically," says Michael Woodward, of American Express Travel Related Services. Woodward believes that the average cost of air fare for the business traveler increased between 8 and 11 percent in 1990.

To streamline expense reporting, Fast Frame's Scott ordered company credit cards from his bank for the half-dozen employees who travel. He also designed a special expense reporting form with an envelope attached to collect the receipts that often disappear. He asked his secretary to serve as travel manager, so she keeps track of who is going where and when. She works with a travel agent who tries hard to find them the best fares.

Scott also subscribes to Prodigy, the on-line computer service, because it offers an airline booking service. Scott says he uses Prodigy to check fares and make sure they are truly getting the best fares available.

Another tip from Scott: He recently took back the credit cards he had loaned to the independent marketing executives who sell Fast Frames franchises. Instead, Scott sets a monthly travel budget based on their expenses in the past two years. If the marketing executives spend more than the monthly travel limit, they have to pay the difference. If they don't spend it all, they keep the difference as a bonus.

Reducing costs and streamlining your travel reporting requirements is not as daunting as you might think. One of the easiest ways to save money and time is to work with a competent travel agency that specializes in serving small businesses.

Many people don't realize travel agents provide most services at no charge. The agency earns its money on commissions paid by the airlines, hotels, car rental companies, and cruise lines, not by charging fees to its customers. "Most people making their own airline reservations don't have the ability to pull up 14 different carriers on a computer screen," says Caryl Steinberg-Bendinger, a 20-year veteran of the travel industry and owner of Master Travel and Tours in Chicago. "We fare-shop and always look for the lowest applicable rates," says Steinberg-Bendinger, who estimates 60 percent of her business is devoted to serving small companies.

She says most small-business owners rely on her staff to get them the best value for their travel dollars. But, she claims it is becoming harder and harder to find low fares because business travelers are bearing the financial burden of airline fare deregulation.

While air fares and hotel rates are going up, the IRS is cracking down on travel expense reporting. Many small-business owners may be unaware of changes brought about by a little-noticed amendment to the Family Support Act of 1988. The rules established new requirements for cash advances, per diem, car mileage programs, and expense reimbursements. The IRS now requires companies to have what the government considers an "accountable plan" for tracking travel expenses.

According to a brochure published by American Express, an accountable plan has four basic elements. First, any reimbursement or cash advance you provide to an employee must be used only in connection with his or her duties. Next, all expenses must be documented according to existing IRS rules, and the advances must be drawn within a reasonable period of time before the expenses are incurred, usually 30 days. Finally, any unspent funds must be returned to the company within 120 days. If the money is not returned on time, it can be considered income and must be taxed.

Companies that allow their employees to spend more money each day than the per diem amounts set for federal employees may also be subject to extra taxes.

The IRS sets a uniform "high" rate, or maximum, which changes periodically. Check with your accountant for details.

You should also be sure to check the current allowable mileage rate for automobile travel.

TRAVEL TIPS FOR SMALL-BUSINESS OWNERS

- Find an experienced travel agent who specializes in planning business trips.
- Designate one person in your company to be responsible for keeping track of travel expense reports, even if everyone makes their own travel arrangements.
- Review all employee travel expense reports at least once a month.
- Try not to schedule any last-minute trips, because they always cost more.
- Always ask for the best rates available on hotel rooms and rental cars. Note: The "corporate rate" is not always the cheapest.
- Follow the new IRS regulations on travel expenses to avoid problems.

81. SHOULD I REGISTER A TRADEMARK FOR MY BRAND NAMES?

Buoyed by the popularity of their trendy hair salon in the Chicago suburb of Hinsdale, Raymond Koubek and Salvatore Segretto created a line of shampoos, conditioners, and gels under the name Zazu salon brand.

They registered "Zazu" with the Illinois trademark office in 1980 and began selling the products to clients on a limited basis in 1985. In 1986, Koubek and Segretto were astonished to see national magazine ads for a line of temporary hair-color products called Zazu, placed by L'Oreal, a major Paris-based cosmetics company.

"We were as careful as a small-business owner could be and went through the trouble of protecting ourselves," says Koubek, who immediately contacted L'Oreal and told them to stop using his trademark. L'Oreal officials told him it was too late to stop distribution of what turned out to be a short-lived product.

The angry entrepreneurs sued L'Oreal and in September 1988, a federal judge in Chicago awarded Zazu's founders $2.1 million in damages. After ruling, the judge agreed to accept additional evidence at the request of Cosmair Inc., which represents L'Oreal in the United States. But even with the additional evidence, the judge reaffirmed his ruling in early 1991 and ordered Cosmair to pay up. In August 1991, Cosmair appealed the ruling and it is still pending.

Although Zazu's owners are still waiting for the money and are faced with staggering legal bills, they feel vindicated because the judge agreed that L'Oreal flagrantly violated Zazu's trademark registration.

John D. Sullivan, corporate counsel for Cosmair Inc., which licenses the L'Oreal line, says the ruling was "extraordinarily unusual." He asserts that Cosmair will continue fighting because it contends "Zazu" was not a federally registered trademark. "If you don't register your trademark in every state you don't automatically get protection," warns Sullivan.

Many small-business owners who think filing for a trademark is too expensive or time-consuming will be surprised to learn it usually costs less than $2,000 and can save you endless grief. "The money you spend in the beginning to protect your name is going to pay itself back 100 times," advises James Warren, head of the intellectual property group at the San Francisco law firm of Pillsbury, Madison & Sutro.

Warren, who has been hired to protect the New Kids on the Block rock group name, among other big and small company trademarks, advises that even the tiniest company can benefit from trademark protection. Your company may be small now, but if your products or services take off, you don't want imitators to threaten your success. On the other hand, of course, if you use a name that belongs to someone else, you can be put out of business immediately if they find out.

It is possible to conduct a trademark search on your own to save money, but hiring a competent trademark attorney is not as expensive as you might think.

Once you've chosen a name you like, the first step is to see if anyone else is using it or anything that sounds or looks like it. This kind of first-level search is usually done by paralegals and costs about $100, depending on where you live. If nothing turns up at that level, the next step is to complete a national search of data bases, telephone books, trade magazines, and other published sources. The second phase can cost $250 or more, depending on the complexity and comprehensiveness of the search.

If the name you choose is available, the next step is to file an application with the U.S. Patent and Trademark Office. In the past, you had to actually produce and sell a product before you could trademark its name. No more. Now you can apply for a trademark in the planning stages and increase your protection.

The government charges an application fee, currently under $200, for each class of goods or service your product falls into. To qualify for a federal trademark registration, your products have to be sold in more than one state. After your application arrives at the Patent Office, it is turned over to an attorney who determines whether there is anything "confusingly similar" between your trademark and others. (Names are not the only thing you can register as a trademark. Logos and other graphic designs can also be protected.) If your trademark application clears this hurdle, notice of your intent to register the mark is published four times in a weekly publication called the *Official Gazette*, so others can be alerted.

If no one files a notice of opposition, the registration certificate is usually issued by the Patent Office within four to six months.

West Hollywood, California, entrepreneur Ken Girouard learned the hard way how vigilantly giant corporations monitor their trademarks. Fruit of the Loom, the giant apparel maker, filed suit against Girouard and his company, Two Left Feet, over his "Fruit Flops" hand-decorated rubber beach sandals. Girouard, a former Madison Avenue ad executive, contends the giant apparel maker does not have a monopoly on the word *fruit* and retained an attorney to defend him in Los Angeles federal court.

When he ran out of money for legal fees, Girouard ended up representing himself in federal court and won a victory against Fruit of the Loom in September 1991. A federal judge ruled that Girouard could use the Fruit Flops name, but the costly and exhausting legal battle practically drove him out of business.

"The companies that have spent millions and billions of dollars creating, protecting, and promoting their trademarks are very vigilant," says Michael Finn, spokesman for the United States Trademark Association in New York City.

Finn says there are about 650,000 active, federally registered trademarks, plus thousands of others registered with states. While big corporations have entire legal departments devoted to protecting trademarks, small-business owners usually have to rely on vendors and customers to tell them if another company is infringing on their product name. But in our computerized society, Finn says, anyone who tries to get away with using someone else's name will eventually get caught.

Through the years, Finn claims, many product names have lost their protected status because they were commonly used by the press and the public. Corn flakes, nylon, escalator, dry ice, kerosene, and raisin bran are among those products that have been victims of "genericide," or generic use, according to Finn.

He said his trade association, which has about 2,200 members, offers several publications to help business owners deal with trademark issues.

"A Trademark Is Not a Patent or Copyright," "Protecting Your Trademarks Abroad," "Trademark Checklist," "The Guide to Proper Trademark Use," and "Trademarks . . . A Winning Combination" are among the publications available for a modest fee from the association. To obtain a publications price list, send a self-addressed stamped envelope to: U.S. Trademark Association, 6 East 45th Street, New York, NY 10017.

An additional resource:

U.S. Patent and Trademark Office
(703)557-3158
automated voice-mail information

---

82. HOW DO I FIND THE INFORMATION I NEED TO MAKE SMART BUSINESS DECISIONS?

If you think you have all the information you need to make a critical business decision today, read no further. But—be honest, now!—if you feel you could make much smarter decisions if you had more information, read on.

Most small-business owners know there are information resources available beyond the local library, but have no idea about how to tap them. Or, are sure they can't afford them. But knowing how to obtain affordable, strategic information is essential to your financial success.

Big businesses have the financial resources to absorb the occasional marketing mistake, but small businesses do not have that luxury, according to Seena Sharp, owner of Sharp Information Research in Hermosa Beach, California. That's why current, accurate information can be one of the biggest bargains available to small-business owners. "One of the great things about information is that it is just as available to small businesses as large ones," says Sharp, who specializes in ferreting out information from direct and published sources rather than from computer data bases.

Sharp has collected information on everything from the market potential for upscale furniture to the potential success of a "mystery shopper" quality-control service.

"For the man who bought the upscale furniture store, I found three current market surveys—all free," says Sharp. "Most information is free and out there. The trick is to access it."

Each week she reads about 15 publications, including *AdWeek* and *Newsweek*. However, Sharp contends, she gets the highest quality of information by calling on experts directly, asking them for their opinions, and research data.

Andrew Garvin, president of FIND/SVP, a Manhattan-based information retrieval service, agrees that when money is scarce small-business owners are reluctant to buy information, but argues they should consider it a wise investment. "Almost any question you have can be answered in its simplest form for under $500," says Garvin.

Garvin's company serves both large and small clients who can pay annual retainers ranging from $2,000 to $5,000 or pay by the question. His business is based on a similar service he discovered while working as a journalist in Paris. Today, his staff of researchers answers about 6,000 questions a month and also completes more in-depth research reports for clients in a variety of businesses.

Cookie Lewis, founder of Infomania in Sherman Oaks, California, is a law librarian who branched out to serve as an information broker for all kinds of businesses. She says the right information can reduce the risks of a new venture. "It doesn't make sense for a small-business owner to put their life savings into something that a big company has already begun marketing," says Lewis rightly.

One of her most challenging assignments was to compile all the environmental regulations affecting 12 communities for a company who was acquiring a firm that did business in those locations. "I had two days to complete the assignment. I almost had a nervous breakdown, but I did it," boasts Lewis.

She said information brokers, whose fees range from $60 to $150 an hour plus expenses, can tap into thousands of computerized data bases, both government and private. One of the better-known data bases is Nexis, which provides full-text articles gleaned from more than 150 U.S. and international publications. StateNet monitors legislative developments in all 50 states and Legislate tracks what's going on in Congress. Lexis and Westlaw serve the legal community.

Finding competent information brokers can be a challenge in smaller cities across the country. But your local reference librarian, Chamber of Commerce director, or other business owners may have suggestions.

Before hiring an information broker, check his or her references and find out whether the fee is per hour or per project. Next, find out whether there is an extra charge for computer time, how the information will be sent to you, and whether the firm offers both rush and nonrush rates.

For a comprehensive view of the industry, you can turn to the *Directory of Fee-Based Information Services*, published by Burwell Enterprises in Houston, Texas. Helen Burwell, publisher, said the 1984 edition featured 334 companies and individuals. By 1990, the directory had grown to more than 800 entries.

The directory is available by writing to: Burwell Enterprises, 3724 F.M. 1960 West, suite 214, Houston, TX 77068. Her company also publishes the *Information Broker* newsletter.

Lewis's Infomania is located at 14141 Dickens Street, suite 113, Sherman Oaks, CA 91423.

The address for FIND/SVP is 625 Avenue of the Americas, New York, NY 10011.

Sharp Information Research, P.O. Box 335, Hermosa Beach, CA 90254.

DO-IT-YOURSELF INFORMATION GATHERING

- Ask yourself every week, "What information do I need to make better business decisions?"
- Ask your employees to help you collect information about your industry, your competitors, your suppliers, and your vendors.
- Read as many general interest publications as you can, in addition to trade magazines.
- Join industry organizations and subscribe to industry publications and newsletters.
- Attend conferences, seminars, and workshops. In addition to meeting people, collect and read all the brochures and pamphlets available.

- Tune in to radio talk shows to keep up with local and national trends and issues.

- Don't be afraid to call up an expert quoted in a publication or interviewed on television. People generally love to talk about their special interest or field.

- Clip, copy, and circulate pertinent articles, advertisements, and brochures.

83. HOW DO I FIND AFFORDABLE HELP FOR MY BUSINESS PROBLEMS?

Perhaps the most important rule for entrepreneurs is this: Don't let your pride get in the way when you need help. The most successful business owners I know admit they need help and get it as soon as possible.

Here's how one group of small-business owners link up to help each other. On the second Thursday of each month, Gerald Winkelmann, owner of All-Type Containers, Inc., leaves his closed-out merchandise business behind and heads to a four-hour meeting in Creve Coeur near St. Louis, Missouri. "On the way over there, I'm thinking, 'I've got 15 things I must do today,'" says Winkelmann. "But, before the first break, I've got answers to six of the things I need to deal with."

Winkelmann is not spending his morning with an expensive management consultant. He's sitting around a table with about a dozen fellow small-business owners who belong to The Alternative Board, or TAB, as it is known. TAB groups, forming around the country, serve as unpaid, informal advisory boards for small-business owners.

"You've got to be willing to spill your guts or it's no good," Winkelmann says. "You can't tell the group half the story."

Missouri businessman Allen Fishman ended an early retirement to create TAB. Membership is limited to owners or chief executive officers of noncompeting businesses. Each group is organized to bring like-sized businesses together. Members pay between $1,000 and $3,000 a year, based on their annual company revenues, for the privilege of sharing their experiences and learning from one another's mistakes.

"The key is getting the advice from your peers," says Fishman, who retired to Aspen in 1987 after selling a multimillion-dollar electronics company. "Peer pressure also helps people follow through with the solutions proposed."

TAB's headquarters in St. Louis can be reached at (800)727-0126, 8:30 A.M. to 5:30 P.M. CDT.

The Executive Committee, or TEC, as it is known, has a similar roundtable program for executives. TEC is headquartered in San Diego, California.

All kinds of other networking groups are popping up all over the country. Le Tip and Women's Referral Service are just two of them. Local chambers of commerce and trade associations are also terrific resources for small-business owners.

Try to get out of the office to meet with people at least once a week. Isolation can kill a small-business owner's spirit quicker than a lack of cash.

If joining a group doesn't suit your style, you can still fix what's ailing your business without spending a lot of money.

The U.S. Small Business Administration's Small Business Institute program functions in cooperation with universities around the United States. Virtually every business school in the country has programs designed to match eager students with small-business owners. In Los Angeles, for example, business students at Loyola Marymount University are available to research and write a detailed analysis of your business—at no charge. One typical semester, 43 students spent hundreds of hours delving into the financial statements and business histories of a plumbing business, a beauty salon, a print shop, a card store, a computer store, and an office products store, among others. The team of students also analyzed the competition and made suggestions to improve operations.

"Most of the businesses we deal with have between one and

five employees," said Dr. George Hess, a Loyola College of Business professor who coordinates the program. Hess suggests business owners contact the SBA office nearest them for an application form. UCLA's Entrepreneurial Studies Center runs a Small Business Consulting Service, which enables students to work with business owners for pay or academic credit. Another program, the Venture Fellows internship, places five or six graduate students with venture capital firms or companies in which venture capitalists have invested money.

For those interested in going back to school, the Center also offers management development courses targeted to different industries. For instance, Pacific Bell recently sponsored a course for people in the telecommunications field, according to Karen Feinberg, assistant to the director of the Entrepreneurial Studies Center.

The UCLA Center can be reached at (213)825-2985.

At USC, recently graduated business students offer eight weeks of free assistance to business owners as part of their summer honors program.

Companies in Los Angeles and Orange County that have a substantive summer project for an intern can call (213)740-0641.

USC also has a variety of academic programs designed for busy business owners.

If student help doesn't appeal to you, how about advice and counsel from a veteran businessperson?

The SBA's SCORE program, which stands for Service Corps of Retired Executives, has hundreds of volunteers working out of SBA offices around the United States.

SCORE advice is always free, and many SCORE counselors are willing to form a long-term relationship with the owners they help. SCORE also sponsors a myriad of low-cost classes and seminars on topics ranging from writing a business plan to running a home-based business.

> Contact your local SBA district office or call the SBA Answer Desk at (800)827-5722.

If you prefer to stay home and solve your problems, check out the New American Business System, a 350-page, illustrated step-by-step program outlining a practical, small-business management plan. "Most newcomers ignore the experiences of businesspeople who have already done it, so they make the same mistakes," says Charles Chickadel, the San Francisco-based author, consultant, and publisher who created the system. Purchased alone, the easy-to-understand program, delivered in a notebook format, costs $49.95. If you want the filing system designed to go along with it, the cost is $64.95.

> For information call: (800)462-2699, ext. 77.

84. HOW DO I KEEP UP WITH ECONOMIC TRENDS?

Far too many small businesses fail because the owner is operating in a vacuum. You can't possibly make intelligent decisions if you haven't a clue about what is going on in the world around you.

The biggest excuse I hear from poorly informed business owners is that they are too busy to read a newspaper, listen to the radio, or watch the news on TV. These same folks let their industry trade magazines pile up without opening them, and barely skim the newsletters and other magazines they subscribe to.

Big mistake!

Here's how one successful business owner keeps on top of what's going on without spending a lot of her time or money:

Like most small-business owners, Barbara Rodstein listens to the news and reads the business pages.

But when she really wants to figure out how the economy will affect her decorative bathroom-fixture business, she drives over to Randy's Donuts in Inglewood, California, for a cup of coffee and an earful of news. "I guess I don't believe the government indicators," says Rodstein, who founded Harden Industries with her late husband, Harvey. "I want a more immediate response to what's happening in the world."

In boom times, businesses can flourish even if their owners ignore international events and pay little mind to short-term economic trends. But in today's unstable world, accurate information is critical to success. If you are about to ship motors to Mozambique, wouldn't you like to know the government has collapsed *before* you ship them, rather than after?

Instead of hiding under a pile of paperwork and worrying about your day-to-day troubles, get out and visit a nearby truck stop or popular coffee shop. What you pick up in an hour will be more valuable than reading 10 business magazines or listening to all the prognostications of respected economists. "There are a lot of defense companies around here, so I hear about layoffs possibly a bit earlier than most people," says Larry Weintraub, who has owned Randy's Donuts with his brother, Ron, since 1979.

Situated five miles from Los Angeles International Airport, Randy's, with its distinctive, huge rooftop doughnut, serves a busy traveling public. And every customer going to or from the airport is a potential bearer of important economic and international news.

When Rodstein is not cruising through the industrial area that surrounds her southwest Los Angeles plant in her cream-colored Rolls Royce, she frequently strolls around Beverly Hills noting the amount of retail space for rent. She considers business in Beverly Hills a good economic barometer because the people who frequent the pricey Rodeo Drive boutiques are the same ones who buy her upscale bathroom fixtures. "I'm mostly concerned with the amount of consumable income people have to spend on luxury items," admits Rodstein, who also peeks into grocery carts to see what people are buying.

When she can't leave her office, she visits the parking lot during breaks to ask the catering truck driver whether business is up or down and which companies are laying off workers. "I know things are bad when the truck drivers tell me people are buying fewer things to eat and drink."

Rodstein, who took over the multimillion-dollar company when her husband died, says her never-ending quest for useful economic information helps her make critical business decisions.

Rodstein believes, "If you are ignorant of something, there is no way you can take action." Historically, Harden focused solely on the high end of the brass bathroom-fixture market. In response to the flagging economy, she moved into the middle market by producing lower-priced fixtures. This change of strategy is aimed at boosting sales to consumers who cannot afford a $600 faucet.

Across the country, in Milford, Connecticut, another successful entrepreneur is on the road one week out of the month, collecting information. Fred DeLuca, founder of the widely franchised Subway sandwich shops, says he comes up with some of his best ideas while traveling.

DeLuca, who started the company 25 years ago with Pete Buck, a retired nuclear physicist, has about 5,000 franchised Subway stores in operation. By 1995, he hopes to have 8,000 across the United States and abroad.

One of the secrets of his success came to him years ago while he was visiting one of the first Subway sandwich stores in the Southeast. "I stopped in to visit the owner of a store in a small town outside Charlotte, North Carolina," DeLuca recalls. "When I got there, an employee told me the owner was at the Greyhound bus station picking up bread, which he did three times a week because the closest bakery was 40 miles away."

Sensing an immediate disaster if the bus was late or if the workers at the distant bakery went on strike, DeLuca decided right then that Subway owners had to start baking their own bread in the stores. When he went back to Connecticut and explained his plan to his colleagues, they thought he was crazy. But he persisted because he knew it was the right move. "I visited that North Carolina store in June 1983," DeLuca says. "By August, we were testing our first frozen bread dough."

Today, every Subway store bakes its own bread to maintain consistent quality and taste throughout the system. And, DeLuca said with a smile, one of the things customers like is the freshness of the bread.

BECOME YOUR OWN ECONOMIC FORECASTER

■ Get out of your office at least once a day to visit another business.

■ Talk to as many people as possible wherever you go.

■ Chat with truck drivers and delivery people to gather information on whether business is good or bad in your area.

- Drive around to count the number of for-rent, for-lease, and for-sale signs in your area.
- Listen carefully to any information passed along by your suppliers and vendors.

85. WHAT CAN A PRODUCTIVITY EXPERT DO TO HELP MY BUSINESS?

No one was happy when things began to slow down at the Chico Medical Group. Everything, from seeing patients to collecting money, bogged down. So the two dozen or so physicians who owned the corporation hired a productivity consultant to help them figure out ways to work smarter.

Sharon Stone, medical group administrator, says the doctors called in the consultant because they sought to improve patient service while keeping labor costs down.

For four months, an analyst from Western Productivity Group in Palo Alto spent about eight hours a day observing every aspect of life at the Chico Medical Group. Before improvements could be made, the analyst had to figure out how patients moved through the system, how they paid for their care, and how the doctors and other health-care providers communicated with staff members.

"A productivity consultant gives you some statistics to make sound business judgments," says Stone. "She asked lots of questions. She and the others who worked with us explained that they were here to help us work smarter, not faster."

Based on the $60,000 study, the medical group implemented several of the consultants' suggestions, including improvements in the patient check-in area, billing department, medical transcription department, and data processing. The consultants even recommended a change in the type of notepads used for telephone messages to ensure their getting to the right people.

Ray Dillard, president of Western Productivity Group in Palo Alto, says the Chico Medical Group could save between $250,000 and $300,000 by implementing his recommendations.

Productivity consultants offer various services to small-business owners. Some firms specialize in analyzing specific tasks, such as how long it takes a secretary to type a report. Others take a bigger-picture approach, studying how systems work.

For manufacturers, a productivity consultant can figure out how long it takes employees to do a certain task. Then the measurements are used to develop standards and to figure out how many people to hire.

"Because not every person can meet the standards, we try to look at the group doing the task and not the individual," says Joe Lima, director of instrument operations at Lifescan, which makes blood glucose monitors in Milpitas, California.

Lima believes that small-business owners should choose a productivity consultant carefully. Some consultants charge more than $100 per hour; others as little as $50 to $60 per hour. "Be sure to ask exactly what will be delivered under the contract," says Lima. "Ask if the consultant will supply the standards and train someone to teach employees."

When interviewing productivity consultants, be sure to check references and call other clients for firsthand information. Then be sure to meet with the person who will be doing the actual work, rather than just the president or marketing director for the consulting firm.

Dwight Shackelford is a "white-collar" productivity consultant who helps businesses solve their paperwork problems. "There are a lot of things that can be done to help small-business owners," says Shackelford. He says owners can respond quickly to productivity problems if they watch for the symptoms. "Extensive overtime means something is wrong," he says. "Other signs would be paper flow backing up, and workers missing deadlines, or walking around the office more than necessary. If they're moving, they aren't working," says Shackelford.

Dillard says small-business owners can help boost productivity themselves by keeping a close watch on the company's operations to spot trouble before it gets out of hand. "You need to continually adjust your costs as your sales change," advises Dillard. "Don't wait until the end of the month for results; you need to have this kind of information at your fingertips."

When things are not going well and you are losing money, it's difficult to think about spending *more* money to get help. But *do* it. Consultants who specialize in boosting productivity can do a quick study, as well as the more detailed one they did for the Chico Medical Group. The money you spend to save your business will be well spent.

So, how do you find a productivity consultant? Try asking your banker, your accountant, or your attorney to recommend one. You might also check with business associates to see if they have worked with anyone they would recommend. Most general management consultants can also refer you to a person who specializes in boosting productivity.

86. HOW CAN I TELL IF MY BUSINESS IS IN SERIOUS TROUBLE?

"Most entrepreneurs wear rose-colored glasses at all times, never seeing a problem until it's overwhelming," says M. Freddie Reiss, partner in charge of the reorganization and bankruptcy practice for Price Waterhouse's western region.

Reiss, who has steered large and small companies out of choppy waters, says financial troubles don't just blossom overnight. There are very clear warning signals, but most small-business owners refuse to recognize them until it's too late. "You should always be watching your cash flow," advises Reiss. "It's the single most important element to keep an eye on."

Related to cash flow is the necessity of paying close attention to your accounts receivable. Every week, ask yourself if your customers are taking longer to pay you—and why.

Are you stretching your payables from 30 to 45, or 60 to 90 days because you don't have the cash to pay your bills? If so, you are in very deep trouble. "Too many people go into business with razor-thin equity," says Reiss. "You have one bad month and suddenly you can't withstand the impact."

Conversely, Reiss says he has seen too many small businesses go under not for a lack of business, but because of an inability to cope with success. Reiss says he has watched too many businesses "grow into oblivion."

Maui and Sons, a very hot beachwear manufacturer, is a good example of how success can kill a small business.

"They went into shoes and other items because they wanted to sell things all year long," relates Reiss. "They tried to expand beyond T-shirts and shorts." But when the new products flopped, they lost money and their financing. Maui and Sons was forced into bankruptcy and ultimately sold by its creditors to a licensee.

Another example is a chain of dental offices that grew very fast, went public, and then crashed. "Their bank hastened their demise by giving them too much money," says Reiss. Although the management team was unable to handle the pressure of opening in 15 locations over 12 to 14 months, they forged ahead. The chain's rapid expansion devoured all the cash and two years later the firm filed for bankruptcy.

If you think you are heading into financial trouble, take the following quiz developed by management consultant and professor Eric Flamholtz.

It may be the most valuable few minutes you can spend today.

GROWING PAINS QUIZ

Management consultant and professor Eric G. Flamholtz has pinpointed the "Ten Most Common Organizational Growing Pains."

If your company is suffering from more than two of these symptoms, you need help *fast*.

Answer yes or no to these symptoms:

_____ 1. People feel there are not enough hours in the day.
_____ 2. People spend too much time putting out fires.
_____ 3. People are not aware of what other people are doing.
_____ 4. People lack understanding about where the firm is headed.
_____ 5. There are too few good managers.
_____ 6. People feel that "I have to do it myself if I want it to get done correctly."
_____ 7. Most people feel that meetings are a waste of time.

_____ 8. When plans are made, there is very little follow-up, so things just don't get done.

_____ 9. Some people feel insecure about their place in the firm.

_____10. The firm continues to grow in sales but not in profits.

Reprinted with permission from Eric Flamholtz. His book, *Growing Pains: How to Make the Transition from an Entrepreneurship to a Professionally Managed Firm*, costs $27.95. It's published by Jossey-Bass, 350 Sansome Street, San Francisco, CA 94101.

87. HOW CAN A TURNAROUND EXPERT SAVE MY BUSINESS?

Every year, thousands of small businesses fail because their entrepreneurial owners are too stubborn to acknowledge that things are falling apart. Yet admitting you need help is the *first* step toward saving your business from an early death.

Art publisher Gary Hinte's company was gasping for cash, down to three employees, and losing customers when he finally called turnaround expert Ward Wieman for help. "We were virtually bankrupt," admits Hinte, founder and former president of Arion Studios in Carson, California.

One of the first things Wieman did when he got to Arion was to roll up his sleeves and help assemble a press that boosted Arion's printing capacity. Next, he sorted out a myriad of financial problems. Wieman, founder of Management Overload in Playa del Rey, California, says that at one point he invested his own money in Arion and temporarily held an equity position—because he believed in the company.

Because he was willing to admit he needed help, Hinte saved his business. Hinte eventually sold Arion, but when he left, the company was on solid ground.

Unfortunately, too many troubled small-business owners are afraid to call for help because they think they can't afford it. But the few thousand dollars paid to a skilled turnaround expert is much less than the cost of losing everything you have created.

Wieman admits that his major problem is getting in the door

to talk to a stubborn entrepreneur; in most cases, worried bankers, concerned investors, or a panicky board of directors are the ones who insist on bringing in an objective rescuer. No matter who calls for the help, the owner or manager is forced out of power, at least temporarily.

So who are these turnaround experts to whom you are expected to relinquish control of your company?

Most good ones have served as top executives of other companies or have gotten into turnaround and workouts through law or accounting. The best turnaround experts are cool-headed, diplomatic, and expert negotiators. Most charge $100 and up per hour and expect to be paid in full and often in advance, week by week.

"When we walk in, our clients are out of time and out of money," says Gerald P. Buccino, president of Chicago-based Buccino & Associates. By the time he or a member of his firm steps in, key employees are fleeing, suppliers have cut off credit, and customers are taking their business elsewhere.

"We have to do some Herculean things," says Buccino. Salaries are slashed and payrolls are often switched from weekly to biweekly to conserve cash. Excessive inventories are sold off to raise money. Company cars are eliminated, country club memberships terminated. A good consultant also negotiates with employees and union officials to restore support for your company during the crisis.

"We know very shortly if a company can be saved or not," says Buccino.

SYMPTOMS OF A TROUBLED COMPANY

by Walter Kaye, Pasadena attorney and turnaround consultant

Take a few minutes to see if your company is suffering from any of these problems. If you have checked off more than three, you need *help* fast.

■ Do you have stale, missing, or inaccurate financial data?

■ Is your sales volume declining over successive periods of time?

■ Are your sales expenses increasing as a percentage of sales?

■ Is your interest expense growing at a faster rate than sales?

■ Are you financing your operations deficits with loans or trade credit?

■ Is your attention dominated by putting out fires and dealing with unhappy vendors?

■ Are you ignoring sales trends?

■ Are your accounts receivable turning into notes receivable?

■ Are you writing down inventories?

■ Are your bank accounts or credit lines overdrawn?

■ Do you have negative working capital?

■ Are you resorting to the "suicide diversion," by not paying payroll tax? (This is not only illegal but it becomes a permanent, personal liability.)

Here are Kaye's suggestions to get yourself back on track:

■ Find a "point person." Put someone between you and the problem. *You* caused the problems . . . *you* cannot fix them. The point person can use his or her expertise and reputation for your benefit.

■ Quickly reestablish credibility with creditors, bankers, suppliers. The ill-will of trade creditors can often ruin the best recovery plan.

■ Inform your creditors that you have a problem before they find out about your problems from someone else. Creditors hate surprises. The worst thing to do is nothing. Remember, you need your creditors to be part of your recovery.

■ Work on debt restructuring, personal guarantees, secured or unsecured loans, asset-based financing.

■ Discuss the liquidation alternative with creditors. Tell them, "If you do not go along with this work-out, you will get nothing." This is a hard-ball strategy.

■ Become judgment proof. Assign payables for the benefit of creditors.

■ Determine what you can really do without.

- Work on employee, wage, benefit, and perk concessions.
- Consider the pros and cons of filing for Chapter 11 reorganization.
- Consider the pros and cons of a Chapter 7 liquidation.
- Realize that not *all* companies are salvageable. But don't wait too long to get the right kind of help. Don't let your pride or vanity put your company beyond help.

Because troubled companies are in a state of chaos, one of the first things a turnaround expert does is plow through the piles of mail and paperwork to search for important mail, including purchase orders and uncashed checks. Bruce Ballenger once found about $1 million worth of uncashed checks in the office of an ailing hotel. "The accounts receivable clerks weren't cashing the checks if they couldn't find an invoice to match," says Ballenger, the partner in charge of Ernst & Young's corporate services management consulting group in Century City, California.

Losing track of incoming checks is just one warning sign of impending disaster. Companies that lose track of cash flow and operate without a tight budget are candidates for failure.

How do you find a good turnaround consultant? Ask a bankruptcy lawyer or your accountant to recommend a few firms. Be sure to choose someone you feel comfortable confiding in and someone you respect. Remember, this person will be filling your shoes for an indefinite period of time.

Once the person arrives, be prepared for the pain of stepping aside. You may actually be asked to stay out of the office for a while.

It will hurt. It will be humiliating. But, in the long run, it may save your company and all your employees from an untimely demise.

DISASTER WARNINGS

If your company is suffering from more than one of these symptoms, seek help immediately:

■ You frequently turn in late or heavily revised monthly financial statements.

■ You have piles of uncollected accounts receivable.

■ Your banker refuses to extend any more credit or threatens to call in a loan.

■ You have excess inventory on hand all the time.

■ Your expenses for perks are out of control.

■ You have no monthly budget or long-range business plan.

■ Your business is overly dependent on one supplier, vendor, or customer.

■ Your cash flow fluctuates and you feel a lack of control over expenses.

■

88. CAN A MERGER SAVE MY BUSINESS?

Although you may find the thought of joining forces with your competitors distasteful, more and more small-business owners are using mergers as a way to flourish during the current economic slowdown.

"It is much more difficult for companies to remain independent and grow in a recession," says Jim Freedman, managing director of Barrington Associates, a Brentwood, California, investment banking firm. "In tough times, companies need size, bargaining power, increased distribution, and decreased costs."

If your company is not ranked number three or better in your particular industry, you might consider making the right kind of alliance with a competitor, suggests Michael Corrigan, head of Price Waterhouse's corporate finance group in Los Angeles. "In any recession, the weakest tend to go to the wall," says Corrigan.

Phil Tremonti, a Price Waterhouse partner who works with Corrigan on mergers, says the biggest problem in bringing two small companies together is getting their typically strong-willed owners to cooperate. "While I use financial logic, the entrepreneurs let their egos get in the way," says Tremonti.

If you think that a merger might be the way to go, sit down and make a list of competitors whose products or services might mesh well with yours. Decide whether the owner is someone you could work with. If you absolutely hate the person, or they have a bad reputation, don't even *consider* making an approach.

Once you've decided on a candidate, it is usually preferable to have a third party make the initial contact. It's often just too painful to be offering your company to someone else, at least at the beginning.

Remember, orchestrating a successful merger is like getting married. You may be attracted to each other and have similar interests, but everyone has a different way of doing things. After you find a company that may be compatible, ask yourself these questions:

■ What is the synergy between our companies? Do we serve the same customers? Are our products and services similar?

■ How could our combined companies increase sales?

■ Are our management styles compatible?

■ Which company has a better facility or location?

■ If we merge, should we move to a bigger space or new location?

■ Who will be president and who will be vice-president?

■ How would we eliminate duplication of jobs and let employees go?

■ What should the merged company be called?

■ Should we have employment contracts to keep each other around for a while?

■ Where can we find the best advisers to structure the deal?

If things look optimistic, and you begin to negotiate, retain the best advisers you can. You'll need a competent attorney who does merger work, a sharp accountant, and perhaps a good marketing person who can envision the best way to present the newly merged company to the public.

Try not to let your ego get in the way. If you and your merger partner take on different areas of responsibility, and agree on who has the final say on what, you'll stay out of each other's hair—and you can end up in a stronger and more stable position than before.

89. HOW DO I DEAL WITH A BUSINESS CATASTROPHE?

No one wants to think about tragedy befalling their business, but calamities do occur. The best way to prevent a disaster from doing your business in is to be prepared with a crisis-management plan.

If you are well-prepared for coping with a crisis, you increase your chances of surviving. Although he didn't have a crisis plan, Wade Pope, a Louisiana retailer, was lucky. Here's what happened to him:

Wade Pope was reading the newspaper around 9 P.M. on a steamy August night, when his wife called him to the telephone. It was someone from the Bossier City, Louisiana, police department, asking Pope to return to his upscale clothing store immediately.

His worst nightmare was about to come true: His store was on fire. "I figured they'd have the fire out by the time I got there," recalls Pope. "But when I pulled off the interstate and saw the smoke billowing out the roof, I was just sick over it."

Pope learned that fire is the number one U.S. business catastrophe. Storm damage, explosions, collapses, and earthquakes follow on the list.

The fire, believed to be caused by an electrical short in a tailor's sewing machine, destroyed the two-story, antique-filled building. The blaze not only caused about $1.5 million in damage, but jeopardized Pope's traditionally busy Christmas shopping season. A veteran retailer, Pope knew he had to get his doors open again—and fast.

His instincts were right. Forty-three percent of businesses closed down by a catastrophe never reopen, and 28 percent of those that do face financial problems within three to five years of re-opening, according to Nelson Bean, president of Evans American Corp., a Houston-based construction company that specializes in disaster recovery. "Within about three weeks after a business catastrophe, customers have to go elsewhere," says Bean, whose firm has rebuilt oil refineries, grocery stores, and a host of other businesses. "There is a whole series of hidden costs, including the layoff costs of employees."

A fast recovery is essential to save your company from certain death. That's why catastrophe specialists like Evans American and Quality Construction/Inrecon in Dearborn, Michigan, work 24 hours a day, cutting construction time to days and weeks instead of months and years. Too many small-business owners, still in shock over the disaster, make the mistake of trying to handle everything themselves. "The key is for the business owner to be properly insured; don't be penny wise and pound foolish," says Randy Fenton, president of Quality Construction.

Here's the right way to go: Before trouble strikes, you should have a written plan for dealing with disaster. The plan should designate a spokesperson responsible for dealing with city officials, law enforcement officers, the press, customers, and vendors.

After calling your insurance agent and dealing with the immediate safety issues, call your customers and vendors to assure them you have a plan to get back in business as soon as possible.

"Perception is a large part of the game during a crisis," says Sandy Evans Levine, a media crisis management specialist in Poolesville, Maryland. "If the public perceives you are doing everything you can to make things better, they will give you the benefit of the doubt and stick with you."

Levine suggests setting up a special consumer hot line to answer questions. She says most customers and vendors are happy to cooperate and help you get through the crisis if you are open and honest about what's going on. "If you have a crisis and have to deal with the public, it's a great time to boost the company's positive image," says Levine. "It's an opportunity to replace fears of impending doom with reminders of what is good about your company."

Fire and physical calamities aren't the only disasters to befall small-business owners. When one of Levine's clients, a financially troubled machine tool company, had serious money problems, company officials set up a temporary system for its major supplier to deal directly with its customers. This solution kept the customers and the supplier happy until the company could turn itself around.

Although the fire that devastated Pope's business caused a personal and financial trauma, he says that many customers expressed their support and hoped that the store would reopen in time for their Christmas shopping. Evans American won the bid to rebuild Pope's building even though it was slightly higher than competitors' bids. Why? Because it promised to rebuild the structure faster. "About 12 days after the fire, they turned the building back over to us to finish things up," says Pope, who was grateful that the workers labored steadily, 24 hours a day, to complete the job.

Pope's reopened for business around Halloween. Pope and his employees scrambled to redecorate and restock the merchandise. Their efforts paid off in a record Christmas season. Pope had to lay off a few workers, but he put many others to work in different jobs, including taking inventory of new merchandise, handling accounts payable, and restocking the shelves.

A few final points:

- If possible, try to keep your employees busy during the reconstruction period. Paying unemployment benefits is costly, and your recovery will be delayed if you have to hire and train new workers.
- If your building is destroyed, rent or borrow temporary office space and get your computers and phone lines up and running as soon as possible.

DEALING WITH DISASTER

No matter how small, no business is immune to disaster.

- If your business is damaged or destroyed, take care of safety issues first. Make sure the gas and electricity are shut off and rope off the building to keep the public away.

■ Hire a company to board up any damaged windows, walls, or the roof.

■ Remove excess water and humidity as soon as possible.

■ Move salvageable goods out to a safe location.

■ Don't hide from the public. Be available to officials, reporters, and customers.

■ If you can't answer a question, promise to get the information and call back.

■ Draft a crisis-management plan before you need one. Include a chain of command and set some ground rules.

■ Make sure your insurance coverage is adequate and up to date.

■ Consider advertising to let your customers know what happened and what you are doing to bring the business back to life.

■

90. HOW DO I DEAL WITH THE MEDIA DURING A BUSINESS CRISIS?

When federal investigators turned up the heat on their investigation into Drexel Burnham Lambert's "junk bond" trading, the firm's reaction was to hunker down and refuse to say much of anything to the press.

I know this from personal experience. Assigned to a team covering the mergers and acquisitions binge of the 1980s, I tried for days to speak with someone at Drexel. My efforts were fruitless. Finally, my frustrated editor sent me out after hours to knock on doors in search of any Drexel executive. I headed into some of the most glamorous neighborhoods in Los Angeles and the San Fernando Valley, armed only with a few addresses.

Every house I approached was dark, buttoned up, and silent. Funny how all the Drexel executives seemed to be out of town at the same time.

Frustrated and tired, my last stop was at Michael Milken's house. Milken was Drexel's brilliant bond trader and the brains behind its phenomenal growth and power. His personal contacts and influence changed the face of corporate America. It also landed him in jail. But, in his heyday, he was revered by friends and foes alike. He led an insular, protected life, working long hours on the trading floor in Drexel's Beverly Hills office. His home was nestled at the end of a wooded drive in Encino, an upscale but unpretentious suburb. It was nearly 10 P.M. when I approached the house—

really much too late to be knocking on doors. But I had come this far.

The gate to the private drive was open. No ferocious guard dogs. No armed sentries. I walked to the front door and tapped lightly.

After a few minutes, as I was turning away, the door swung open. There stood his wife, Lori, in a robe, looking sleepy and worried.

"I'm so sorry to bother you this late," I said after I showed her my press credentials. "We have tried for days to reach someone at the company."

"My husband isn't here," she said quietly. She smiled and shut the door.

I headed back downtown.

The pursuit of Drexel executives went on this way, until Drexel finally realized that *not* dealing with the press was doing more harm than releasing a few well-chosen statements. Years later, with Milken serving time in federal prison, I think back to that night and how much damage was done to Drexel's public image by the arrogant way they initially handled both the press and the public.

You, as a small-business owner, can learn from the mistakes of others when it comes to handling a crisis. After all, while you may not be dealing with multimillion-dollar fraud charges, you might have to deal with a toxic spill, a labor strike, or an explosion that kills a worker. Any of these things will thrust you and your company into the public eye. And, unless you are prepared, you risk losing more than your credibility.

One of the best books I've read on crisis management is *The First 24 Hours: A Comprehensive Guide to Successful Crisis Communications*, by Dieudonee Ten Berge (see "Books" in Resources guide). A Dutch journalist and foreign correspondent, Ten Berge takes you inside some of the biggest corporate crises ever, including the Tylenol cyanide poisonings and the *Exxon Valdez* oil spill.

She emphasizes the importance of being prepared to handle a crisis before one actually happens. You don't need an elaborate, written plan, but you do need some sort of plan and a chain of command. You also need to designate a public spokesperson, so conflicting information is not given out by different people.

Once you choose an official company spokesperson, insist employees not speak to the press—or even to their families, if necessary. Ten Berge also suggests suspending your advertising for a short period of time after the crisis so it won't be associated with the bad news.

Create a crisis-management team that meets at least twice a year to figure out exactly what to do if something bad hits. Then, plan a drill and a rehearsal to test the plan.

You need to identify your constituencies and figure out the best way to address your customers, vendors, and even competitors who will try to capitalize on your misfortune.

Most business owners don't realize the kind of impossible deadlines reporters face. If word of the problem hits the newswires at 2 P.M. and the deadline is 5 P.M., that reporter must have all the information possible to write a coherent story. So, when reporters call in, ask for their deadline times and respond to them in order of urgency.

"Get the bad news out fast and get it out completely," says Ten Berge. "Explain what you are going to do about the problem. Tell the truth. Remember that silence implies guilt." Saying "no comment" is the worst response. If you truly don't know the answer to a question or can't answer on the advice of your attorney, explain that.

Make sure you get the reporter's name and telephone number before you begin the interview, so you may contact them again as the situation changes. If you say you are going to call back at a certain time, *do it*.

A good rule to live by is that nothing is really "off the record." No matter how much you trust the reporter, don't say anything that you do not want to see in print—if not that first day, then down the line.

Determine the key points that you want to make and continue stressing them, no matter how confusing the questions become. Putting together a fact sheet or position paper is a good idea, especially if you are dealing with a group of reporters in a news conference.

If your business has experienced a natural disaster, such as a fire or flood, the coverage will certainly have a different slant than if your generator caught fire and burned six workers.

You will increase your credibility if you call the media, rather than wait for them to call you. As part of your crisis-management plan, draw up a list of people to call at your local newspaper, television, and radio stations. You might also note the numbers of the local Associated Press or Reuters office to reach these wire services.

Depending on what the emergency entails, you may have to notify the police department, fire department, county health department, sheriff's office, hospitals, or the highway patrol. It is better to call these public servants first, rather than let them hear the news on the radio or television.

Being prepared is the most important thing, so run through an emergency scenario once or twice. You hope the real thing never happens, but if it does, you will be well prepared.

One final note on crisis management:

I spent nearly five years covering a much beleaguered Orange County oil services company called Smith International. Through wildly fluctuating profits, through a hostile takeover attempt of a competitor, through a massive patent infringement lawsuit and a bankruptcy filing, Smith executives were open, accessible, and honest.

Smith chairman Jerry Neely took time for lengthy interviews after long, stressful days. He always returned my telephone calls. He cooperated because he knew I was working very hard to cover the company's troubles in a clear, insightful way. Although the news about Smith was seldom good, by being open with me and other reporters, the company came out looking much better than Drexel ever did.

91. WHAT SHOULD I CONSIDER BEFORE FILING FOR BANKRUPTCY?

Until recently, the stigma of filing for bankruptcy was enough to keep many small-business owners afloat, no matter the cost to their psyches and health. But today, thousands of troubled business owners are heading to the federal bankruptcy court to buy themselves some peace of mind and to keep their creditors at bay.

"Chapter 11 has become a financial planning device," says Carolyn Fergoda, a bankruptcy attorney in Pasadena, California, who represents mostly small-business owners. "The trend in Chapter 11 filings is called the 'prepackaged filing,' where you go in with a deal already worked out with your creditors."

Fergoda says the myth that bankruptcy destroys your credit is really that—a myth—because bankruptcy usually has the effect of clearing a bad credit history. Instead of a long list of foreclosures, late payments, and debts, your credit history will contain a notation of your bankruptcy petition being discharged or approved by the court.

In other words, declaring bankruptcy no longer means your credit is ruined or that you can never buy property again. Yes, most of the people you will deal with after filing for bankruptcy will want to know the circumstances surrounding the filing—and you should always tell them the truth—but the stigma is gone.

There are several kinds of bankruptcy filings, and the type of filing you make depends on the facts surrounding your financial situation. A Chapter 11 filing permits a business to keep operating while it tries to solve its financial problems. But Chapter 11's are expensive and risky. The filing fee for a Chapter 11 proceeding costs about $500, not counting the thousands of dollars you will probably need to pay a competent bankruptcy attorney. And about 80 percent of the businesses that file for Chapter 11 protection fail to emerge from the court intact.

"A Chapter 11 filing does buy time," says Fergoda. "It stops the IRS from foreclosing and stops creditors from attaching your assets."

A Chapter 7 liquidation can be very effective for a small business with few debtors and no serious tax problems. The goal of a Chapter 7 is to sell off every possible asset and raise cash. It is the best filing when the business is beyond hope.

After you file for protection, you have 120 days to propose a plan to the bankruptcy court for repaying your debtors.

Following are some tips from bankruptcy experts to help you figure out if filing for bankruptcy protection is the best thing to do.

TIPS

- Don't wait until your creditors are banging on your door and the lights have been turned off. Talk with your creditors as soon as possible and try to work out an extended payment plan or new terms.
- Hire a competent bankruptcy attorney to review your case. *Note:* Bankruptcy attorneys generally require you to place their retainer in a trust account administered by the bankruptcy court.
- Ask your lawyer to outline the various options and filings so you can decide which is best for you.
- Try to line up financing from an asset-based lender or other high-risk lender before you file any papers. It's much easier to find money before you file, than after.
- Conserve cash and slash all your expenses.
- Consider setting up an arbitration proceeding to work out a plan with your creditors in a neutral setting.
- Payroll taxes are *not* dischargeable through bankruptcy.

Even if you file bankruptcy on behalf of your business, you will be personally liable for the amount owed. In fact, you will not only have to pay the payroll taxes, you may be subject to a 100 percent penalty as well.

92. SHOULD I CONSIDER EXPORTING MY PRODUCTS?

Although the world's political conditions are tumultuous at best, there are true opportunities for small-business owners willing to be patient and persistent. It will always take longer and cost more than you expect to put a foreign deal together, but if you know what you are getting into and work with qualified consultants, you should eventually begin to make money.

A lack of information is the main reason most small-business owners shy away from exporting their goods or services. "The reason 70 percent of smaller companies don't export is because they believe there is no single accessible source for export information," says John Rennie, author of *Exportise: An International Trade Source Book for Smaller Company Executives*. (See the Resources guide for additional export information.)

Rennie, a veteran exporter who is also chairman and chief executive of Pacer Systems, a Massachusetts aerospace firm, says there *is* a wealth of information and support for small-business owners willing to spend time finding it. Every year, the federal government, individual states, and even some cities and counties sponsor hundreds of trade missions that welcome small-business participation. The U.S. Small Business Administration and the Commerce Department jointly sponsor about 100 "matchmaker" trade missions each year. The SBA usually provides $500 for the first 10 qualified business owners who sign up.

The SBA and the U.S. Export-Import Bank (known as the "Eximbank") offer government guaranteed export financing. Most states also provide financing assistance to support exports.

If you are interested in exploring the international market, attend one of the dozens of seminars and workshops taking place every week to acquaint business owners with export opportunities. Most cities have an Export Managers Association, a Port Authority, or a state world trade commission. The Foreign Trade Association also has chapters around the country.

To learn more about the SBA's matchmaker trade missions contact your local SBA office or call the Commerce Department at (202)377-4806.

Exportise, published by the Small Business Foundation of America in Washington, D.C., costs $49.50. You can order this readable and comprehensive book by calling the Foundation's Export Opportunity Hotline. The hot line is staffed by people who can answer your export questions. The number is (800)243-7232.

Eximbank works with small and medium-sized firms to encourage exports. In fiscal 1990, the bank authorized $2.1 billion in support for small-business exports. Export credit insurance protects you against foreign buyers failing to pay you. Working capital guarantees encourage commercial lenders who need money to make goods for export.

The bank also provides loans to foreign buyers of U.S. goods, and conducts free programs for companies interested in exporting. For the schedule and registration information, call the bank at (202)566-4490.

The Foreign Credit Insurance Association represents a group of insurance companies that work with Eximbank to insure exporters against foreign creditors failing to pay their debts. The coverage protects against commercial and political risks, including war and revolution. The association also has special policies for new exporters, offering enhanced commercial risk protection for the first two years and requiring no deductible.

To get started you need to figure out whether what you have to sell is needed by the people in the country you want to sell to. Trade specialists at the Department of Commerce's International

Trade Administration (ITA) can help you connect with their counterparts posted in American embassies and consulates around the world. ITA representatives can answer questions about the local market and point you in the right direction for assistance.

For very nominal fees, the ITA will distribute your company's catalogs or videotapes to customers in distant countries, provide mailing lists, or evaluate the financial and political stability of a foreign nation.

You may want to work with an attorney or export consultant who specializes in dealing with the country you want to sell to. A specialist can help answer questions ranging from how to obtain a letter of credit to how to insure and ship your goods. The passage of the "fast-track" trade legislation aimed at boosting trade between the United States, Canada, and Mexico should make it easier and easier to do business with our neighbors.

Thomas Teofilo, president of the World Trade Services Group in Long Beach, California, is a veteran export consultant who helps small companies manuever through the maze of marketing and regulatory challenges. Teofilo's office is close to the International Business Incubator in Long Beach, a modern incubator that combines traditional executive suite services with the expertise of on-site export consultants. "Our objective is to help a domestic company go international and help foreign companies come into the United States," says Teofilo.

> Teofilo says many small-business owners are eager to ship goods to the Eastern Bloc, because they see how lacking in material goods people there are. But his advice—at least for the short-term—is "Don't do it." Most people don't realize that although the people you see on the nightly news *need* just about everything, they have *no* hard currency to spend. Unless you are willing to work out a barter arrangement, or wait years for your cash, think twice about doing business in the splintered Soviet Union. Huge American corporations have done some business there, mainly because they can accept certain goods in trade, as Pepsi-Cola did with a major vodka company a few years ago.

In addition to export consultants, some companies skilled in international trade are willing to invest in certain deals in exchange for an equity position in them.

Harvey Morris, president and chief executive of the '76-'92 Group of Sea Bright, New Jersey, said his company, which was founded in London in 1979, has worked with companies exporting equipment, chemicals, and computer products. The company often helps put the deal together in exchange for a slice of the profits.

Once you've located a consultant and are assured there is a market for your products, don't be afraid to do business in a foreign currency.

On the other hand, Tim Murphy, president of the Export Managers Association of California, says it is important to match your method of financing to the preferred means of doing business in the country you are dealing with.

A resource list from Eximbank and the Foreign Credit Insurance Association follows.

CONTACTING EXIMBANK

	EXIMBANK HEADQUARTERS	EXIMBANK WEST COAST OFFICE
Mail:	811 Vermont Avenue, N.W. Washington, DC 20571	11000 Wilshire Blvd., suite 9103 Los Angeles, CA 90024
Telephone:	(202)566-2117	(213)575-7425
Telefax:	(202)566-7524	(213)575-7428
Telex:	TRT197681(EXIM UT)	
Cable:	"EXIMBANK"	
TDD:		(202)535-3913
Export Financing Hotline:		(800)424-5201
Electronic Bulletin Board:		(202)566-4699

PROGRAM CONTACTS

DIRECT LOANS, INTERMEDIARY LOANS, AND GUARANTEES
(Contact the appropriate area division, based on the buyer's country):

Africa and Middle East Division	(202)566-8011
Asia Division	(202)566-8885
Europe and Canada Division	(202)566-8813
Latin America Division	(202)566-8943

WORKING CAPITAL GUARANTEES
United States Division   (202)566-8819

EXPORT CREDIT INSURANCE (Contact the nearest FCIA office):

New York:	40 Rector Street New York, NY 10006	(212)227-7020
Chicago:	20 North Clark Street, suite 910 Chicago, IL 60602	(312)641-1915
Houston:	Texas Commerce Tower 600 Travis, suite 2860 Houston, TX 77002	(713)227-0987
Los Angeles:	222 North Sepulveda Blvd., suite 1515 El Segundo, CA 90245	(213)322-1152
Miami:	World Trade Center 80 Southwest 8th Street Miami, FL 33130	(305)372-8540

COURTESY, EXIMBANK

93. CAN I DO BUSINESS FOLLOWING THE "SECOND RUSSIAN REVOLUTION"?

The failed Soviet coup and the subsequent collapse of the Soviet Union has left many American business owners wary about the possibilities of *ever* doing business in Russia. But business consultants who work closely with the Soviets are optimistic about the entrepreneurial spirit of the Russian people and their hunger for American products.

"Soviet business people are more like Americans than anyone else I have dealt with," says Dan Corcoran, whose Riverside, California–based InterOccidental consulting firm puts together joint ventures for Soviet companies. "I am continually impressed and amazed by the way the Soviet business people are creating opportunities where others see only adversity." Corcoran says Americans are amazed at the Soviet business owners' total lack of business experience. But remember, private enterprise was officially prohibited for decades and the government has done all it can to suppress any capitalistic leanings, despite a flourishing black market.

Corcoran and others believe persistent and patient American entrepreneurs can teach their Russian counterparts how to succeed and eventually make money by doing so. But it will not be easy. Political instability and a lack of hard currency thwart most efforts to do any kind of business deal in Russia. Still, "The Soviet people understand that the free market and democracy are the only ways to save the country from total collapse," says Jeff Ostrovsky, a Russian immigrant who founded the Staten Island, New York–

based Atlantic J&S Corp. to set up joint ventures with the Soviet Union.

Ostrovsky, whose firm is involved in oil and gas ventures, plastic production, and metal recycling, says the demand for products is "absolutely tremendous," adding that business owners willing to be patient and creative about getting their money out will be rewarded by profits. Because it is nearly impossible to convert rubles to hard currency, he advises clients to invest them in projects such as hotel construction or in the production of items destined for export, which will generate exchange.

"Doing business over there is a long-term game; you won't experience fast returns," says David Kern Peteler, a Los Angeles attorney who specializes in business transactions with the Soviets.

Peteler says American businesses continue to be frustrated by the Soviet monetary system. "The Russian government has gold and dollars, but it is difficult to get them to spend them," says Peteler, who believes that the ruble will become a convertible currency by the end of the century—if the Soviets are serious about joining the world economy.

He says American entrepreneurs are often surprised at how their Soviet counterparts act during negotiations. "Russians tend to use bluster to cover up embarrassment over their troubled economy," Peteler says. "But they are seeking help, and having a Western partner gives them credibility."

Deal-making can also be costly in the Soviet Union, with legal fees ranging to around $50,000 for a complicated transaction.

One New Jersey business owner has become legendary for his successful dealings with the Soviets. By working closely with local government leaders in Moscow, Shelley Zeiger has brought pizza and apple pie to Muscovites. He constantly encourages American business owners to pursue opportunities in Russia and personally leads small business trade missions to Moscow for the U.S. Department of Commerce.

A native of the Ukraine, Zeiger has been doing business in the Soviet Union since the mid-1970s. Through the years, he has imported everything from natural fragrances to wooden nesting dolls. His greatest triumph was opening the Trenmos restaurant about a mile from the Kremlin. Named for Trenton and Moscow, the upscale restaurant accepts both rubles and hard currency for such fare as steak and ice cream and apple pie.

Zeiger's Soviet partner is the Lenin District Food Catering Trust. Zeiger's son, Jeff, spends three out of every four months in Moscow, running the Trenmos restaurant and keeping an eye on the family's other business ventures.

Although he has succeeded in making money in the Soviet Union, Zeiger admits doing business there is rough. "They want to have a free market system, but when it comes to digging into their pockets or having to deal with supply and demand, they can't," Zeiger says.

Although the bureaucratic red tape discourages even the most energetic American entrepreneurs, Zeiger remains optimistic because "we are dealing with 300 million people who need anything and everything except guns." Right now, demand is high for the most basic consumer goods—blue jeans, underwear, sneakers, and other kinds of clothing and shoes.

If you decide to try to do business with the Soviets, you are pretty much on your own. You can try to obtain foreign credit insurance and financing from the U.S. Export-Import Bank. (See 92. Should I Consider Exporting My Products?)

"You have to do it yourself," Zeiger says. "You won't get much help from state or federal commerce department officials." He says applying for an export license to sell your goods is the simplest way for a small business to enter the Soviet market.

But despite the problems, Zeiger says "dealing with the Soviets is very attractive for those with the courage and guts to take the risks."

Zeiger's own greatest challenge has been teaching Soviet employees to be polite to their customers.

He recalls the first day he began selling pizza from a mobile kitchen in Moscow. Although hundreds of Soviets were clamoring to buy pizza from his Astro Pizza truck, Shelley Zeiger firmly asked the young salesclerk to stop selling. "She was taking their money and throwing it in a bag rather than saying, 'Thank you' and using the cash register," recalls Zeiger.

"I asked her to put the money in the cash register and say, 'Spacebo,' which means 'Thank you.' You should have seen the looks on the people's faces. That's when I knew I had brought a little bit of America to the Soviet people."

94. HOW DO I KNOW IF MY BUSINESS IS READY FOR FRANCHISING?

Ask successful entrepreneurs if they've thought of franchising their business and watch their eyes twinkle. With the franchise boom continuing, it's tempting to think of cloning your small business. But franchising is much harder than you think.

The pitfalls are many. You need to figure out how to keep running your business while gearing up to help others open their doors. You need money for training, advertising, and marketing. You will be surprised to find that there are very few financing options for buyers of new, unproven franchises.

And, you have to be prepared to deal with a state and federal regulatory maze now governing new franchises. "Thou shalt not franchise what hasn't proven successful on its own," says Stephen Raines, founder of National Franchise Associates in Atlanta, Georgia.

To crack the competitive franchise market, Raines says, your business must have a profitable track record, be easily taught to someone else, and have the potential to work in cities and towns across the country. In other words, just because your business is successful, doesn't mean it should be franchised.

If you are determined to go ahead, Raines says, remember that franchising carries a moral obligation to protect your franchisees from financial ruin. Many buyers invest their life savings; you must remember that you are toying with somebody else's economic future.

Ask yourself these questions before you jump into a franchising plan:

- Is your business at least two years old and profitable?
- Have you worked *all* the bugs out of your daily operations?
- Do you serve a specific market niche?
- Can your business concept be as successful in Des Moines as it is in Los Angeles?
- Can you teach the basics of your business to anyone?
- Are you patient and willing to train people?
- Do you have enough money set aside to pay for legal fees, marketing, advertising, and training?

If you can answer yes to most of these questions, sit down with a franchise consultant and get a second opinion. Remember, expanding a business is a huge step and should not be taken lightly.

95. SHOULD I RELOCATE MY BUSINESS TO A "FRIENDLIER" STATE?

A few years ago, when state marketing representatives began hitting the road to bring new business to their states, they wined and dined only corporate executives. Today, with the recognition that small businesses create two-thirds of new jobs and constitute the engine that drives the U.S. economy, states and counties are wooing companies that balance having only a handful of employees with good potential for growth. "The traditional approach was to go after the Fortune 500 companies that appeared to be growing and expanding," says Bob Henningsen, chief marketing representative for the state of Iowa. "But the truth is, the small- and medium-sized businesses are the ones with all the growth."

Iowa, which touts itself as "The Smart State for Business," offers a range of financial incentives for small-business owners. The state's venture capital resources fund has about $11 million available for young, growing businesses. Iowa also has $4.6 million in its "community economic betterment" account—for companies that come in and create jobs.

To make things easy for newcomers, the state operates a business information center in Des Moines. The center, which fields about 6,000 calls a year from business owners, helps people interested in moving their companies to Iowa as well as those simply trying to do business there.

South Dakota is also out to woo you with a program that boasts no corporate income tax, no personal income tax, no personal property tax, and no business inventory tax.

Low taxes are just one of the advantages that states are using to promote themselves as business locations. And South Dakota is one of the states spending millions of dollars to entice small- and medium-sized companies to move in.

Nevada, South Carolina, and Pennsylvania are also wooing business, according to Andrew Shotland, a marketing consultant for Development Counsellors International in New York. "States realize that one way to diversify their economy is to attract small businesses," he says.

Nevada is one of the more aggressive states when it comes to small-business recruitment. "We target businesses with about 10 employees," says Jim Spoo, executive director of the Nevada Economic Development Commission in Carson City. "Moving small companies is easy. Moving big companies is very hard; you might as well try to move a branch of the federal government."

Spoo says 40 to 60 percent of Nevada's new businesses are coming across the border from California. In the past year, about 65 newly relocated companies created 2,549 jobs in Nevada. "They are coming here largely because of what Nevada is, not because of the goodies we dangle in the air," Spoo says. Lack of personal income, corporate, and inventory taxes have turned Nevada into a mecca for warehouses and distribution centers, Spoo asserts.

Every week, a dozen recruiters from other states are traveling across California, enticing business owners to move out. The out-of-state recruiters emphasize that California's steep workers' compensation insurance rates, high taxes, and stringent air-pollution control laws make it difficult to make a profit.

"We don't take these recruiters lightly," says Warren Rashleigh, spokesman for the California Department of Commerce. "California has its work cut out for it." Rashleigh said California, which had no formal marketing program until 1984, is focusing on retaining businesses already there. The state has 19 enterprise zones that offer businesses tax incentives to locate in certain areas.

Although California officials don't keep track of how many businesses move out, Rashleigh says expansions by companies that stay make up for the losses and keep the economy strong.

Cities and counties across America also have economic development offices that will be glad to provide all kinds of incentives and information to small-business owners.

Caution is in order, however: Before you pack up, be sure to do all the research and feel confident you are making the right move.

96. HOW DO I CREATE A STRATEGIC ALLIANCE WITH A BIGGER COMPANY?

Sometimes the best way to get your product out on the market is to join forces with an established company and take advantage of their distribution channels. Establishing a working relationship with a larger, successful company in your field often means the difference between success and failure for a fledgling company. Cash is not the only benefit: The larger company can provide you with expertise, access to customers, and patented technologies.

It is possible to find a mentor company in virtually any industry if you join a trade association, attend a national conference, or advertise in a respected trade magazine or newsletter.

Here's how one successful biotechnology firm helps smaller companies gain a foothold in the fiercely competitive biotech field: South San Francisco–based Genentech, Inc., which flourished by licensing its own products to large pharmaceutical companies, is now on the other side of the equation, putting together research and development deals with small biotechnology firms.

"Biotechnology is probably the most difficult business to succeed in for a start-up company," says Gary Lyons, vice-president of business development for Genentech in South San Francisco. "The best relationship is where they have something we want and we have something they want."

These liaisons are especially critical for struggling biotechnology firms, which usually face an 8- to 10-year delay between discovery and distribution of a new drug. "Now more than ever, small biotechnology companies need the market access of larger companies," says Larraine Segil, founding partner of the Lared Group in Century City, California.

Segil, whose company has structured dozens of strategic alliances between big and small companies around the world, says a successful match has tremendous benefits for both partners. "For a big company, the smaller entrepreneurial company is able to contribute its creativity and innovation," she says. The smaller company benefits from an infusion of money and support that enables its research to continue.

Stephen Sherwin, president and chief executive of Cell Genesys Inc., is well acquainted with the benefits of working with a big biotechnology company. Sherwin, former vice-president of clinical research for Genentech, left to form his own company a few miles away. "Our goal is to establish partnerships with larger biotechnology and pharmaceutical companies," says Sherwin, whose company is pioneering new ways to treat disease and genetic disorders.

Unlike many biotechnology start-ups, Cell Genesys, located in Foster City, California, has been lucky. It has raised about $8.5 million from several venture capital funds and Stanford University.

Sherwin and his colleagues are exploring a technique called "homologous recombination." This new technology enables scientists to replace, activate, and deactivate selected genes within cells. The goal of homologous recombination is to make permanent changes in cells, enabling them to serve as new ways to carry drugs or to combat disease themselves. So far, one promising area for this technology is in the reversal or prevention of blindness associated with old age and certain diseases. Sherwin said his scientists are trying to engineer cells to replace deteriorated cells in the retina.

Brian Atwood, vice-president of operations at Glycomed, Inc., in Alameda, California, has crafted three research and development deals with bigger companies, including a $15-million venture with Genentech. Together, Genentech and Glycomed plan to develop a new line of anti-inflammatory drugs. "The key to a successful relationship is to open up a broad front of communication," advises Atwood. "Each of us here talks to a different person in the organization we are working with."

Segil agrees that communication is essential, especially since the initial excitement of a new working relationship often masks serious conflicts. "A number of strategic partnerships we put together three or four years ago have experienced problems," says Segil. "We find the commitment of energy and commitment to learn from each other changes with time."

The danger of a lopsided commitment, according to Segil, is that "one side or the other feels taken advantage of."

Although linking up with a big company may sound like the perfect solution to your money problems, there are dangers. Entrepreneurs who thrive on the excitement of running their own companies often chafe under the restrictions imposed by a strategic alliance.

Often, the larger company's policies and bureaucratic regulations begin to snuff out the creativity of the people at the smaller firm. Every management team also has its own view about taking risks, and sometimes this creates conflict.

"We tell clients, it's not a one-way street, there cannot be learning in only one direction," says Segil.

FORGING AN ALLIANCE

- Seek out a partner with similar long-term goals.
- Strive to make equal contributions to the deal.
- Money talks, but the partner without money should have a voice, too.
- Keep the lines of communication open.
- Periodically review how the project is progressing.
- Be open to restructuring or modifying things if problems arise.

97. HOW DO I MAKE SURE MY PENSION PLAN MEETS FEDERAL STANDARDS?

If you treat managing your company's pension plan as just one of your many responsibilities, you are asking for trouble: Meeting all the rules and regulations enforced by the Department of Labor and the Internal Revenue Service can be a full-time job. And right now, these federal agencies are actively pursuing small-business owners whose pension plans violate the federal laws aimed at protecting employee funds.

The Department of Labor, which is responsible for enforcing the federal Employee Retirement Income Security Act (ERISA) added 100 people to its enforcement unit in 1991, bringing the total to 400, according to David Ball, Assistant Secretary of Labor. "Enforcement has never been more vigorous than it is today," says Ball.

Criminal indictments and civil penalties filed against small-business owners are on the increase. In fact, Ball says, many small-business owners who purchased annuities from California's collapsed Executive Life Insurance Co. are in trouble for jeopardizing their employees' financial security.

Although ignorance of the law is no excuse for violations, the Labor Department does have a voluntary compliance program which allows business owners to make restitution to their plans and clean up their act without harsh penalties. "The cheapest insurance you can buy is to use professional help in the administration of your plan," advises Ball.

Millions of American workers have no pension plans. One reason is that many smaller companies have neither the time nor the money to create them. But in April 1991, the Labor Department unveiled a proposal to set up a new kind of portable individual retirement account for workers. This initiative was designed to help small-business owners provide coverage to millions more employees with a minimum of paperwork, Ball says.

No matter what kind of pension benefits you offer, however, if you act as the plan's trustee, you are legally and financially responsible for the money and everything that happens to it. Every plan must have written investment objectives that detail the goals and objectives of the plan, in addition to the plan document itself. The plan administrator must monitor performance of the plan and its investments based on the objectives set. The regulations also require a trustee to thoroughly investigate the qualifications of any investment management firm it hires, according to Robert DiMeo, a financial account executive for Kidder, Peabody & Co., in Chicago.

DiMeo recently fine-tuned and brought into compliance a profit-sharing plan operated by the architectural firm of O'Donnell, Wicklund, Pigozzi & Peterson, in Deerfield, Illinois. Kathy Jessen, OWP&P's controller, retained DiMeo after reading some articles that alerted her to potential problems with the firm's 20-year-old profit-sharing plan. "I became aware of certain regulations and saw we had a potential problem with the type of investment funds we were offering to employees," recalls Jessen.

Although she was familiar with how the plan worked, Jessen said she did not feel qualified to make the changes. "Bob [DiMeo] helped develop our fund management policies and found an appropriate third investment fund," says Jessen. "He also suggested three qualified investment managers and helped us interview all three before we hired one."

David West, a specialist in employee benefits and a partner at Gibson, Dunn & Crutcher, in Los Angeles, notes that under ERISA, plan trustees must not only act in a prudent manner, but manage the fund as well as an expert would. "Good intentions just don't count," says West.

And any business owner who taps into the pension fund is asking for big trouble, including stiff penalties from the Department of Labor and the IRS. "When a business owner gets into a pinch, he or she may think, 'I'll just borrow a little money from the plan and put it back,' " says West. "I suggest that you not touch the money until your advisers tell you it is legal to do so."

The IRS works closely with the Labor Department on pension fund enforcement issues. In fact, the pension plan reports you file with the IRS are dutifully logged into the Department of Labor's data base, according to Ball. He says violations not picked up from the computerized data base are often red-flagged during manual audits performed in regional offices around the country.

Ball's advice to business owners tempted to borrow money from their pension funds when times are tough: "Get professional help—and keep your hand out of the cookie jar."

TIPS

Richard A. Sirus, an attorney who specializes in employee benefits cases at the Chicago law firm of Pope, Ballard, Shepard & Fowle Ltd., offers these tips on avoiding problems when acting as a fiduciary for your pension plan:

- Confirm that plan documents are in order and contain the necessary provisions for proposed actions.
- Carefully document all fiduciary decisions. This paper trail should include resolutions, minutes, advice received from professionals, studies performed, and so on.
- Hire competent professionals experienced in the field to consult on plan and fiduciary duties.
- Set up procedures for evaluating and monitoring fiduciaries working under contract. Review the investment manager's performance at least once a year. Review plan administrators to make sure they are keeping accurate records and keeping track of benefit payments.
- Obtain fiduciary liability insurance to increase your protection.

98. HOW DO I PASS MY BUSINESS TO THE NEXT GENERATION?

Succession problems are tough, but they can be solved with open communication and expert help. Meet a smart family who decided they didn't want their business to die:

Ted Twardzik spent 36 years making pierogies, a stuffed Polish-style pasta pocket. From his mother's kitchen table in Shenandoah, Pennsylvania, Twardzik had built a thriving enterprise that soon outranked coal mining as the town's largest employer. Each week, he watched Ateeco Inc.'s 200 workers produce about 4 million frozen pierogies for shipment across the country.

A few years ago, with sales approaching $15 million, Twardzik felt it was time to cash in and retire. Although his two younger sons had expressed an interest in taking over the business, the senior Twardzik was not convinced Tim and Tom were ready to step into his shoes. The Twardziks faced what thousands of small, family-owned businesses face every day: how to pass the company along to the children.

Children uninterested in the business squabble over who will take over, and heavy federal and state estate taxes all work against the perpetuation of family business in America. Yet, families like the Twardziks, who turned to estate-planning experts for advice, have been able to work out the difficulties.

No longer up for sale, Ateeco (which stands for "a Twardzik company") is remaining in the family. After watching his sons dealing with attorneys, accountants, and potential buyers, Twardzik was convinced they were ready to run the business. Several years ago, Twardzik stepped aside and promoted himself to chairman. Tom, at 29, was named president and Tim, at 31, became vice-president of marketing. To ensure his sons would take control, Twardzik moved out of the Mrs. T's office on East Center Street and set up shop in the former Elks Club building he owns about a mile away.

With the help of tax specialists and insurance agents, the Twardziks fine-tuned their succession plan. A key element of their strategy was to buy a life insurance policy that will help cover the 55 to 60 percent estate taxes that will be due when the senior Twardziks die. "Without that insurance protection, we would have to sell the business to pay the taxes," says Tim Twardzik.

Dealing with tax issues is just one part of a total succession plan, according to Ron Hartwick, an attorney who specializes in estate planning at U.S. Trust of California. Without the right strategy, your children could be faced with an enormous, unpayable tax burden.

Hartwick, who has prepared estate plans for more than 200 small-business owners, said too many families focus on minimizing taxes, rather than looking at the broader issues of who will run the business and how to prepare that child or children for the transition.

The task is so onerous that fewer than one-third of family businesses make it to the second generation, according to Léon Danco, author and founder of the Cleveland-based Center for Family Business. "The estate plan is fuel for the dream," says Danco. "And the family-owned business is the epitome of the American Dream."

"The classic plan is to leave the business to the wife," says Hartwick. "But if all you have is that pure vanilla pablum plan, it can be a disaster."

He recommends sitting down with your family and discussing the future of your family business the same way you would sit down and plan a vacation. "It's important to create a plan that the next generation will not tear apart," says Hartwick. "The inheritance business brings out the worst in people."

Hartwick also encourages his clients to be generous while they are still alive. Each year, every taxpayer is allowed to give away $10,000 each to an unlimited number of individuals, tax free. And, under current federal tax laws, everyone is entitled to pass along $600,000 tax free to their children or anyone else. If properly planned for, you and your spouse could transfer $1.2 million worth of property estate tax free.

Because nobody likes to think about dying, most business owners put off any discussion of a succession plan. But having no plan could result in the loss of your business to Uncle Sam rather than Son Bob or Daughter Sue. Benson and other estate-planning experts agree that not having a will is the surest way to make your family hate you when you've gone.

Benjamin Benson, one of the authors of *Your Family Business* (see "Books" in Resources guide), suggests asking yourself these questions before creating a succession plan:

- How can I protect my spouse?
- How can I be fair to my heirs?
- Does fairness necessarily demand equality?
- Who should own the stock in my business in the next generation?
- Who should have the controlling interest?
- How can I arrange my affairs so my heirs are not burdened with excessive estate taxes?

Your family attorney and accountant may not be the best ones to create an estate plan. Ask other family business owners to recommend an estate-planning specialist, and be prepared to spend between $3,000 and $15,000 for a complete plan.

Because buying a very large life insurance policy is a key element of many succession plans, it is best to work with an insurance agent who is a Chartered Life Underwriter. This title means he or she is a member of a professional society that sponsors tough examinations and requires members to continue their education.

With enough of the right insurance, the heirs should have the money to fund buy-sell agreements with any family member who wants to cash out. The money can also pay estate taxes and administration costs, provide cash to heirs who are not active in the business, and build financial security for the surviving spouse.

HERE'S HOW TO BEGIN PLANNING FOR THE FUTURE OF YOUR SMALL BUSINESS:

■ Be sure you and your spouse have properly written and updated wills.

■ Create an estate-planning team comprised of experienced people you can trust.

■ Sit down with your family and discuss your personal goals for the future of your business.

■ Evaluate the cost benefits of buying life insurance to cover estate taxes and other expenses.

■ Choose people you trust to manage your affairs after your death.

■ If no relatives are interested in carrying on the business, spend the next few years preparing to sell your business to an outsider.

---

99. HOW DO I KNOW IF I'M READY TO SELL MY BUSINESS?

Selling a successful business you have created and nurtured is like helping a grown child pack for college: You feel proud and happy, but realize nothing will ever be the same again.

Letting go can be especially tough for women business owners, who often need to work twice as hard as men to achieve success.

"It is very difficult to make the transition from being God to being a junior angel," says Ellen Boughn, who sold After Image, her Los Angeles stock photo agency, to a British company in 1989 and stayed on until February 1992.

Born on her kitchen table in 1976, After Image grew and flourished by providing book and magazine editors access to a collection of 400,000 photographic images from around the world. Needing capital to expand when sales surpassed $1 million, Boughn decided to sell the company to London-based Tony Stone Worldwide for a handsome price. Although it was difficult to relinquish total control, she served as president of the Los Angeles regional office until early 1992.

Why do successful entrepreneurs like Ellen Boughn decide to sell their small businesses?

Burnout is the number one reason, according to merger and acquisition experts. The owner, who began with a dream and has ended up with a thriving enterprise, just wakes up one day and is too exhausted to get out of bed.

Often the death of a spouse or partner precipitates a sale. Many

widows who inherit their husband's business are just too overwhelmed to run the operation and desperately seek to unload it.

"Before doing anything, sellers really need to look inside at
the emotional reasons for wanting to get out," says Gene Siciliano,
a financial management consultant in Playa Del Rey, California.
"Figure out what you like, what you don't like, and what it is you
are walking away from."

Maybe the reason for selling is a financial one. Are you financially overextended? Do you need an infusion of cash to pay off
loans, personal or otherwise? Maybe you are running several businesses at once and feel like a plate spinner at the circus—but with
plates crashing all around you.

Boredom is another reason to sell out. A true entrepreneur
lives for the thrill and the risk, often starting three or more businesses in a lifetime. The day-to-day operations may become too
tedious for such high-fliers.

You may also want out if you've heard that a competitor is
about to launch a better line of products or open a new store
nearby. Or maybe you believe your particular industry is about to
hit the skids and want to make a clean exit.

Whatever the reason for selling your business, there are definitely right and wrong ways to plan, negotiate, and finalize the sale.

First you need to decide whether you want to sell out completely, sell a percentage to someone else, or bring in a partner. A
word of caution, though: Selling a piece of the business may bring
in needed cash, but can also create major headaches if you are used
to running the show. Finding money may be easier than finding a
compatible person to share the power with.

Once you decide to sell all or part of your business, you need
to get the word out—but at the same time, you must be discreet.
If you advertise the fact that your business is for sale, clients may
stop paying you, vendors will become skittish, and competitors will
relish telling your customers you are about to go under.

Only a few key advisers—your attorney, accountant, and
banker—should be involved in the transaction. It's best to leave
employees out of the loop until a serious buyer makes an offer.

Why? Because no matter how loyal your employees are, résumés will start flying out the door as soon as they hear the business
is for sale.

"If you don't have professional representation when you are selling your business, you are asking for trouble," says Melvin Poteshman, managing partner of Levine, Cooper & Spiegel, a Los Angeles accounting firm specializing in advising small and midsize businesses. The professional may be an attorney or your accountant, depending on who knows your business best. "I also advise clients using a business broker to only tell the broker what they want the other side to know," Poteshman says.

Before you can entertain offers, you have to figure out what your business is worth. You may have a vague idea based on the balance sheet, but emotions will color any calculations you do yourself. An experienced valuation professional can help you figure out exactly what price to ask and expect for your business. These experts, who usually charge between $100 and $300 an hour, depending on where you live, will interview you in depth about your business and objectively review your financial statements. They will add up your assets, check your liabilities and inventories, compare your business with similar ones in the industry, and prepare a detailed report for you and your potential buyers.

You may spend between $5,000 and $15,000 for the valuation, but a detailed report can alleviate any doubts or regrets you might have about not getting a fair price for your baby—your business. "The price you set depends on the size and complexity of the business," says Davis Blaine, chairman of the Mentor Group, a valuation firm with offices in southern California and Texas. "The expression, 'your price and my terms,' is appropriate for the sale of small companies."

The most serious challenge involved in selling a small, privately-held business is dealing with a balance sheet that rarely reflects reality. If you are like most business owners, you use your business to provide yourself and your family with a comfortable lifestyle. You probably siphon off as much cash as possible, spending it on cars, club memberships, entertainment, travel expenses, and salaries, rather than putting the profits back into the business.

Although this popular small-business strategy may reduce your tax bill, it weakens your financial statement and makes your business look anemic when it comes time to sell. Not surprisingly, then, mergers and acquisitions experts who specialize in selling small businesses spend a lot of time restating financial statements to present prospective buyers with a more accurate picture of your company's financial health.

Once you have restated the numbers to look attractive, established a price, and have a negotiating team in place, the next step is rounding up some potential buyers. Soliciting interest from members of your trade association or professional society is often a good place to start, since they know you and your business.

Because the sale itself is emotionally wrenching, you will want to distance yourself as much as possible from the day-to-day hassles. Depending on where you live and what kind of business you own, you can either hire a business broker or ask your accountant or attorney to approach likely candidates. This is especially important when the most likely buyer for your business may be your most hated competitor.

To avoid wasting time with people who are not qualified buyers, your advisers should check out the creditworthiness of any prospective buyer before revealing key financial information.

"Carefully check the person's credit before beginning any serious negotiation," advises John Taylor, president of Robert Q. Parsons & Co. Inc., in Brentwood, California. Don't be afraid to demand current bank references and personal financial statements from prospective buyers.

"Be sure to sign a confidentiality agreement before you release any information about the business," says Taylor. He also suggests the owner decide on a case-by-case basis who gets to look at the company's financial statements. "I would also limit tours of your business to only the most serious prospective buyers," says Taylor. "You don't want your employees to get nervous."

If it appears that the sale is going through, call a meeting of your employees, or your department heads, and tell them what is going on. Be prepared to answer their questions and allay their fears. In most cases, the new owner will keep employees on, but there is a risk that your loyal workers will be tossed out of their jobs when the company changes hands.

In today's world, many cash-strapped buyers expect the sellers to help finance the deal by accepting a note. If you agree to do this, be sure the note is secured by substantial collateral, such as a second trust deed on the buyer's home or other assets. Never let the business itself be used to secure the note. If something goes wrong, you could be forced to foreclose on what was once a profitable business and end up owning nothing.

Remember, the kind of business you operate ultimately dictates the price. For instance, if you own an engineering or architectural firm, the major elements of value would be your talented employees, your track record, and rapport with clients—which may not be transferable or duplicable. If you own a trucking or manufacturing business, your equipment and customer list are the key elements. For a retail business, your inventory and leases play a major role in setting the price.

Whether or not you own the building or property underneath your business also affects the sales price. Be sure to set a value on intangible assets such as patents, technology, favorable industry contacts, and long-term contracts.

"You should be realistic about your inventory," says Parsons & Co.'s Taylor. If the buyer is nervous about buying it outright, you could offer it to them on consignment, or arrange for payments to be made over 18 months. In other words, haggling over the price you get for your inventory should not be a deal-breaker.

Taylor, who has handled scores of transactions, warns that you shouldn't be offended if a buyer comes in with what you consider a ridiculously low offer. Many serious buyers he has dealt with have started the negotiations with a lowball offer just to test the seller's mettle.

Once your representatives bring you a serious offer to consider, take a deep breath before reviewing it carefully and slowly. Of course, you want to negotiate in good faith, but nothing says you have to accept the first offer that comes in. "Sellers want a price that reflects their sweat equity and the benefits the buyer will enjoy in the near future," says the Mentor Group's Blaine.

To gain perspective on the offer, Blaine suggests talking with other business owners who have sold a similar type of business. You don't need to know the exact dollar figures involved, but any insights into what contributed to a successful deal will be invaluable.

Meanwhile, Ellen Boughn says she has never regretted selling After Image despite the emotional roller coaster she has been on since selling out.

The sale enabled her to change her lifestyle dramatically. During the week, she lives in an apartment in Los Angeles. But every

Friday night, she and her cat, Zak, jump in her Mercedes to escape to Ojai, a pastoral haven for artists located about 90 miles north of the city. "Selling the business gave me a much richer life, socially and emotionally," says Boughn. "The sale allowed me to experience the ultimate rich-girl fantasy—I backed my pickup truck into my Mercedes."

The financial rewards have also allowed her to move her invalid mother to a board and care home near her weekend home so they can spend more time together. And, she immediately gained community acceptance by donating a generous sum to the local land conservancy and accepted a seat on the group's board of directors. This move and donation settled her deep into the social fabric of the 7,000-resident rural community.

On a business note, Boughn recommends entrepreneurs demand some kind of formal transition plan to help the buyer and seller make a better marriage. Even if you don't intend to stay on under the new ownership, such a plan is essential, Boughn says.

"We did a good job, but it was totally done by the seat of our pants."

TIPS FOR SELLING YOUR COMPANY

- Figure out why you want to sell your business.
- Bring in professional help to value the business.
- Assemble a trusted team of advisers to negotiate the sale.
- Be discreet while seeking potential buyers.
- Don't discuss your plans with employees; it will make them nervous.
- Talk to other business owners who have successfully sold businesses to gain valuable insights.
- Rely on a good accountant to structure the deal to your advantage, tax-wise.
- If you accept a note from the seller, make sure it is secured by assets other than the business.
- Spend some time figuring out what you are going to do next, so you don't fall into a depression after the business is sold.

HOW TO SELL OUT, BUT STAY ON

- Find out everything you can about the company you plan to sell your business to. Interview its employees, vendors, suppliers, analysts, competitors.

- Hire the best professional advisers you can to plan and negotiate the deal.

- Decide what you need to get out of the deal, besides money.

- Once you've sold your business, don't expect things to remain the same. Realize that under its new owners your company's culture will be dramatically changed, no matter how similar your business goals are.

- Negotiate a short-term employment contract so you don't lock yourself in if things don't work out as you expected.

100. CAN I STAY ON AFTER I'VE SOLD MY BUSINESS?

Five years after Ed Kramar and his partners founded Cypress Electronics in Santa Clara, California, they knew that they needed more cash to expand their wholesale electronics distribution firm. They borrowed some money, then began casting about for a buyer, figuring that they would stay on or go depending on who bought the company. In 1985, Cypress agreed to be acquired for $4 million by Brajdas Corp., a public company based in Woodland Hills, California. Kramar agreed to stay on as president and asked his attorney to draft what is known in the world of mergers and acquisitions as an "earnout agreement."

Under an earnout agreement, the seller accepts a lump sum up front, and more cash down the road, with the amount usually pegged to the company's future profits.

As small-business owners find venture capital and private funding sources more difficult to tap, financial advisers familiar with earnouts predict that they will greatly increase in popularity. "An earnout fills the gap in price between the buyer and the seller," says Gary Mendoza, an attorney who specializes in mergers and acquisitions for Riordan & McKinzie, in Los Angeles.

In a well-drafted earnout, the buyer of a growing company benefits by having to put up less cash in the beginning. The earnout agreement also keeps key people around for a few years, increasing the chance of a smooth transition. Most earnouts serve as incentives for the previous owners to work hard—because their future compensation is hinged to the company's profit.

Because earnouts are complex legal agreements, they are best drafted by a skilled attorney working with a good tax accountant. The accountant must consider all the tax ramifications of the lump sum payment and be sure the future compensation package is structured to give his or her client the best tax advantages. "Most earnouts are set up to last between two and five years," says Robert Untracht, the partner in charge of the diversified industries group at Ernst & Young, in Century City, California. Untracht, an attorney and a CPA, has structured several earnout agreements for big and small companies.

An earnout agreement should include ways it can be undone if the deal doesn't seem to be working out. "You should have an unwind provision that specifies whether the seller gets the company back—and at what price—if things don't work out," says Mendoza. "If you sold good goods, you don't want to buy back bad goods. "

Cypress's Kramar asked Brajdas to reduce his earnout agreement from three years to two because he was facing certain ethical dilemmas related to the future of the company's operations. For example, Kramar said, he was torn between spending money to hire people and open new offices to bring in new business, and cutting back on expenses to improve the company's profitability. If he cut expenses, he could increase the amount of money he would receive under the earnout agreement. "But what might have been the best for me personally was not the best thing for the company," Kramar said.

Allan Klein, chief financial officer of Brajdas, says the ethical situation that Kramar was in illustrates a problem with earnouts. The buyer must be careful to structure the deal so that the earnout does not interfere with the company's growth.

But overall, Klein says, Brajdas was pleased with the way the Cypress earnout has worked, especially since Kramar was still part of the management team three years after the earnout expired. Kramar left the company about two years ago.

"We were very fortunate that the former owners wanted to be part of a growth scenario," says Klein, who was responsible for presenting the former owners with monthly financial reports.

For Kramar personally, the first year after selling out was the hardest. "Before the sale, if I wanted to spend $200,000, I just did it," he says. After the sale, he had to ask the new president for his approval on major issues, although day-to-day operations were left to Kramar. "If we had sold the company to a more hands-on person, I probably wouldn't have lasted more than a year," admits Kramar.

Even the most well-written agreements can end in disaster if buyers and sellers have different ideas about how the company should be run. There also tend to be more problems when the seller is given a big chunk of cash up front and a paltry compensation package. With this approach, there is little incentive for the former owner to stay on and work hard for the company.

Untracht says earnouts work especially well for professionals, such as doctors or dentists, who want to bring in a young partner to take over the business. "Don't sell your business the day you want to retire," he advises. "Begin to get ready three or four years ahead."

UP FOR AN EARNOUT?

Before considering an earnout agreement, ask yourself these questions:

■ Will you be able to relinquish control and work with the new owner?

■ Are you willing to accept part of the sale price up front and the rest at a future date?

■ Will you be motivated to keep working after you put the initial payment in the bank?

■ Would you want the company back if the arrangement didn't work to your satisfaction?

■ Can you find a skilled accountant and attorney to draft an earnout agreement?

101. WHAT SHOULD I DO WHEN I FEEL LIKE GIVING UP?

No matter how well things are going, there will be many, many times when you'll feel hopeless, out of control, and depressed. Being responsible for your family's financial welfare and the welfare of your employees and their families is terrifying, especially when times are tough.

But entrepreneurs are strong, resilient, and optimistic. You wouldn't be reading this book if you weren't. And, if you didn't thrive on meeting adversity head on, you would still be working for someone else. It's okay to be afraid as long as you admit it and take action.

I learned how to overcome fear and adversity under the worst circumstances. I learned to cope with crisis and tragedy in my personal life, later applying the painful lessons to my business.

Always a risk-taker, I was totally convinced the delicate open-heart surgery planned for our eldest daughter, Julie, would be a rousing success. She was born prematurely, with a major heart defect. Standing by my side in the intensive care nursery, her doctor told me I was lucky to have twin daughters because only one was going home with us.

But, at 3¼ pounds, Julie fought her way to recovery from one high-risk surgery. A year later, she fought her way through another. At three, she fell in love with the film *The Wizard of Oz* and cherished a pair of ruby slippers I made her for Halloween. She thrived and flourished and proudly graduated from nursery school.

When she was at her strongest, a vibrant, 4½-year-old pixie, we were advised to take her to a world-renowned heart surgeon at UCLA Medical Center. An arrogant and revered man, he was touted as the "best of the best." Although he explained the risks, he believed he could fix Julie's heart and she would live a long and happy life.

The surgery was a disaster.

Julie struggled and suffered and died a month later, never leaving the intensive care unit.

After Julie died in my arms, I realized I was no longer afraid of anything. The dark years that followed her death calloused me to defeat. The experience taught me to question authority and never be intimidated by people—because people are human and make terrible mistakes.

I learned how to forgive and how to be kind to myself and others. Forgiving yourself for your failings and forgiving the failings of others keep you going. If you don't learn to forgive and keep these disappointments in perspective, you will often feel overwhelmed and slowly begin to lose faith in yourself.

You *are* your business, and it is natural to take every setback personally. But you are only human and people will appreciate that you are doing the best you can.

My adopted motto, "No guts, no glory," is a good one for anyone in business for themselves.

If you are going to take big risks, you must accept that you can't control everything. My best friend and husband, Joe, always tells me that the only thing we can be sure of is that we can't be sure of how things will turn out.

But this uncertainty is what gives entrepreneurs their sparkle and quickly addicts us to that adrenaline rush. Knowing you alone are responsible for your actions is terrifying and exhilarating at the same time.

If you feel like everything is falling apart, take a break. Get away from your office or factory or workshop. Take yourself on a long walk up the road, along the beach, or into the woods.

Tell yourself you are a good person, that you are doing the best you can with what you have. Then, turn to others, reach out, and find solutions for your problems. Fix one small piece of the problem at a time. Try replacing the spark plugs before you tear apart the engine.

Listen to my grandfather George and tell yourself, "This too shall pass."

And know that it will. And know that you will go on because your dreams are too precious to abandon.

RESOURCES FOR SMALL-BUSINESS OWNERS

AGENCIES/OFFICES

U.S. Small Business Administration (SBA)

The SBA provides the primary source of federal government assistance for small business. The agency helps small-business owners primarily by providing financial assistance through loan guarantee programs, distributing publications, hosting workshops, and offering management assistance through its Business Development Program.

The SBA is located at 409 Third Street, S.W., Washington, DC 20416. There are also local and regional offices in major cities across the country.

REGION 1
155 Federal Street
9th Floor
Boston, MA 02110
(617)451-2023

REGION 2
26 Federal Plaza
Room 31-08
New York, NY 10278
(212)264-7772

REGION 3

475 Allendale Road
Suite 201
King of Prussia, PA 19406
(215)962-3700

REGION 4

1375 Peachtree Street, NE
5th Floor
Atlanta, GA 30367-8102
(404)347-2797

REGION 5

230 South Dearborn Street
Room 510
Chicago, IL 60604-1593
(312)353-0359

REGION 6

8625 King George Drive
Building C
Dallas, TX 75235-3391
(214)767-7643

REGION 7

911 Walnut Street
13th Floor
Kansas City, MO 64106
(816)426-3607

REGION 8

999 18th Street
Suite 701
Denver, CO 80202
(303)294-7001

REGION 9

450 Golden Gate Avenue
San Francisco, CA 94102
(415)556-7487

REGION 10

2615 4th Avenue
Room 440
Seattle, WA 98121
(206)442-8544

SBA DISTRICT OFFICES
ALABAMA

2121 8th Avenue North
Suite 200
Birmingham, AL 35203-2398
(205)731-1344

ALASKA

222 West 8th Avenue
Room A36
Anchorage, AK 99501
(907)271-4022

ARIZONA

2005 North Central Avenue
5th Floor
Phoenix, AZ 85004-4599
(602)379-3737

ARKANSAS

320 West Capitol Avenue
Suite 601
Little Rock, AR 72201
(501)378-5871

CALIFORNIA

2719 North Air Fresno Drive
Fresno, CA 93727-1547
(209)487-5189

330 North Brand Boulevard
Glendale, CA 91203
(213)894-2956

880 Front Street
Suite 4-S-29
San Diego, CA 92188-0270
(619)557-5440

211 Main Street
4th Floor
San Francisco, CA 94105-1988
(415)974-0649

901 West Civic Center Drive
Room 160
Santa Ana, CA 92703
(714)836-2494

COLORADO

721 19th Street
Room 407
Denver, CO 80202-0660
(303)844-6501

CONNECTICUT

330 Main Street
2nd Floor
Hartford, CT 06106
(203)240-4700

DELAWARE

Branch Office
920 North King Street
Room 412
Wilmington, DE 19801
(302)573-6295

DISTRICT OF COLUMBIA

1111 18th Street, NW
Sixth Floor
Washington, DC 20036
(202)634-1500

FLORIDA

1320 South Dixie Highway
Suite 501
Coral Gables, FL 33146
(305)536-5521

The Center Building
Suite 100-B
7825 Baymeadows Way
Jacksonville, FL 32256-7504
(904)443-1900

GEORGIA

1720 Peachtree Road, NW
6th Floor
Atlanta, GA 30309
(404)347-2441

HAWAII

300 Ala Moana Boulevard
Room 2213
Honolulu, HI 96850
(808)541-2990

IDAHO

1020 Main Street
Suite 290
Boise, ID 83702
(208)334-1696

ILLINOIS

219 South Dearborn Street
Room 437
Chicago, IL 60604-1779
(312)353-4528

INDIANA

575 North Pennsylvania Street
Room 578
Indianapolis, IN 46204-1584
(317)226-7272

IOWA

373 Collins Road, NE
Room 100
Cedar Rapids, IA 52402-3118
(319)393-8630

219 Walnut Street, Room 749
Des Moines, IA 50309
(515)284-4422

KANSAS

110 East Waterman Street
1st Floor
Wichita, KS 67202
(316)269-6571

KENTUCKY

600 Martin Luther King Place
Room 188
Louisville, KY 40202
(502)582-5976

LOUISIANA

1661 Canal Street
Suite 2000
New Orleans, LA 70112
(504)589-6685

MAINE

40 Western Avenue
Room 512
Augusta, ME 04330
(207)622-8378

MARYLAND

10 North Calvert Street
3rd Floor
Baltimore, MD 21202
(301)962-4392

MASSACHUSETTS

10 Causeway Street
Room 265
Boston, MA 02222-1093
(617)565-5590

MICHIGAN

477 Michigan Avenue
Room 515
Detroit, MI 48226
(313)226-6075

MINNESOTA

100 North 6th Street
Room 610
Minneapolis, MN 55403-1563
(612)370-2324

MISSISSIPPI

101 West Capitol Street
Suite 400
Jackson, MS 39201
(601)965-4378

MISSOURI

1103 Grand Avenue
6th Floor
Kansas City, MO 64106
(816)374-6708

620 South Glenstone
Suite 110
Springfield, MO 65802-3200
(417)864-7670

815 Olive Street
Room 242
St. Louis, MO 63101
(314)539-6600

MONTANA

301 South Park Street
Room 528
Helena, MT 59626
(406)449-5381

NEBRASKA

11145 Mill Valley Road
Omaha, NE 68154
(402)221-4691

NEVADA

301 East Stewart Street
Room 301
Las Vegas, NV 89125
(702)388-6611

NEW HAMPSHIRE

55 Pleasant Street
Room 210
Concord, NH 03302-1257
(603)225-1400

NEW JERSEY

60 Park Place
4th Floor
Newark, NJ 07102
(201)645-2434

NEW MEXICO

625 Silver Avenue, SW
Suite 320
Albuquerque, NM 87102
(505)755-1868

NEW YORK

111 West Huron Street
Room 1311
Buffalo, NY 14202
(716)846-4301

26 Federal Plaza
Room 3100
New York, NY 10278
(212)264-4355

Room 1071
100 South Clinton Street
Syracuse, NY 13260
(315)423-5383

NORTH CAROLINA

222 South Church Street
Room 300
Charlotte, NC 28202
(704)371-6563

NORTH DAKOTA

657 Second Avenue, North
Room 218
Fargo, ND 58108-3086
(701)239-5131

OHIO

1240 East 9th Street
Room 317
Cleveland, OH 44199
(216)522-4180

85 Marconi Boulevard
Room 512
Columbus, OH 43215
(614)469-6860

OKLAHOMA

200 NW 5th Street
Suite 670
Oklahoma City, OK 73102
(405)231-4301

OREGON

222 SW Columbia Street
Suite 500
Portland, OR 97201-6605
(503)326-2682

PENNSYLVANIA

Suite 201
475 Allendale Road
King of Prussia, PA 19406
(215)962-3846

960 Penn Avenue
5th Floor
Pittsburgh, PA 15222
(412)644-2780

PUERTO RICO/ VIRGIN ISLANDS

Federico Degatau Federal
  Building
Room 691
Carlos Chardon Avenue
Hato Rey, PR 00918
(809)766-4002

RHODE ISLAND

380 Westminister Mall
5th Floor
Providence, RI 02903
(401)528-4561

SOUTH CAROLINA

1835 Assembly Street
Room 358
Columbia, SC 29202
(803)765-5376

SOUTH DAKOTA

101 South Main Avenue
Suite 101
Security Building
Sioux Falls, SD 57102-0527
(605)336-4231

TENNESSEE

50 Vantage Way
Suite 201
Nashville, TN 37228-1504
(615)736-5850

TEXAS

1100 Commerce Street
Room 3C-36
Dallas, TX 75242
(214)767-0605

10737 Gateway West
Suite 320
El Paso, TX 79935
(915)541-7586

222 East Van Buren Street
Suite 500
Harlingen, TX 78550
(512)427-8533

2525 Murworth
Suite 112
Houston, TX 77054
(713)660-4401

1611 10th Street
Suite 200
Lubbock, TX 79401
(806)743-7462

7400 Blanco Road
Suite 200
San Antonio, TX 78216
(512)229-4535

UTAH

125 South State Street
Room 2237
Salt Lake City, UT 84138-1195
(801)524-5800

VERMONT

87 State Street
Room 205
Montpelier, VT 05602
(802)828-4474

VIRGINIA

400 North 8th Street
Room 3015
Richmond, VA 23240
(804)771-2617

WASHINGTON

915 2nd Avenue
Federal Building
Room 1792
Seattle, WA 98174-1088
(206)442-5534

Tenth Floor East
West 601 1st Avenue
Spokane, WA 99204
(509)353-2807

WEST VIRGINIA

168 West Main Street
5th Floor
Clarksburg, WV 26301
(304)623-5631

WISCONSIN

212 East Washington Avenue
Room 213
Madison, WI 53703
(608)264-5261

WYOMING

100 East B Street
Room 4001
Casper, WY 82601-2839
(307)261-5761

Some of the resources offered to small-business owners are listed below.

- Small Business Directory

Lists SBA publications and videotapes on starting and managing a small business. To order write: Small Business Directory, Ft. Worth, TX 76119.

- Answer Desk Hotline

Sponsored by the SBA Office of Advocacy. Offers direct referrals to appropriate sources of information. Toll-free. (800)827-5722.

- SBA-Sponsored Services:
  - Service Corps of Retired Executives (SCORE)
    Small Business Institutes(SBI)
    Small Business Development Centers (SBDC)

U.S. Chamber of Commerce

The Chamber has about 2,700 offices located in cities across the country. You can call the Chamber hotline at (800)638-6582 or consult your telephone directory for your local office.

Council of Better Business Bureaus

The Council's Philanthropic Advisory Service has free or low-cost "Tips On . . ." booklets on numerous issues, including "Tips on Charitable Giving" (free) and "Tips on Tax Deductions for Charitable Contributions" ($1). To order call (703)276-0100.

ASSOCIATIONS/ ORGANIZATIONS

American Small Business Association   Serves the interests of small businesses and the self-employed. Membership includes a subscription to *ASBA Today*, a bimonthly publication. For information call (800)880-2722.

American Women's Economic Development Corporation Provides training and assistance to women in business. For information write the organization at 60 East 42nd Street, New York, NY 10165 or call (800)222-AWED.

International Association for Financial Planners Offers free brochures, including "Financial Planning Consumer Bill of Rights" and "Consumer Guide to Financial Independence." For information write to Two Concourse Parkway, suite 800, Atlanta, GA 30328 or call (404)395-1605.

International Franchising Association Provides information for both current and potential franchise owners. Members get the "Franchise Opportunities Guide" as well as *Franchising World*, a bimonthly magazine. For information contact the IFA at 1350 New York Avenue, N.W., suite 900, Washington, DC 20005 or at (202)628-8000.

National Association of Women Business Owners Offers support and information for women in business. For more information write to 600 South Federal Street, suite 400, Chicago, IL 60605 or call (312)922-0465 or (800) 222-3838.

National Federation of Independent Business The largest business organization in the U.S. with 550,000 members. The advocacy group works to shape policy to fit small-business needs. 600 Maryland Avenue, S.W., suite 700, Washington DC, 20024. Minimum annual membership: $75. Membership includes a subscription to *Independent Business* magazine. For information call (202)554-9000.

National Small Business United An activist organization for business owners interested in participating in the political process. NSBU holds conferences to discuss key small-business issues, among other events. Membership includes subscription to *Small Business USA* newsletter. For information write to NSBU, 1155 15th Street, N.W., suite 710, Washington, DC 20005 or call (202)293-8830 or (800) 541-5768.

The Office of Women's Business Ownership   Sponsored by the U.S. Small Business Administration. Provides tips on obtaining funding for prospective small-business owners. For information write to 409 Third Street, S.W., Washington, DC 20416.

National Restaurant Association   Contact the Association for information on how to start a restaurant and other publications of interest, at 1200 17th Street, N.W., Washington, DC 20036-3097; phone: (202)331-2429.

The Trade Show Bureau   The Bureau is a nonprofit group that provides information on the trade show industry. Write for a free information packet which includes an order form and information about the Bureau's publications. Their address is 1660 Lincoln Street, suite 2080, Denver, CO 80264; phone: (303)860-7626.

AUDIO CASSETTES

The Course in Winning   Motivational cassette package. Includes messages from Norman Vincent Peale, Arnold Palmer, Norman Cousins, and Tom Peters. To order write Nightingale-Courant Corp., 120 Brighton Road, P.O. Box 5008, Clifton, NJ 07015.

How to Manage Your Telephone for Bigger Profits   One-hour tape from the "Telephone Doctor," Nancy Friedman; $24.95 plus $2 for shipping and handling. To order call (800)882-991 or write to P.O. Box 777, St. Louis, MO 63044.

BOOKS

Achievers Never Quit, by Robert O. Redd. Thornapple Publishing Co., Box 56, Ada, Michigan 49301; $6.95.

The Advertising Handbook: Make a Big Impact with a Small Business Budget, by Dell Dennison and Linda Tobey. Contains information on advertising aspects including creating ads, hiring an agency, and buying media space; $8.95 plus $2.50 for postage and handling.

To order, write to Self-Counsel Press, Inc., 1704 North State Street, Bellingham, WA 98225.

Anatomy of a Start-Up From *Inc.* magazine. Explores real-life case studies of 27 start-ups; $24.95 plus $2.50 for shipping. To order, write *Inc.* magazine, 38 Commercial Wharf, Boston, MA 02110.

Big Marketing Ideas for Small Service Businesses, by Marilyn and Tom Rose. This comprehensive book includes direct-mail tips, advertising campaigns, and ways to generate free publicity. The book is published by Business One-Irvin. It is available at bookstores or by sending $27.95 to ABI, Box 1500-SS, Buena Vista, CO 81211. It can also be ordered by credit card by calling (719)395-2459.

Business Plans That Win $$$, by Stanley Rich and David Gumpert. Harper & Row; $9.95.

The Complete Book of Small Business Legal Forms, by Daniel Sitarz; $17.95. Nova Publishing, distributed by National Book Network (800)462-6420.

Do What You Love, The Money Will Follow, by Marsha Sinetar. Dell; $8.95.

Exportise. An international trade source book for smaller company executives; $49.95. The Small Business Foundation of America, 1990. For copies, write the SBF of America, 1155 Fifteenth Street, N.W., Washington, DC 20005.

Expose Yourself: Using the Power of Public Relations to Promote Your Business and Yourself, by Melba Beals; $18.95. Chronicle Books, San Francisco.

Finding Private Venture Capital for Your Firm, by Robert J. Gaston. John Wiley & Sons; $55.00.

555 Ways to Earn Extra Money, by Jay Conrad Levinson. Henry Holt; $12.95.

The First 24 Hours: A Comprehensive Guide to Successful Crisis Communications, by Dieudonee Ten Berge. Basil Blackwell, Cambridge, MA; $42.95.

Free Help from Uncle Sam to Start Your Own Business (or Expand the One You Have), by William Alarid and Gustav Berle. 1989; $11.95. For information, write Puma Publishing Company, 1670 Coral Drive, Santa Maria, CA 93454 or call (805)925-3216.

From Concept to Market, by Gary Lynn. John Wiley & Sons; $17.95.

Growing Pains: How to Make the Transition from an Entrepreneurship to a Professionally Managed Firm, by Eric Flamholtz, a professor of management at UCLA. 1990; $27.95. For information, write Jossey-Bass Publishers, 350 Sansome Street, San Francisco, CA 94104.

Guerrilla Financing, by Jay Conrad Levinson, with Bruce Blechman. Houghton Mifflin, Boston, 1991. To order, call (800)748-6444.

Guerrilla Marketing Attack, by Jay Conrad Levinson. Houghton Mifflin, Boston, 1989. To order, call (800)748-6444.

How to Acquire the Perfect Business for Your Company, by Joseph Krallinger. John Wiley & Co; $65.00.

How to Conquer Clutter, by Stephanie Culp. Writer's Digest Books; $10.95.

How to Really Create a Successful Business Plan, by David Gumpert. *Inc.* magazine, Boston; $14.95.

How to Start Your Own Business and Succeed: A Guide to Being Your Own Boss, by Ripley Hotch. Stackpole Books, 1991; $14.95. For information, write Stackpole Books, Cameron & Keller Streets, P.O. Box 1831, Harrisburg, PA 17105 or call (800) READ-NOW.

The Marketing Sourcebook for Small Business, by Jeffrey P. Davidson. Davidson, a management consultant, explains how to define your company's niche in the marketplace and find the right image for your company. He also describes how to become a favored vendor to large corporations. Published by John Wiley & Sons, 605 Third Avenue, New York, NY 10158-0012; $24.95.

Mining Group Gold, by Thomas A. Kayser. Serif Publishing, a subsidiary of Xerox Corp., El Segundo, CA; $12.95.

The New Small Business Survival Guide, by Bob Coleman. How-to guide featuring case histories that relate to issues ranging from permits and licenses to winning the legal wars. W.W. Norton, 1991; $10.95.

The 90-Minute Hour, by Jay Conrad Levinson. Time-saving techniques for businesspeople. Dutton, 1990. To order, call (800)748-6444.

Running a Family Business, by Joseph R. Mancuso and Nat Shulman. Prentice Hall Press; $12.95. To order, call the Simon & Schuster Consumer Group at (212)373-8141.

Shenson on Consulting/Success Strategies from the "Consultant's Consultant," by Howard L. Shenson. A practical guide filled with research-based strategies on today's consulting business, ranging from building a consulting practice to effectively marketing one's services; John Wiley & Sons in association with University Associates, Inc.; $24.95. (Shenson has several other excellent books available.)

Starting a Business After 50, by Samuel Small. Pilot Books, 103 Cooper Street, Babylon, NY 11702; $3.95 plus $1.50 for postage and handling.

Street Smart Marketing, by Jeff Slutsky, with Mark Slutsky. This chatty, informative guide is filled with creative, low-cost marketing tips for businesses. It is published by John Wiley & Sons, 605 Third Avenue, New York, NY 10158-0012; $14.95.

301 Great Management Ideas. Contains hands-on ideas from small companies organized into 36 management areas; $24.95 and $2.50 for shipping. For information, contact *Inc.* magazine, 38 Commercial Wharf, Boston, MA 02110.

Total Customer Service: The Ultimate Weapon, by William Davidow and Bro Uttal. Harper Perennial, 1989; $9.95.

Working from Home, by Paul and Sarah Edwards. Jeremy P. Tarcher, Los Angeles; $14.95. (The Edwardses have other books, too.)

Working with the Ones You Love, by Dennis Jaffee. Conari Press, Berkeley, CA; $19.95.

Workouts & Turnarounds, edited by Dominic DiNapoli, Sanford C. Sigoloff, Robert F. Cushman. Business One Irwin, Homewood, IL; $75.00. Paperback available through Price Waterhouse.

Your Family Business, by Benjamin Benson, with Edwin T. Crego and Ronald H. Drucker. Dow Jones-Irwin (now Business One Irwin, Homewood, IL); $29.95.

DIRECTORIES/GUIDES/BOOKLETS

The 1991 Directory of Franchising Organizations. From Pilot Books. Lists more than 750 franchise opportunities offering information on each listing and the approximate investment required; $5 and $1 for postage and handling. To order, write 103 Cooper Street, Babylon, NY 11702.

Directory of Members, Institute of Management Consultants. To order, write the IMC at 230 Park Avenue, New York, NY 10169 or call (212)697-8262.

Directory of the National Association of Temporary Services. An annual update of the temporary help industry. National directory on sale for $135. The association will send a list of members by state upon receipt of a self-addressed stamped envelope. For information, call (703)549-6287.

Federally Funded Programs for Small Businesses. Offers information on grants and loans available to small-business owners. To order, send check or money order for $19.95 to Gibbs Publishing of California, Box 207, Dept. Z-07, Vacaville, CA 95696 or call (707)447-3053.

The 1992 Franchise Annual. A complete guide to North American franchises. Send $39.95 to Info Franchise News, Inc., 728 Center Street, Lewiston, NY 14092 or call (716)754-4669.

The Fringe Benefits Business Owners and Their Families Are Now Entitled To By Law, by Prentice-Hall Professional Newsletters. Includes information on subjects ranging from "How to Take Tax-Free Rent from the Business" to "How Your Company Can Buy Cars for Your Family at Minimum." For information, contact Prentice-Hall Tax and Professional Practice, Englewood Cliffs, NJ 07632.

Guide to Health Insurance for the Small Business Owner. Free from Celtic Life Insurance Company. Offers information to help small-business owners compare health insurance plans and ask the right questions about cost and quality of coverage. To order, write 208 South LaSalle Street, Chicago, IL 60604 or call (312)332-5401.

How to Buy a Personal Computer for Your Small Business (The Little Blue Book). From IBM. Ask any IBM dealer for a copy.

How to Comply with Federal Employee Laws, by Sheldon I. London. Provides employers with information on labor law issues ranging from overtime pay rules to drug/alcohol testing; $19.95. For information, contact London Publishing Company, 1156 15th Street, N.W., Washington, DC 20005.

Inc. Magazine's "Small Business Success" products. *Inc*. offers a wide variety of video and audio tapes and other resource materials for business owners. For a free list, call *Inc*. Business Products,

(800)372-0018, or write to *Inc.*, P.O. Box 1365, Wilkes-Barre, PA 18703-1365.

Simplified Employee Pensions. This booklet offers information for companies of 25 employees or less on setting up an easy, low-cost retirement plan for the company; $1. To order, call (202)783-3238, pick up at a local U.S. government bookstore, or write to Superintendent of Documents, Washington, DC 20402-9325.

The Small Business Resource Guide. From the SBA and AT&T. Comprehensive guide listing public and private resources needed by small-business owners. To order, write Braddock Communications, 1001 Connecticut Avenue, N.W., Washington, DC 20036.

The Small Business Resource Guide: What You Need to Know About Starting and Running Your Business. From the editors of the "Direct Line" column in *Nation's Business* magazine. Features a compilation of answers to questions on areas ranging from import/export to retail; $5.95, plus $1 for shipping and handling. To order, write *Nation's Business* Circulation Department, 1615 H Street, N.W., Washington, DC 20062.

Starting & Succeeding in Business: A Guide for California Entrepreneurs; $1.75 for postage. Call (916)445-8994.

Venture Capital: Where to Find It. Directory listing venture capital sources for entrepreneurs who are looking for financing to start or expand a small business. Includes contact names, preferred level of loans or investments, investment policies and types and industry and geographical preferences for more than 200 venture capital and related firms that invest in small business; $10. For copies write to NASBIC Directory, P.O. Box 2039, Merrifield, VA 22116.

For a free copy of the "Succeeding in Small Business" How-to Booklet catalog, send a self-addressed, stamped envelope to The Applegate Group, P.O. Box 637, Sun Valley, CA 91353-0637.

GENERAL INFORMATION

An American Guide to Doing Business in Australia.   Includes listings of complimentary business literature from leading accounting and law firms, banks, export, technology, and investment publications and Australian business periodicals. To order, send $25 to PacRim Publishing, 150 South Glenoaks Boulevard, suite 8054, Burbank, CA 91510 or call (213)620-1928.

The Naming Guide.   A booklet on how to name a new business offered through *Independent Business* magazine. For information, call The Salinon Corp. at (214)692-9091.

The New American Business System.   From Meridian Learning Systems. A step-by-step approach on how to start a small business; 312-page reference binder with seven tabbed sections and 25 business briefings. To order, call (800)462-2699.

27 Performance Tips for Troubled Times.   From businessVision, a business consulting firm. For more information, write 23704-5 El Toro Road, suite 123, El Toro, CA 92630 or call (714)855-6060.

35 Timely Tips to Get the Most from Your Mailings.   From Pitney Bowes. Free booklet on how a small business can use a metered mail machine. To order, call (800)MR BOWES.

HOT LINES/TELEPHONES

The Export Opportunity Hotline   Offers answers to export questions, information on trade-related events throughout the country and referrals to appropriate sources of trade assistance. Sponsored by the Small Business Foundation of America in Washington, D.C. For information call (800)243-7232.

Small Business Hotline   Sponsored by *Black Enterprise* magazine; (900)446-4423. (Per-minute charge) $1.95, 1st minute, 95¢ each additional minute.

Telemap   Offers directions by phone or fax to more than 10,000 cities across the country. Open 24 hours/day, 7 days/week. For 1 to 10 subscribers, annual cost is $24; for 11 to 100, $20. For information, call (800)843-1000.

Use Your Phone to Build Your Business   From U.S. Message Corporation. Offers 50 tips on managing phone communications and strengthening customer service. Free informational booklet available. To order call the "50 Tips" hot line at (800)535-7306.

MAGAZINES

Black Enterprise 130 Fifth Avenue, New York, NY, 10011.

D & B Reports The Dun & Bradstreet magazine for small-business management.

Entrepreneur and *Entrepreneurial Woman* 2392 Morse Avenue, Irvine, CA 92714.

Independent Business 875 South Westlake Boulevard, suite 211, Westlake Village, CA 91361.

Inc. 38 Commercial Wharf, Boston, MA 02110.

Nation's Business Published by the U.S. Chamber of Commerce. 1615 H Street, N.W., Washington, DC 20062.

Your Company American Express Co.'s magazine, published exclusively for AMEX Corporate Cardmembers who are small-business owners. Part of AMEX's Small Business Services division. Cosponsored by IBM, UPS, Cigna, and Buick.

NEWSLETTERS

A Cottage Business Association P.O. Box 2802, Decatur, IL 62524-2802.

Four Corners An electronic newsletter devoted to small-business public relations. Published bimonthly over on-line services. To order, call Four Corners Communications at (212)924-4735.

Greener Pastures Gazette Relocation Research, P.O. Box 1122, Sierra Madre, CA 91025.

The Guerrilla Marketing Newsletter. To order, write Guerrilla Marketing International, Box 1336, Mill Valley, CA 94942 or call (800)748-6444. Subscriptions $49 per year.

Home Based & Small Business Network P.O. Box 232, Cambridge, MN 55008.

Home Based Business Operators P.O. Box 476, South Elgin, IL 60177.

Small Business Direct A bimonthly newsletter of United Group Information Services. Serves as an informational source for direct marketers. For information, call (603)673-1294.

White Collar Crime Fighter Published by Jane Kusic, founder of White Collar Crime Prevention, Inc., and an expert on financial crime prevention. Subscription fees are $36 for one year and $70 for two years. To order, write 12030 Sunrise Valley Drive, suite 440, Reston, VA 22091-3409 or call (703)620-1610.

STATE AGENCIES DEALING WITH SMALL-BUSINESS ISSUES

ALABAMA

Alabama Development Office
Small Business Office
401 Adams Avenue
Montgomery, AL 36130
(205)242-0400

ALASKA

Department of Commerce &
Economic Development
P.O. Box 110804
Juneau, AK 99811-0804
(907)465-2017

ARIZONA

Office of Community Finance
Department of Commerce
1700 West Washington Street,
  4th floor
Phoenix, AZ 85007
(602)280-1300

ARKANSAS

Small Business Information
  Center
Industrial Development
Commission
1 State Capitol Mall,
  room 4C-300
Little Rock, AR 72201
(501)682-1121

CALIFORNIA

Office of Small Business
Department of Commerce
1121 L Street, suite 600
Sacramento, CA 95814
(916)445-6545

COLORADO

Business Information Center
Office of Regulatory Reform
1560 Broadway, suite 1530
Denver, CO 80202
(303)894-7839

CONNECTICUT

Small Business Services
Department of Economic
  Development
210 Washington Street
Hartford, CT 06106
(203)258-4200

DELAWARE

Development Office
99 King's Highway
P.O. Box 1401
Dover, DE 19903
(302)739-4271

DISTRICT OF COLUMBIA

Office of Business and Economic
  Development
10th floor
717 Fourteenth Street, N.W.
Washington, DC 20005
(202)727-6600

FLORIDA

Bureau of Business Assistance
Department of Commerce
107 West Gaines Street, room 443
Tallahassee, FL 32399-2000
In-state: (800)342-0771
(904)488-9357

GEORGIA

Georgia Department of Industry
and Trade
285 Peachtree Center Avenue,
suite 1100
Atlanta, GA 30303
(404)656-3584

HAWAII

Small Business Information
Service
P.O. Box 2359
737 Bishop Street
Honolulu, HI 96804
(808)586-2600

IDAHO

Economic Development Division
Department of Commerce
700 West State Street
Statehouse Mail
Boise, ID 83720-2700
(208)334-2411

ILLINOIS

Small Business Assistance
Bureau
Department of Commerce and
Community Affairs
620 East Adams Street
Springfield, IL 62701
(217)782-7500

INDIANA

Division of Business Expansion
Department of Commerce
One North Capital, suite 700
Indianapolis, IN 46204-2288
(317)232-8888

IOWA

Department of Economic
Development
200 East Grand Avenue
Des Moines, IA 50309
(515)242-4730

KANSAS

Division of Existing Industry
Development
400 SW Eighth Street, 5th floor
Topeka, KS 66603
(913)296-5298

KENTUCKY

Small Business Division
Commerce Cabinet
Capitol Plaza Tower, 23rd floor
Frankfort, KY 40601
In-state: (800)626-2250
(502)564-4252

LOUISIANA

Development Division
Office of Commerce and
Industry
P.O. Box 94185
Baton Rouge, LA 70804-9185
(504)342-5365

MAINE

Business Development Division
State Development Office
State House
187 State Street
Station No. 59
Augusta, ME 04333
In-state: (800)872-3838
(207)289-2659

MASSACHUSETTS

Small Business Assistance
Division
Department of Commerce
100 Cambridge Street, 13th floor
Boston, MA 02202
(617)727-4005

MICHIGAN

Michigan Business Ombudsman
Department of Commerce
SBDC
Biz Info Hotline
2727 2nd Avenue
Detroit, MI 48201
In-state: (800)232-2727
(313)577-4848

MINNESOTA

Small Business Assistance Office
Department of Trade and
Economic Development
900 American Center
150 East Kellogg Boulevard
St. Paul, MN 55101
In-state: (800)652-9747
(612)296-3871

MISSISSIPPI

U.S. Small Business
Administration
101 West Capitol
Jackson, MI 39201
(601)965-4378

MISSOURI

Small Business Development
Office
Department of Economic
Development
P.O. Box 118
Jefferson City, MO 65102
(314)751-4982
(314)751-8411

MONTANA

Business Assistance Division
Department of Commerce
1424 Ninth Avenue
Helena, MT 59620
In-state: (800)221-8015
(406)444-3923

NEBRASKA

Small Business Division
Department of Economic
Development
P.O. Box 94666
301 Centennial Mall South
Lincoln, NE 68509
(402)471-4167

NEVADA

Commission on Economic
Development
Office of Small Business
5151 South Carson Street
Carson City, NV 89710
(702)687-4325

NEW HAMPSHIRE

Office of Industrial Development
P.O. Box 856
172 Penbrook Road
Concord, NH 03302-0856
(603)271-2591

NEW JERSEY

Office of Small Business
Assistance
Department of Commerce and
Economic Development
1 West State Street, CN 835
Trenton, NJ 08625
(609)984-4442

NEW MEXICO
Economic Development Division
Department of Economic Development and Tourism
1100 St. Francis Drive
Santa Fe, NM 87503
In-state: (800)545-2040
(505)827-0300

NEW YORK
Division for Small Business
Department of Economic
   Development
230 Park Avenue
New York, NY 10169
(212)827-6100

NORTH CAROLINA
Small Business Development
   Division
Department of Commerce
Dobbs Building, room 2019
430 North Salisbury Street
Raleigh, NC 27611
(919)571-4155

NORTH DAKOTA
Small Business Coordinator
Economic Development
   Commission
1833 East Bismarck Expressway
Bismarck, ND 58504
In-state: (800)472-2100
(701)224-2810

OHIO
Small & Developing Business
   Division
Ohio Department of
   Development
77 High Street Vern Riffe Tower
Columbus, OH 43215

In-state: (800)282-1085
(614)466-1876

OKLAHOMA
Oklahoma Department of
Commerce
6601 Broadway Extension, Building 5
P.O. Box 26980
Oklahoma City, OK 73126-0980
(405)843-9770

OREGON
Economic Development
   Department
775 Commerce Street NE
Salem, OR 97310
In-state: (800)233-3306
(800)547-7842
(503)373-1200

PENNSYLVANIA
Bureau of Small Business
Department of Commerce
461 Forum Building
Harrisburg, PA 17120
(717)783-5700

PUERTO RICO
Commonwealth, Department of
   Commerce
Box S
4275 Old San Juan Station
San Juan, PR 00905
(809)721-3290

RHODE ISLAND
Small Business Development
   Division
Department of Economic
   Development
7 Jackson Walkway
Providence, RI 02903
(401)277-2601

SOUTH CAROLINA

Business Development and
   Assistance Division
State Development Board
P.O. Box 927
Columbia, SC 29202
In-state: (800)922-6684
(803)737-0400

SOUTH DAKOTA

Governor's Office of Economic
   Development
711 East Wells Avenue
Pierre, SD 57501-3359
(800)952-3625
(605)773-5032

TENNESSEE

Small Business Office
Department of Economic and
   Community Development
320 6th Avenue North, 8th floor,
Rachel Jackson Building
Nashville, TN 37243-0405
In-state: (800)872-7201
(615)741-2626

TEXAS

Small Business Division
Department of Commerce
   Economic Development
   Commission
P.O. Box 12728, Capitol Station
410 East Fifth Street
Austin, TX 78711
(512)472-5059

UTAH

Small Business Development
   Center
100 West 500 South, suite 315
Salt Lake City, UT 84101
(801)581-7905
(801)533-5325 (International
   Trade)

VERMONT

Agency of Development and
   Community Affairs
The Pavillion
109 State Street
Montpelier, VT 05602
In-state: (800)622-4553
(802)828-3221

VIRGINIA

Small Business & Financial
   Services
Department of Economic
   Development
P.O. Box 798
Richmond, VA 23206-0798
(804)786-3791

WASHINGTON

Small Business Development
   Center
245 Todd Hall
Washington State University
Pullman, WA 99164-4747
(509)335-1576
(206)464-7076 (International
   Trade)

WEST VIRGINIA

Small Business Development
  Center Division
Governor's Office of Community
  and Industrial Development
Capitol Complex
1115 Virginia Street East
Charleston, WV 25301
(304)348-2960

WISCONSIN

Small Business Ombudsman
Department of Development
123 West Washington Avenue
P.O. Box 7970
Madison, WI 53707
In-state: (800)435-7287
(608)266-0562

WYOMING

Economic Development and
  Stabilization Board
Herschler Building, 2nd floor,
  West Wing
Cheyenne, WY 82002
(307)777-7287
(307)777-7574 (International
  Trade)

VIDEOS

"The *Black Enterprise* Video Guide to Starting Your Own Business." Co-sponsored by IBM. $39.95 plus $2.50 for handling. Contact *Black Enterprise* magazine, 130 Fifth Avenue, New York, NY 10011.

"The Business Plan: Your Road Map to Success." From the SBA and Bell Atlantic. Includes information on setting a strategic vision for a company, obtaining working capital, and motivating key employees; $30. To order, write U.S. Small Business Administration, "Business Plan" Video-Dept. A, P.O. Box 30, Denver, CO 80202-0030, or call the SBA in Denver at (303)534-7518. (There are other titles, as well.)

"How to Survive and Profit in Tough Times." Management experts discuss how to survive in tough times. Subjects include cutting costs while increasing productivity and utilizing customer service to increase business; $99 plus $2.50 for shipping. For information contact *Inc.* magazine, 38 Commercial Wharf, Boston, MA 02110.

"Small Business Video from Apple." Demonstrates how the Apple Macintosh can help a small business run more efficiently; free. To order call (800)441-3001, ext. 650.

ACKNOWLEDGMENTS

Thanks to all the entrepreneurs who shared their dreams, secrets, and time with me. Thanks, too, to all the professional advisers who generously contributed their knowledge and insight.

I also want to thank the business section editors at the *Los Angeles Times* for editing and packaging my weekly column and the *Los Angeles Times Syndicate* staff for enthusiastically representing my work.

Special thanks to John Clendening, the Applegate Group's marketing director, for his support and research assistance, and to Josette Crisostomo, my hard-working associate, for keeping my business and family running smoothly so I could finish this book.

Two special friends and advisers contributed to this book shortly before they died. The keen insights of Joan Sheridan and Howard Shenson will be missed by small-business owners everywhere.

You would not be reading this book if not for the enthusiasm and support of my editor, Alexia Dorszynski, and my literary agent, Dominick Abel.

PLUME

BUSINESS SAVVY